The Psyche Revealed
Through
The I Ching

The Psyche Revealed
Through
The I Ching

by
Carol K. Anthony and Hanna Moog

ICHINGBOOKS

ICHINGBOOKS
distributed by Anthony Publishing Company, Inc.
206 Gleasondale Road
Stow, Massachusetts 01775, U.S.A.
www.ichingbooks.com, or www.ichingoracle.com
Library of Congress Number: 2009910650
ISBN 1-890764-06-X   13 digit: 9781890764067
Printed in the United States of America
Cover Design by Gabriele Wilson
First Edition

Illustration on page 39 by Tilman Michalski, reprinted from
Sibylle Sailer (Ed.) Ich hör dir zu und denk mir was, ©2003 by
Arena Verlag GmbH, Würzburg, Germany

Photograph on page 23 courtesy of Sandra Aldana, London,
England

Contents

Table of Contents

Acknowledgements

We greatly appreciate and thank our editor, Brian Donohue, for the improvements made in our manuscript due to his expertise and forthright critiques. It made us happy that as editor of our earlier book, *I Ching, The Oracle of the Cosmic Way*, he once more accepted the job of doing the substantive editing.

We feel deeply grateful for Dr. Polly Bloomberg's generous willingness to read and comment on our manuscript. She provided invaluable help and encouragement.

Additional thanks go to David Kirchhof, D.C., for generously giving us his feedback.

This book has greatly benefited from the contributions of unnamed users of our previous books, and their willingness to share their experiences.

We thank Gabriele Wilson for yet another beautiful cover design.

Mike Zaino and Mark Kogut have our full gratitude for their continuous support in matters of production and printing.

Introduction

It is taken for granted that the Austrian psychoanalyst, Sigmund Freud, first founded the discipline of psychology in the Western world, just before the turn of the 19th Century. However, largely unrecognized is the fact that the ancient Chinese oracle known as the *I Ching*, gave the world a psychology more than three millennia ago.

Carl G. Jung of Switzerland, Freud's student and contemporary, was first to recognize the psychological value of the *I Ching*. He learned about it through his friend Richard Wilhelm, translator of the most famous translation of the book from Chinese into German in the 1910's. Jung was the first to notice that when consulted as an oracle, the *I Ching* reflected the unconscious. His interest in the *I Ching* opened the minds of hundreds of thousands of people throughout the Western world.[1]

For those of our readers who are familiar with Dr. Jung's work, we want to mention that just as we were in the process of completing this book, Jung's "Red Book" was published, revealing his journey into his own psyche. Written in the early part of the last century, it was withheld from the public eye until now, due to his family's realization that it might be grossly misunderstood. Seen in the light of our book, the demonic forms Dr. Jung experienced during his inner journey owe their existence to words and beliefs that are in conflict with our true nature. This book shows how we can, with Cosmic help, free our psyche of them by removing these words and beliefs.

As an interested student consulting the *I Ching* in the 1970's to resolve my personal problems, I, Carol Anthony, soon realized that my daily consultations with the oracle revealed the *I Ching* to be an ancient system of psychology.

I soon learned from it a method of meditating that allowed the voice that speaks through the *I Ching* to make itself known

---

1 *The I Ching, or Book of Changes*, The Richard Wilhelm Translation rendered into English by Cary F. Baynes, Bollingen Foundation Inc, New York, N.Y. 1950, and Princeton University Press, 1977.

to me as a Cosmic Teacher. I came to call it the "Sage." The *I Ching* describes the relationship between the student and this teacher in the hexagram called "Youthful Folly,"[2] noting that it answers only to the person who comes to the oracle with an open mind, and a sincere desire to learn. Since ancient times, the purpose of consulting an oracle has been defined as learning how to bring one's thinking and attitudes into harmony with the Greater Cosmos.

When Hanna Moog joined my publishing company in 1998, she came with seventeen years of experience as an editor, author, lecturer, and seminar-giver on the *I Ching*. She had worked for the German publisher who had first published Richard Wilhelm's translation in 1924. During her employment with this publisher, Hanna had also translated my first four books on the *I Ching*.[3] We two began our day by consulting the *I Ching* together. Our very different backgrounds proved to be an essential ingredient in our common learning process.

Our learning from the Sage was greatly enhanced by a method of communicating I had discovered in 1994. This method allowed us to put hypotheses to the Sage in which we suggested in our own words what the *I Ching* text was saying to us. The toss of the coins gave us yes and no answers that indicated whether we understood correctly or not. I called this method the "Retrospective-Three-Coin Method," or *rtcm*. It enabled us to have a continuous and meaningful dialogue with the Sage with the assurance that we were understanding the *I Ching*'s numerous metaphors. An example of such a metaphor is "the Devil's Country."[4] The Sage made me aware that in one instance it referred to a wrong path I had chosen. In another instance it referred to beliefs I held that were actually in conflict with the Cosmos. Because these beliefs had been passed down from generation to generation, they had never been questioned and therefore had never been corrected.

---

2 A hexagram is a sign composed of six lines. The *I Ching* is composed of 64 hexagrams, each of which has six lines with specific meanings.
3 *A Guide to the I Ching*, 1980, *The Philosophy of the I Ching*, 1981, *The Other Way, Meditation Experiences Based on the I Ching*, 1990, and *Love, An Inner Connection, Based on Principles Drawn from the I Ching*, 1994.
4 See Hexagram 64. Line 4.

The use of the *rtcm* to communicate with the Sage led to great shifts in our ability to see things from the Cosmic perspective. For us, it was comparable to the recognition, in the 16th Century, that the Earth is not the center of the universe. In its gentle way, the Sage made us aware that humans have falsely been viewing themselves as the center of the universe, and that this view is at the root of all conflict and suffering humans have inflicted upon themselves and on their relationships with the natural world, the Earth, and with the invisible side of the Cosmos.

Once we step outside the human-centered view we have inherited from the past, we are able to see ourselves as an integral part of the greater whole we call the "Cosmos." This enlarging of our perspective, rather than undermining our social order, frees it from the ideas that keep it in conflict with the Cosmos. By noticing and writing about the many mistaken ideas and beliefs that have been accepted and promoted by social, cultural and religious institutions, we are not saying that these institutions are the cause of the disorders we describe, but that they also have been under the influence of these faulty ideas from the past that can be corrected.

Recognizing the falseness of the human-centered view will open a completely new window to our understanding the conditions that create harmony, peace, and prosperity for us humans and for the world at large. These conditions already exist in the DNA of all life on Earth. We only need to remember that we humans share most of the genome of the other animal species and that we all have a common origin in the invisible side of the Cosmos. Long before scientists discovered what they called *DNA*, the *I Ching* described this storehouse of inner wisdom and called it our "inner truth." Embedded in every cell of our body, it contains a collection of everything we need to know to live our lives happily and joyfully, and it provides us with the feeling knowledge of what it means to be in accord with Cosmic harmony. Our mental, emotional, and physical health is dependent on whether our thinking and our attitudes agree with the Cosmic Principles of Harmony that are the basis of our very existence.

The important role our thinking plays in creating our reality was first shown in our book, *I Ching, The Oracle of the Cosmic Way*,[5] and further demonstrated in its practical application in our next book, *Healing Yourself the Cosmic Way*.[6] This latter book is dedicated to showing ideas and beliefs that cause physical illnesses, and to showing how we can free ourselves from illness by rejecting the validity of these ideas. The sick-making ideas, we were to learn, are stored in the psyche, where they act like a negative 'program' that overrides our *feeling program of inner truth* that would otherwise keep us healthy. The fact that these harmful ideas can be identified, with the Sage's help, and removed from the psyche once and for all, drew our attention to certain functions of the psyche that were involved in storing the negative programs on the one hand, and that could be engaged in freeing ourselves from them, on the other.

The overall role our psyche plays in the healthy personality is the subject of this, our third book. It shows the psyche as the meeting place for our mind and body. In this meeting place, our body brings to our mind its feeling experiences of life and the wisdom of our inner truth, while our mind brings to our body its ability *to express in words the inner truth* our body conveys through its feelings.

Our psyche has wonderful functions to make this interface between our body and mind possible. Many of these functions are described in this book. Besides being the body-mind meeting place, our psyche weaves the meaningful threads in such a way that on looking back over our lives, we can see the pattern that developed, which gives our life meaning.

Unfortunately, shocking and traumatic experiences that have not been processed prevent our fulfilling the meaning of our lives. Their presence in this unprocessed form creates in us unconscious patterns of behavior that harm our lives and spoil

---

5 *I Ching, The Oracle of the Cosmic Way*, by Carol K. Anthony and Hanna Moog, ICHINGBOOKS, Stow, Massachusetts, 2002.
6 *Healing Yourself the Cosmic Way*, by Carol K. Anthony and Hanna Moog, ICHINGBOOKS, Stow, Massachusetts, 2006.

the Cosmic gifts we are born with. Fortunately, just as we can free ourselves from the harmful ideas that cause illness, we can also free ourselves from these wounds to our personality. With Cosmic help we can completely free the psyche from them.

Another critical development in our understanding was the realization that the *I Ching* is not based on "changes," as has been thought for centuries. This view of the *I Ching* led in China to a philosophy of passive acceptance of adversity as the correct way to adapt to the "ups and downs" of life. As we learned, it is the Cosmic Principle of Transformation that governs all life, and enables its renewal. These transformations take place on the cellular level and are set in motion by consciousness that is in harmony with the Cosmos. The basis for this book and our two previous books is the understanding that we can heal illness, resolve conflict, and return to inner peace only by engaging transformations. By contrast, the idea that life is governed by changes causes us to attempt to make things happen through mechanical means. These means address the symptoms rather than the causes of dysfunction and are the result of mistakenly viewing the universe as a system of mechanics.

As we, Carol and Hanna, experienced for ourselves, people usually come in touch with the *I Ching* at a time of great need: when a relationship has failed, an illness has struck, a financial crisis has occurred, or when they have become alienated from who they are. It is then that they are ready to look for the true cause of their misfortune. It is an interesting fact that the Chinese ideogram for "crisis" has the second meaning of "opportunity." In a time of great crisis, the Sage approaches us in various possible guises to reveal to us the positive potential the crisis contains, while at the same time showing us the mindset that has caused our dilemma. In order to uncover the positive potential, we need to start on an inner journey into our psyche, where we are faced with the ideas and beliefs that have caused our crisis.

Although this book presents an understanding of the human psyche that took us many years to acquire, it need not take the same amount of time for the reader to ferret out the false programs that have taken residence in his psyche, and which have been ruling his life. We present here many of the road signs that indicate the direction in which his inner freedom can be found.

Our original intention was to put all the materials we had collected on this subject in one book. However, as the chapters grew in number, we realized this was not possible. The present book gives a comprehensive understanding of the psyche in its relation to our mind and body, and to our existence as an integral part of the Cosmos. It enables the reader to resolve many common emotional problems.

A second book will be dedicated to understanding the causes of those internal conflicts that have manifested in more severe mental and emotional disturbances, or psychological disorders. It will also provide the reader who has thoroughly understood the fundamental concepts presented in this book with a greater ability to free himself, or others, from those disturbances.

We make no apology or defense for what we have presented in this book. It is based on our personal experiences in working with the *I Ching* over many years. We have written it to share with those who are open to it, what we learned first-hand, by experience. Just as the *I Ching* came into our lives at a time of our greatest personal crisis, this book happens to be published during a great financial crisis, when many people have lost their jobs, their homes, and their savings. Our experience has been that not all was lost, and that our time of crisis proved to be a time of great opportunity. By focusing on attaining harmony in our inner lives, we found fulfillment and success in our outer lives.

This book is about restoring inner harmony and inner freedom within ourselves, which are the true source of all outer harmony and freedom. It is about finding our true home and security within ourselves, whereby we also find ourselves at home in the Cosmos. We carry this inner home with us wherever we go, and therefore are at home wherever we are.

Joy comes softly

— I Ching, The Oracle of the Cosmic Way —
(Hexagram 47, Line 5)

1.
In the Darkest Hour Friends Come

This book had its beginning in our personal journeys into our psyche with the help of the ancient Chinese oracle, the *I Ching*. The book came into our lives at the moment of greatest need. We had lost the sense of who we were, and the sense that our lives had meaning.

How did the *I Ching* guide us out of our difficulties? We were to learn that the true purpose of an oracle is to reflect to us the thoughts and images we harbor in our psyche that are contrary to our true nature, and therefore lead to misfortune. It also showed us how to return to our true nature and to our wholeness.

We have written this book to share what we learned with those who are open to it. It is to let them know that the transition to joy and inner peace can happen, and that the help we found for ourselves is there for them, too. It requires that we recognize the limits of what we can do all by ourselves, and that we open our minds to the invisible help that is available to us from the loving Cosmos. The *I Ching* provided us a direct access to this help.

We tell our stories here of how the *I Ching* came into our lives at the moment of our deepest need, and showed us the way out of our difficulties.

Our Stories

Looking into the Abyss

In 1981, when I, Hanna, was 35, everything I had strived for came to a halt. My marriage had failed and my professional career had ended, because it was tied to a business run by my husband. Even my mother turned against me after I told her I wanted to leave my marriage. Suddenly, I was no longer the wife of...., the successful business person, the beloved daughter of .... Who then, was I??

A friend who wanted to help me, asked, "What do you really enjoy doing?" Until then I identified myself with my work, and with the social roles I had adopted. I had never asked myself what I "enjoyed." Looking for the answer inside, all I saw was a deep, dark abyss. This realization came as a shock!

Just at that point, another good friend gave me a copy of the *I Ching*. I had seen other friends use the *I Ching* every year on New Year's Eve to get a reading for the coming year, but the words of the oracle sounded like a riddle that needed time to reveal its meaning. Now, with no other solution in sight, I was ready to give it a try. Without asking a specific question, I developed a hexagram.[1] Its name was "Resoluteness/Breakthrough." The image presented was that of dammed up water ready to break through, an image that totally described my feeling at the moment. Indeed, I needed to break through to something completely new. The image of water about to "break through" made me feel that the pitch blackness of the abyss might not be endless, but a tunnel with a light at the end.

I ended my self-employment with my husband without having a new job contract in my pocket. Knowing I needed a break from working — just to rest, and to give myself time to see what I would be attracted to doing, I left without savings to rely on, and no financial support in sight. I was offered a job almost immediately that seemed to be totally tailored to what I was good at: languages, organizational talent, interfacing with people who could establish the necessary connection to advance me in my career. Yet, something did not feel right about that job. I gave myself a few days to reflect on the offer.

Then help came from an unexpected quarter: At the next meeting of my Gestalt therapy group, I was the one to start the session. What followed was one of the most efficient fifteen minute therapy sessions I have ever experienced.

The therapist asked me to tell the group what benefits I saw,

---

1 A hexagram is one of the *I Ching*'s 64 chapters. Each hexagram addresses a specific subject.

if I took the job that was offered.

"A higher salary than I have ever earned," I replied, "a job that could serve me as a springboard to make a career, and give me prestige." Then I added, "On the other hand, it would mean that I would have to buy new clothes, and a car (because the job was outside the city and outside the reach of public transportation); in short, it would force a lifestyle on me that does not feel right."

"Okay," replied the therapist, "now put into words what it would mean for you if you did not take this job offer."

"No money, insecurity, no work," I said.

"Now," he continued, "I want you to rephrase the things you said last into something positive. For example, what would it mean 'not to work'?"

"Vacation," I said without thinking, noticing right away that did not feel right, either. "No," I corrected myself, "it would need to be longer than a vacation."

"How long?" the therapist asked.

"Four months," the answer burst out of my mouth.

"And where would you like to go?"

"To the Canary Islands," I heard myself saying, as the image of sunshine, mountains, and ocean — my dream combination — popped into my mind.

"How are you going to pay for it?" I heard the therapist ask.

"I could sell my few antiques," I replied, as the names of several people sprang to mind to whom I could offer them.

"When are you leaving?" he pressed on.

"In six weeks," I heard myself say.

The image of being without money, without work, and in a place of insecurity had, within minutes, been transformed into possibility — the specific possibility of realizing a long-held dream.

I walked out of the session as if on wings. The inner clarity I felt had wiped away all doubts. I had a goal, I knew it was feasible, and I was resolute to go for it.

"Resoluteness/Breakthrough" — already the answer of the *I Ching* was taking on a practical meaning. The dammed-up water was beginning to find an outlet.

I was to learn more about it in the weeks that followed, as the clarity of what needed to be done to make my dream come true, remained. Instead of using my organizational skills for others, I was now using them to further my own undertaking. This was the first time I allowed myself to do that. And, to my amazement, help came from all quarters: friends agreed to store my furniture, a new renter was found to take my place, I was able to sell my antiques, and to get everything prepared to go on my trip. Exactly six weeks from the day I made the decision, I left.

Although my goal was clear as to the first place I wanted to go to, it was also a backpack trip into the unknown. More than the overweight of my backpack, which I was able to reduce in the first two days, a thought began to accompany me on my journey, and, in no small way, to weigh me down: What would I do when the four months were over? And where would I want to live? For the moment, however, I had to put it aside.

My "lonely" trip took its first unexpected turn on the ferryboat that connects Spain with the Canary Islands. I met four young people who were heading for the same island, but, unlike me, they had no concrete goal. Would I mind, they asked, if they joined me? "No, I would not," I replied.

I was the only one who had a map that showed hiking trails on the island. We decided to hike from the town where the ferry landed to the town I had in mind. We were sure to get there in a day, so we only supplied ourselves with enough water to last for a day.

As our trail crossed a mountain, the sun rose higher in the sky. Just as it was getting hot, we suddenly lost our way. The trails on the map, we realized, had been used by the military in the 1940's (the date on the map!), but had grown over with time. After some searching, we found the trail that allowed us to continue in the right direction. The heat, however, was unrelenting and none of us was used to walking for hours with a heavy backpack. With our water supplies soon exhausted and our stomachs grumbling, the feeling of not knowing how long it would take us to reach our goal cast a dark shadow over our little group.

We had to camp in the open that night, realizing that we had not come very far. Fortunately, we found some drinking water the next morning. We divided what each of us had left to eat between the five of us. It was a sparse breakfast.

By noon we realized that in a whole day and a half we had not met a single soul, nor seen a single house. Amazingly, on first studying the map, we had not paid attention to the topography of the relatively round island, which has an old volcano in the center. Over time, the slopes of the volcano had eroded into deep valleys, called *barrancos.* What looked like the shortest connection between the town where we landed, and the town of our destination, was actually the longest, because we had to go far up one side of a barranco then far down into the next one, then climb up the next slope, etc.

In the afternoon of the second day, when hopelessness had set in, we suddenly saw some houses in the far distance. Quickly, our spirits came back. But, oh, as we drew closer, the houses looked deserted. We remembered reading that many people from the island had left in the 1950's for South America, because they could not make a living any more. The prospect of having come upon a ghost village dampened our mood considerably. However, our path did not leave us any other choice. We had to go through the place, no matter what.

We were still at quite a distance when suddenly we saw a dog come out of a door, followed by an old man. The man made a signal not to be afraid of the dog, and to come over to his house. He gave us a friendly welcome. I thought, the only thing I would like to ask him for is water. Water would be wonderful. What we were given, though, was beyond all expectation: he and his wife insisted that we sit on the only five chairs they had in the house. She brought in a fresh goat cheese as big as a plate, dry crackers, plenty of water, and…a bottle of wine! They urged us to eat and drink.

We had a conversation using our hands and feet, and the little Spanish I had learned at home. What mattered was our communication from heart to heart. I was humbled by the experience. The old man reassured us that we could reach our destination before evening. With the skill of a goat, he led us to our path. He was right. We reached the town before darkness.

The experience of these first two days on the island was a breakthrough to humility. Blown away was the arrogance of thinking that *I* knew the way because I had a map. This bit of humility, I was to learn, was the central thing needed to embark on what became a twenty-year journey to understand myself.

What these experiences and many others to follow showed me was that whatever difficulty arises, I needed to remain resolute to see the possibility of a breakthrough, and that help is there for me.

My Darkest Hour

I, Carol, was 41 when my husband left our marriage, leaving me with four children and no means of support. What was more depressing to me at the time was the personal failure I felt in "losing my marriage." With its collapse, I felt as if the trapdoor of my certainties — what I held most valuable — had fallen out from under me, leaving me dangling at the end of a rope.

I did not know where to turn for help since I could not imagine that either a psychological or a religious counselor had the answers I needed. In despair, I called out to whatever helpful forces there were "out there" to bring me help. When a friend visited me the next day with a copy of the *I Ching* in her hands, I did not realize that this was the answer to my call.

I had heard of the *I Ching* already from two other highly respected friends, but when they told me it was an oracle consulted by tossing coins, I had dismissed it. Now, out of respect for my friend's sincere desire to help, I let her demonstrate how it worked.[2]

Its first words to me were, "In the midst of the greatest obstructions, friends come. Here we see a man who is called to help in an emergency. He should not seek to evade the obstructions, no matter how dangerously they pile up before him. But because he is really called to the task, the power of his spirit is strong

---

2 *The I Ching, or Book of Changes*, the Richard Wilhelm Translation.

enough to attract helpers whom he can effectively organize, so that through the well-directed co-operation of all participants, the obstruction is overcome."

These words shined the light of possibility into my inner darkness. In the next days and years, the *I Ching* addressed one problem after another, showing me how, through learning to meditate in the way it suggested, I could end my sleeplessness, how I could relate to problems that came up with my teenagers, and to my husband, and to the lawyers throughout the period of our divorce. It even guided me in how to run the business opportunity that "coincidentally" came my way. Whenever I look back on this period, I do not see how without its help I could have got through it.

This is not to say that I understood every hexagram. Far from it. I had to feel the meanings of the metaphors. Then a curious thing would happen: an image or idea would come into my consciousness of itself, that clarified what the *I Ching*, in its ancient language, was trying to communicate.

Over time, I had the definite sense that the help I was receiving came from a distinct entity. Hexagram 4, *Youthful Folly*, mentions how to approach the "Sage" that teaches through the *I Ching*. It was then that I realized that this Sage was coming into my consciousness to clarify the messages. It was, in fact, the voice that speaks through the book. It informed me that I, as "the young fool" approaching it, was ignorant of the affairs of "the inner world" of my own self, and that the best way to understand this inner world was to suspend everything I thought I knew about myself.

Two things stand out, on looking back over my more than forty years of learning from this wise and caring Sage. Whenever I was unsure and needed help, it was always there for me. By this I mean, it not only provided the answers I needed, I had the feeling of being loved and cared for, as if I were a member of a larger Cosmic family. But, whenever I began to feel too comfortable and began to question whether I was just "thinking this up," the *I Ching* hexagrams I received became suddenly mysterious and indecipherable, and the feeling of being supported and loved gradually faded until I once more felt alone. These feelings were often accompanied by one or another problem, which the *I Ching* reflected as "misfortune." When I wished to find the cause of this change, I received hexagrams that spoke of my doubting as an "arrogance" that caused the retreat of the Sage, so that gradually I began to understand how my inner thoughts and attitudes were creating my reality.

It took many more years to realize that the *I Ching* is a Cosmic gift to humans, to help them know themselves, and to know the Cosmos as our true and ultimate home. As it puts it in the hexagram called "The Well," the *I Ching* is a source of pure and nourishing refreshment that is available to everyone who comes. What we get when we draw up this water is our own deepest *inner truth*. As the hexagram text makes us aware, before we can reach the source of this pure water, we need to remove the "mud" that has accumulated in the well through the social conditioning that has made it inaccessible. This is a reference to the mistaken beliefs that have made us doubt our inner truth and the infinite resources we possess within us.

My own path has been one of finding and ridding myself of the untruths that have blocked my self-understanding. As I proceeded on this path, the balancing I experienced during the first years, which was like that of walking on a tightrope, changed to the wide road of the inner wanderer, who progresses through life at home within himself, having all his possessions with him.

The Friends that Came

It was quite a long time before we, Carol and Hanna, could look back over our lives and see the consistent fact that once we embarked on our inner journeys, help came from all sources. At the time, neither of us recognized this. For both the help first came through the friends who brought us the *I Ching*. For Hanna, more help came through her group therapist, friends who offered to store her things, a stranger who sublet her apartment, and buyers of her antiques. Once on the island, help came from the old man and his wife. For Carol, help came in learning to meditate in a new way that resolved her sleeplessness and helped her understand the Sage's messages. The help also came as a business opportunity that paid all her bills over the next thirteen years, and enabled her to remain independent. Through 'seeing possibility' we both attracted the helpers mentioned in Carol's first hexagram, with whose help she "could effectively overcome the obstructions." It became clear only years later that these helpers were motivated by the attraction that naturally accompanies sincerity in asking for help. It also became clear that this help is inspired by the Cosmos that functions only on what we later discovered to be the Cosmic Principle of Attraction.

Gaining a Broader Perspective

Just as the *I Ching* acts as a guide to knowing ourselves, it also acts as a guide to knowing the Cosmos. This knowing occurs on a deep inner level in moments of insight. It needs no belief or supporting rationales because its truth is felt. It resonates through our whole being.

That the Cosmos is knowable is an idea that may come as a surprise, since we are taught to view it as the "Unknown." We are even taught to believe that it is "an abyss into which we can fall." Our experience showed us that the Cosmos is reflected in the total goodness of our true nature. We were shown that when our true nature becomes freed from its conditioning, it is loving, kind, and beneficent. That, as the reader will discover, is also the nature of the Cosmos.

Failure to know ourselves had resulted for us in a fate, or what the *I Ching* refers to as "misfortune." The next chapter will show how Fate, too, turned out to be a Cosmic friend that came to help us return to our true nature.

2. "Shock Comes — Oh, Oh! Laughing Words — Ha, Ha!"[1]
Fate —The Consequence of Going Against Our True Nature

As devastating as ending up in a fate sounds, our personal experiences made us revise our view of it. Fate, as we came to learn, was actually Cosmic help in disguise — help given to return us to our true nature, which is in harmony with the Cosmos.

Fate is created whenever we base our lives on ideas and beliefs that are against our true nature. These ideas and beliefs are the result of humans, throughout time, falsely assuming that our language ability makes us special, and that we have an unlimited freedom to think whatever we choose. In reality, our language ability is a Cosmic gift the purpose of which is to express in words the Cosmic truths that govern all life. Because the Cosmos is a system of Principles of Harmony, bringing these truths into our consciousness brings us joy. Whenever we feel fear or experience suffering, it is an indication that we are giving validity to words that have no Cosmic basis.

Fate, the Cosmic Principle of Cause and Effect

The gift of language to humans comes with the freedom to experience the Cosmic Principle of Cause and Effect. In the course of the millennia, humans have learned about the law of cause and effect from the laws of physics. What they have not learned is that the same kind of limits apply when we disregard the principle of cause and effect as it applies to language.

The *I Ching* teaches us that all thought is a form of energy. Thought that is in harmony with the Cosmos has beneficial effects. Thought that does not express Cosmic truths exceeds the limits defined for humans, therefore has destructive effects. Such thoughts are destructive to us both psychologically and physically. When they are projected out onto others, or onto other

1 See Hexagram 51. *Shock*

10

life forms, or onto the Earth, they do harm and create disorder. Because the Cosmos is a self-regulating system based on harmony, the negative energy of disharmonious thoughts invariably returns to us at some point in time, like a boomerang. When the boomerang hits, we experience a fate, when the negative energy we have been putting out returns to us. Fate thus is the manifestation of the Cosmic Principle of Cause and Effect.

The Cosmos maintains its duration through the Principle of Fate. Fate is like an invisible energy-wall, or fence we run into when we go against a Cosmic Principle of Harmony, as when we deny or violate our true nature. That a fate manifests physically shows us that there is a direct connection between our consciousness and the effect it has on the world of form. Modern physics has become aware of the effect of the researchers' thoughts on their experiments, but unfortunately, this insight has not yet been applied broadly to all fields of science.[2]

Fate is also a law of physics. Just as we would fall out of the air if we tried to fly an airplane without wings, we run into this wall when we exceed the Cosmic limits that apply to humans. Because Fate is like an energy-wall, negative energy in us sets it in motion in such a way that our harmful thoughts and deeds bounce back to us like a boomerang.

We violate Cosmic harmony when we use language that falsely describes things. When we project slanders on others, the harm we do to them invariably returns to us in the form of a fate. Fate is also triggered by words and phrases that slander

---

2 David Bohm, On Creativity, Routlege, London, 1998, p. 33. "Thus, in science it was commonly thought that theories and instrumental observations were simply reflections of the world as it is. Later, it became evident that such a simple reflection process cannot give the whole story. Each theory and each instrument selects certain aspects of a world that is infinite, both qualitatively and quantitatively, in its totality. According to modern physics (especially the quantum theory) when one comes down to the atomic and subatomic level of size, the observing instrument is even in principle inseparable from what is to be observed, so that this instrument cannot do other than disturb the observed system in an irreducible way: and indeed it even helps to create and to give form to what is observed. One may compare this situation to a psychological observation, which can likewise disturb the people being studied, and thus take part in the process that one wants to learn about, as well as "create" and shape some of the very phenomena that can be observed."

aspects of the Cosmos (visible or invisible), such as the Nature around us, or our own nature. When we eliminate from our awareness the invisible help that is available to us, our fate is to lose that help. All fundamental untruths we accept as true sooner or later create a fate for us. Understanding Fate helps us to realize that the great gift given to humans — that of speech and the ability to think in words — has limits. We are not free to say or think harmful thoughts. When we make up myths that falsify the nature of things, harmful consequences follow; there is always a price to pay.

Recognizing Disharmonious Thoughts

Feelings of dis-ease are the first warning signs that we harbor disharmonious, destructive ideas. An example is the well-worn phrase, "We humans have to do it all ourselves." We only need to notice how depressed this makes us feel to realize it is disharmonious, and therefore untrue. The cause of this depressed feeling lies in the assumption that no help is available to us from the Cosmos. On holding this depressed view we fail to recognize that it is also self-fulfilling, because it shuts the door to the invisible Helpers of the Cosmos. Then, we are indeed left to our own limited devices. Life thereafter becomes hard, giving rise to the common belief that "life is a vale of tears," which is yet another slander on the loving, caring nature of the Cosmos.

What Had We, Carol and Hanna, Done to Create Our Fates?

In Carol's view, she had fulfilled her role as mother, wife, and good citizen. Ultimately, however, she had to realize that she had adopted a heroic image of herself as 'the one who could endure hardships, insults, injuries, and injustices longer than anyone else for the sake of her family.' This heroic self-image drew her into a marriage relationship that would perfectly match her heroic abilities to endure. When those very hardships occurred, she felt that her willingness to be self-sacrificing was not respected or appreciated. Then she wondered if she had failed through not having endured enough. The *I Ching* helped her to realize that such a pact to endure hardships was contrary to the dignity of her true nature.

The Sage makes us aware that our dignity as an individual is the one and only thing we have that can be called 'inviolable.' The Cosmos does not require that anyone endure hardships as a proof of virtue.

Carol had also devalued herself by failing to protect her personal boundaries from encroachments by others. These encroachments took the form of unreasonable expectations by others, that she sacrifice her values, her energy, and her self-respect for their benefit. Ultimately, she had to realize that the collapse of her marriage was the consequence of this weakness on her part, which she incorrectly had seen as strength. Her husband's fate in the breakup of the marriage was caused by a reservation of attitude that he carried from the beginning to the end of their relationship as to whether Carol was the 'right person for him.'

From Hanna's standpoint, she had been the 'good wife,' devoting all her efforts to furthering her husband's choice of career, and doing nothing selfish. Why then, had she come to such a burnout? There seemed to be something harmful in her image of being the 'supportive wife.' This image was so monumental that it had squeezed her true self out of the picture. She did not realize that such self-sacrifices cannot be sustained. Only through working with the *I Ching* did she later realize that in her teenage years she had entertained the image of 'becoming a saint.' Long forgotten, this image, stored in her psyche, had played a determining role in the collapse of her energy to continue.

The Purposes of Fate

As we were to learn, Fate is a blessing in disguise because it brings to an abrupt halt the negative trajectories we have created by our disharmonious thoughts. These are the trajectories that have led us away from the path of fulfilling our Cosmic destiny. (See Chapter 3.)

The abrupt halt and shock that accompany fates have their value in that they make us ask ourselves which idea or belief has led us to this impasse. Shock also brings us 'back to Earth' from ideas that have exaggerated our self-importance. Being brought back to Earth is experienced as an unaccustomed humility, one that gives us a temporary window through which we can get in touch with our true self. The shock brings with it the recognition that our true self possesses an inner strength that is quite different from the bravado and exaggeration that accompany disharmonious thinking. This humility comes with a sense that we are part of something larger than ourselves, on which we can depend in this moment of crisis. The experience that we can depend on "something solid" is different from the idea of the "threatening unknown" we were taught to fear as children. Humility connects us with the loving, caring Cosmos we once knew, when we were still in the age of innocence.

The Aftermath

Unfortunately, the humility produced by shock is often short-lived. Rationales such as the following are heard in the back of our minds: "You didn't try hard enough. If you had, you would have succeeded." On listening to them, we give them control over us.

A prolonged struggle between our emerging true self and our old, disharmonious way of thinking now begins. The old mindset is surrounded by an array of fears and rationales that defend it in the attempt to keep it in place. These defenses are aroused whenever we consider giving up our old ways of thinking. Consequently, the time when the true self attempts to take its place as leader of our personality, is a time fraught with conflicting inner voices. Fortunately, for those who consult the *I Ching*, they are helped to process their fears by being shown the mistaken ideas and beliefs that have created them. The *I Ching* also helps us distinguish between thoughts coming from the old mindset and those that come from our inner truth.

How is it, one may ask, that a false mindset, once created in us, can become so self-protective that it acts as the boss of everything we do? How can it regain its dominance after having been displaced by the shock of Fate? One might suspect that habit is so powerful that it rules all. In fact, no habit has intrinsic control over us. The old mindset is like a computer program that has been installed in our psyche at a very early age; it operates mechanically, as if a switch in the brain has been turned on. By the time we have reached adulthood, we have grown so accustomed to the switch turning on as a reaction to perceived threats that we think, "that is the way things are."

We gradually realize that the old mindset is completely foreign to our true nature. In fact, it started in our youth by repressing our true nature and taking the place of our true self, as an imposter in our personality. The name of this imposter is "the individual ego."[3] It uses any number of language tricks to fool us about its false nature, one of which is to speak as "I" in the psyche. Since the ego is not part of the Cosmos, it has no energy in and of itself. Rather, it has to constantly steal our life energy for its purposes. This fact also leads to its downfall because the stress of its demands and usurpation of our energy eventually lead to our exhaustion and collapse.

On the road to recovery from its collapse, we need help to protect our frail and uncertain true self as it emerges from its imprisonment in the psyche. Thanks to the *I Ching*, this emergence was possible for us, and it is possible for everyone who has the sincere desire to get to know and free his true self. To achieve this goal it helps to first know more about our true nature and its resources, which meanwhile have either been denied or slandered by the mindset of the ego.

---

3 Note that this definition of ego comes from the *I Ching*, which shows the ego to be composed of a number of self-images that are contrary to our true nature. Once introduced into the psyche, these self-images seek to take over the personality. For a more complete description of how it gets installed in the psyche, how it operates, and how it protects itself, see Chapters 4 and 5.

3 "Possession in Great Measure, Supreme Success"
Our True Nature

The *I Ching* makes us aware that everything that manifests into form exists first as an *image* in the Cosmic Consciousness. Cosmic Consciousness is the name the *I Ching* has given to the invisible side of the Cosmos. We do not tend to think of something invisible as existing because we are trained to take as 'real' only what we see with our eyes. However, the most obvious invisible reality we experience is that of our own consciousness as the invisible side of our being.

Not only is the Cosmic Consciousness the source of all things, it also stores the original image of everything that exists, including the original pure image of every human being. When we come from our invisible home in the Cosmic Consciousness to experience life in a body, this original image is stored in our psyche. Under normal conditions, our DNA is constantly connected with this image and receives from it all the information it needs to build our body cells and bodily systems. This is to ensure that our body expresses our unique original image. When we are in the danger of losing our sense of who we are, as a unique human being, the undamaged image of us that is stored in our psyche serves as a beacon that helps us return to our true nature.

Our true nature is good and whole. It comes with an abundance of Cosmic possessions. This is described in the *I Ching*, in Hexagram 14, *Possession in Great Measure.*[1] By 'good' we mean that our true nature is in accord with the harmonious order of the Cosmos. By 'whole,' we mean it is in a positive symbiotic relationship with its Cosmic source.

Being in harmony with our true nature is experienced as being sovereign, i.e., in possession of ourselves, meaning we feel whole, protected, and furthered by the Cosmos. In this state, the harmonic forces of the Cosmos join us in everything we do,

---

1 See *I Ching, The Oracle of the Cosmic Way.*

carrying us along effortlessly. We feel this positive symbiosis as a oneness with everything. It occurs when we are modest and humble. We fall out of this state when we either see ourselves as superior or inferior to anything else.

Our Cosmic Possessions

The Cosmic possessions we are endowed with at birth include our 'treasure chest of inner truth,' our inner and outer senses of perception, and a group of other senses called the 'metaphorical senses.' Furthermore, our possessions include our Cosmic virtues, our talents, and our automatic access to all the helping energies of the Cosmos, which the *I Ching* calls *Helpers*.[2] Thus we possess all we need to live our lives happily, and to bring to fruition our uniqueness.

Our Treasure Chest of Inner Truth/DNA
What the *I Ching* calls "inner truth" in the hexagram by that name, is the complete body of knowledge contained in every body cell that science calls DNA. As science has discovered, our DNA holds the complete history of our development as human beings, and is such that a single cell holds all the information needed to build our entire body. The inner truth stored in our body cells also contains all we need to know about the Cosmos, our connection with it, and its Principles of Harmony. This is to say that each of us possesses an inner measure that enables us to distinguish thoughts and actions that are in harmony with the Cosmos from those that are not. Also part of our inner truth is our love for the Earth as our home during our life in a body. Furthermore, our inner truth contains the knowledge of our unique Cosmic destiny, and guides us in fulfilling it.

Our inner truth is our perfect Cosmic operating system, that when not interfered with, keeps our body, psyche, and mind working in a perfect cooperation. This operating system is not based on words, ideas, or images, but on *feelings* that are attuned to Cosmic harmony. It connects us with all the Cosmic support,

---

2 See Hexagram 3, *Making a New Beginning*, Line 1.

furtherance, nourishment, and protection we need as individuals to fulfill our Cosmic destiny.[3]

Blessings as Cosmic Gifts

Hexagram 14 also makes us aware that all the blessings we experience during our lives are gifts that come from the Cosmos: a suitable occupation, a suitable place to live, a true love relationship, friends that complement us, and a multitude of other things that come to us when we need them. These blessings show us the gift-giving and helping nature of the Cosmos. This may sound like fantasy to a person who has been born into a dysfunctional family, or who has experienced life devoid of friends, or lacking a true love relationship. The reasons for these latter experiences will become clear as we describe, in later chapters, how human societies have developed in such a way as to separate us as individuals from our unity with the Cosmos, and thus have created conditions of suffering. We will also show how we, as individuals, have the opportunity to correct these conditions within ourselves, and to return to our positive symbiotic relationship with the loving Cosmos.

Our Bodily Senses and Commonsense

Our Cosmic possessions also include one of our greatest treasures, our *commonsense*. It is the consensus of all our bodily senses. These senses include our inner and outer senses of perception, and what we call our metaphorical senses. We commonly recognize only our five outer senses. However, our common language tells us that we also have five corresponding inner senses of perception. These tell us the inner truth of matters: for example, our inner sense of smell tells us when something 'smells rotten,' our inner sense of taste informs us when something leaves us with a bitter taste, and when an act is

---

3 "Let's start with the 100 trillion cells in your body. In nearly every one is coiled more than six feet of DNA containing the collective evolutionary history of humanity, as well as the special recipe of 3.2 billion chemical "letters" that make up the unique you." See "The Genetic Journey: Following DNA from Cell to Society," article by Brian W. Simpson http://magazine.jhsph. edu/2007/Spring/features/dna/

'tasteless'; our inner sense of hearing informs us when something does not 'sound right'; our inner sense of feeling tells us whether something feels 'smooth' or 'rough.' Our inner sense of seeing allows us to have insights through meditations, but first, insight must be awakened in us through Cosmic help. The metaphorical senses are those commonly referred to in language as our senses: of dignity, of wholeness, of appropriateness, of fairness, of caution, of discretion, of limits, of opportunity, and of order.

We experience help from our inner senses of perception when we say that we have to "sleep on a matter." This expression is an acknowledgement by the mind that it needs additional clarity before making a decision. It seems to know that help is available from this source. When the mind has taken this modest position, our inner senses of perception are activated to give us the clarity needed.

All these senses act in a coordinated way to give us a true perception, not only of the visible world, but also of the invisible world around us that is made up of people's inner thoughts. Our commonsense summarizes the information gained through the totality of our senses, and functions as our inner judge. Its final judgment is pronounced as an inner Yes when the situation is harmonious, and an inner No when it is disharmonious. When our commonsense says "Yes," we can safely go ahead with the matter at hand; when it says "No," we need to consciously affirm that No, and retreat from the situation.

Unfortunately, many of these senses, which are all part of our bodily nature, are made dysfunctional when the mind is viewed as superior to the body.

Our Natural Self-Correcting Function
We possess a natural self-correcting function that is based on our true conscience. It causes us to feel remorse when we have gone against our dignity and self-respect, and pulls us back to our inner truth. (Also see Chapter 8.)

Our Cosmic Virtues
The Cosmic virtues we are born with are: our loyalty to our

inner truth, modesty, Innocence of mind, limitation, integrity, and caring. In combination they maintain our wholeness.

The first virtue is our *loyalty to our inner truth.* This loyalty keeps us connected with the Cosmos and its helping energies.

Our *modesty* is the result of the mind's acknowledging that we are an intrinsic part of the Cosmos, equal to every other part. We live in a positive symbiosis with the Cosmos when we recognize our dependence on it as the primary source of our furtherance, protection, sustenance, and general wellbeing. Then we take our true place in the Cosmic order along with all the other animals and life forms. Because modesty disarms the ego in others, it is our best source of protection and furtherance.

Innocence of mind is intimately connected with the first two Cosmic virtues. The mind remains innocent when it respects the virtues of modesty and loyalty to our inner truth. Then it does not self-importantly interfere with the harmonious ways of the Cosmos. Innocence is a neutral state of mind in which we keep tuned to our feelings of inner truth. This attunement allows us to be spontaneously drawn to what is in harmony with the Cosmos, and to retreat from engaging in what is disharmonious. The *I Ching* describes this state of mind as "not projecting and not expecting," meaning that we keep our mind in the present, rather than in the future or in the past.

The virtue of *limitation* comes to expression as an unwillingness to betray our dignity. When confronted with the ego in others, it is an unwillingness to accommodate ego behavior by excusing, tolerating, or going along with it. We inwardly reject it as unacceptable and withdraw from eye contact, while not making any demonstrative effort to impress the others. By withdrawing eye contact, we give the ego in them no energy. Limitation thus redefines our responsibility as humans.

The virtue of *caring* is also intrinsic to our nature. We know this by the natural inhibition we have to do harm, and also by our natural tendency to respond with help when it is needed, without forethought. True caring needs neither to be recognized nor rewarded by others, nor thought of as "heroism." True caring is not to be confounded with altruism, which is a conscious response to fulfill the noble belief that goodness is selfless. True caring is an involuntary response that is triggered by the necessity of the moment. An example is seeing a child run into the road and jumping up to bring him back.

It may be expected that we include *love* in this section. However, love is not a virtue, strictly speaking, because it flows to us as a gift from the Cosmos to unite us with others who are receptive and sensitive. (See Chapter 17, "What Is It That I Feel?")

None of these virtues come from intention; rather they arise spontaneously, without forethought, when others relate to us sincerely, and when our conditioning has not disabled them. They can function freely only within the limits set by our sense of appropriateness and dignity. It is important that our Cosmic virtues not be thrown away on the ego in others.

Our Supporting Personal Helpers and Our Talents

The personal Helper we first meet is the Sage, our inner teacher. Each person is born with a Sage that is available to teach him throughout his life.[4] The Sage uses a number of functions of our psyche to translate the knowledge contained in our inner truth into words our mind can understand. It also introduces us to all the other Helpers we need for given tasks.

Other personal Helpers are: the Helpers of Our Immune System, also called our Personal Army;[5] our Personal Helper that helps us fulfill our Cosmic destiny, as by arranging that we meet the people who will further us along this path, and by creating the helpful circumstances that enable us to develop our talents; also among our personal Helpers is our Feeling Manager that sends the messages needed to our various bodily systems, to keep them coordinated.

Our unique talents are also Helpers. They help us learn

---

4 The ancient cultures of the Mediterranean believed that every person is born with a "tutelary spirit" that accompanies him lifelong. Its name was "genie," root of the word "genius." The Sage confirmed that the Sage exists in the presence of each person lifelong. When the person is sincere and modest, the Sage resides within him. When the ego is in charge, the Sage retreats outside him and waits to be engaged, by the person's asking for its help.

5 Western medicine recognizes "Helper T-Cells," whose function is best illustrated by the illness that arises from their absence, AIDS.

languages and develop all kinds of skills, be they of an artistic, physical, technical, organizational, or intellectual nature. They are also important in helping us discover and invent new things and processes. The Sage made us aware that every person comes with certain talents that have been well developed in previous lives in a body. Child prodigies such as Mozart and Beethoven are examples.[6] Other talents are still in a beginning stage of development and want to progress further during the present lifetime. It is through the development of his unique talents that a person fulfills his Cosmic destiny while at the same time giving expression to his uniqueness.

The fact that so many people ask themselves about the meaning of their lives shows that many of their unique talents have either not been recognized or have been devalued. The social roles given to people are often so constricting that their true talents have no space to unfold. Fortunately, it is often during times of personal or collective crises that we discover these talents as the means that make recovery possible.

An example of the constricting nature of roles is that of the woman whose only purpose is defined as being a 'good mother.' Depending on her background, this definition may be so restrictive that her unique talents never get developed. The whole family suffers as a result. A man's role, too, can prevent him from developing his natural talents. Gender definitions serve only to protect and further feudal values. The constrictions apply to the people at the top no less than at the bottom. The result is conformity rather than a natural diversity. The unique talents of each individual that would benefit the whole are thus stymied. (Many men who have become notable for their achievements, such as Abraham Lincoln and Thomas Edison, credited their 'unusual mothers' for the encouragement and help they received in developing their talents.)

Being aware of our Cosmic possessions makes us appreciate our true nature, gives us self-respect, and leads us to respect the dignity inherent in all things.

---

6 The *I Ching* does not support the belief in *karma*, which proposes that we carry debt obligations into this life. We come with a clean slate.

Also part of our Cosmic possessions is our positive symbiotic relationship with Nature. When in harmony with ourselves, we receive Nature's chi energy, which gives us stamina and emotional strength. Speaking in terms of Helpers, this chi energy comes from the Helper of Nature. There are many other Helpers of Nature that carry out specific tasks, such as the Helpers of Water and Fire, and the Helpers of the multitudinous species of plants, animals, minerals, etc. We refer to all these Helpers as invisible. However, sometimes the Helpers choose to show themselves in digital photos. They always appear as round forms of light (also known as orbs.) According to the Sage, all the orbs in this photo show one and the same Helper: the Helper of Nature.

The Natural Urge to Express Our Uniqueness

Our true nature possesses great potentials and capabilities that for many have never been allowed to develop. Those potentials are contained in our original image. The desire to develop and express them remains with us throughout our lifetime. The great achievements of humans can be seen to come from this source, since the natural motivation to manifest our Cosmic gifts is the source of all creativity. This process is entirely different from the ego motive to achieve the acclaim of the world. As the ancient Chinese maxim put it, "The master potter leaves no trace (of himself)." He does the thing for its own sake.

History provides us with a bounty of evidence that when a person fulfills his potential by following his true inclinations, what he achieves for himself is also of benefit to everyone around him. Nicolaus Copernicus' fascination with astronomy and mathematics led him to discover that the earth revolved around the sun. Similarly, physicist David Bohm's desire to understand certain behaviors within the atom led to his theory that consciousness and matter are fundamentally related.[7] The spin-off of such achievements, though often held in doubt at the time, led to understandings of the Cosmos and of ourselves that have reverberated around the world in a multitude of positive ways.

The reader may, like us, have experienced that his own ability to express his uniqueness has been blocked. This happens because we are culturally conditioned to see ourselves as *permitted* (by some omniscient authority) to pursue only a limited number of occupations validated by our culture. We therefore do not imagine being able to pursue what comes natural to us. The Sage, nevertheless, shows that each of us has our own destiny to fulfill, and that when we follow our basic urge to fulfill it, we are supported and aided by the Cosmos that wants to express its creativity and desire to benefit the whole through us.

The Prerequisites to Fulfilling Our Cosmic Destiny

The first prerequisite is that we recognize that we have a unique Cosmic destiny to fulfill, one that is entirely positive and fulfilling in the true sense of that word. What we need to know about our particular Cosmic destiny is embedded in our inner truth. It is brought to our conscious awareness in many ways: through opportunities brought to us by the Helpers, and through sudden insights, dreams, or meditations. Sometimes, we receive a

---

7 See Bohm, David, *Wholeness and the Implicate Order*, Routledge and Kegan Paul., London, p. 262. Bohm was one of the founders of Quantum Theory.

vision of something that wants to be manifested through us, and then we are shown the way step-by-step if we follow our inner truth. While we are on this path, we are protected by the Cosmos even when we make a mistake. What counts is our sincere desire to fulfill our Cosmic destiny. Through respecting our Cosmic possessions, which give us our dignity, we remain connected with the Cosmos.

However, when we sacrifice our modesty and self-respect by striving for fame, we lose our Cosmic protection and support. The ultimate result is a fate that makes us lose the worldly possessions we have acquired outside the Cosmic harmony. Fate wakes us up so that we may return to the path of our Cosmic destiny. A hexagram in the *I Ching* describes this process as "To and fro goes the way. It furthers one to have somewhere to go."[8] "To have somewhere to go," means going within to learn the inner truth when we have lost our way. In this way, we reconnect with the help that is available to us to return to our true nature. Furthermore, we are helped to learn from our mistakes and to free ourselves from any Cosmic blame. We incur Cosmic blame when we go against our true nature, as by throwing away our dignity to get something, when we resort to using power, and when we acquiesce in or take part in disharmonious acts.

Our Existence is Validated by the Cosmos

By being shown our true nature, we realize that our existence is validated by the Cosmos and needs no further validation by society. The meaning of our lives is found through living in harmony with our true nature and expressing our uniqueness. Everything else of value, our happiness, and what we add to the lives of others, comes from that.

The idea that we must go in search of our life's 'purpose' denies our Cosmic origin, and the fact that the loving and caring Cosmos has provided our true nature with everything we need.

---

8 See Hexagram 24, *Returning*, The Judgment.

The Human Role in the Cosmic Plan

The Cosmic Plan is one of discovery and increase that accrues to the whole. Each individual human has an opportunity to take part in this plan through fulfilling his uniqueness. This is to say that fulfilling our uniqueness is an integral part of the Cosmic Plan. No talent in this plan is superfluous. Each life has the potential to add value and experience to it. Our negative experiences also add value to the whole if we process them and learn the lessons they contain.

The role given to humans in the Cosmic Plan is defined by the unique gifts they possess, with the gifts of verbal language and thinking being among them. These gifts are meant to be used to express our inner truth, as when we call things by names that reflect their true nature. Inventing slanderous names is a disrespect for that Cosmic gift. We will show later in this book that slanderous names prevent things from expressing their uniqueness. (See Chapter 10, "It All Comes Down to Language.")

Our Human Makeup

Our inner truth is our perfect Cosmic operating system adapted to living our life on Earth in harmony with the Cosmos. It allows us to know and to fulfill our Cosmic destiny. Our body, psyche, and mind are perfectly suited to this purpose. Each of these plays an equally important and unique role, with there being no hierarchical order between them.

The cells of our body, in addition to storing our 'library of inner truth,' possess their own consciousness, which is a *feeling*, rather than a thinking intelligence. The intelligence of the individual body cells is collected in the psyche as a *non-verbal bodily awareness.*[9] The mind, in this troika of body-mind-psyche,

---

9 The Wilhelm/Baynes *I Ching* refers to the body intelligence as "the inferiors." This, as we learned, is due to the fact that the intelligence of the body cells is held in a childlike state through not being recognized by the mind and thus not allowed to mature. Carol, in her meditations, saw them in various stages of development that mirrored her own self-development. See her book, *The Other Way, Meditation Experiences Based on the I Ching.*

needs to learn from the body's inherent knowledge, as well as from the experiences the body has as we live our lives. The body, for its part, learns from the observations of the mind. These observations are expressed in words that the body understands through the feelings the words evoke. The body is an expert interpreter of feelings.

The psyche is the meeting place for all the consciousnesses of the body and mind. Carol once saw this as similar to a large airport, where the various terminals feed into a center place where they meet and exchange information. The information from the mind comes in the form of thoughts and images. The information from the body consciousness comes in the form of feelings. The role of the psyche, as the meeting place, is to integrate and translate them into information the other understands. The feelings of the body are translated into words and images the mind can understand, while the impressions and conclusions of the mind are translated into feelings the body can understand. This translating function is one of the psyche's primary functions. Its importance lies in its processing, in the light of the Cosmic Principles of Harmony, the experiences each has had, and what each has learned from them. The processed material contributes toward the fulfillment of our Cosmic destiny.

Once the translating and processing functions are made inoperative through childhood conditioning, the Sage, our Cosmic Teacher, takes over their functions to prevent humans from destroying themselves mentally, psychologically, and physically.

That these functions can be interfered with indicates that we do not automatically remain whole during our lives. As we will explain in the next chapter, the first act that takes place in our childhood conditioning is the dividing of our wholeness, resulting in our being separated from our Cosmic source.

1. Four False Words
The Suppression of Our True Nature
Through Conditioning

In the previous chapter, we have shown that our true nature is complete in all respects: it fits perfectly into the harmonious order of the Cosmos, from which it receives the nourishment, support, and blessings needed to enable us as individuals to fulfill our Cosmic destiny. What then, we have to ask ourselves, causes us to fall out of this harmonious situation, and become alienated from our true nature and our Cosmic origin? The *I Ching* hints at the cause by stating how important it is that our words have substance; only then, it says, does our life have duration.[1]

For words to have substance they need to be based on our true feelings, which connect us with our inner truth/DNA.

The Purpose of the Gift of Language to Humans

We have mentioned in the previous chapter that the Cosmic gift of language to humans needs to be seen as part of the Cosmic Plan of Evolution. The role given to humans in this plan is to express Cosmic truth in words. When the words we use to name things express their true nature, the words give joy to the things being recognized and to us. Suffering and destruction result when we call things by names that slander their nature.

The frequent misuse of language proves that humankind is as yet inexperienced in the use of this wonderful gift. The misuse is not a crime as long as we are willing to learn from the negative consequences it produces and correct our use of language. Making mistakes in using a new gift is similar to a child's learning to walk, where clumsy moves and falling are part of the process. Learning to use language in such a way that it brings joy involves that we correct those words that cause harm and suffering. Our life on the Earth is a continuous lesson in finding the words that express Cosmic truths, and eliminating the use of words

1 See Hexagram 37, *The Family*.

that stray from what we know, in our deepest inner truth. The *I Ching* informs us that the Cosmos supports us in every way to learn these lessons. In fact, the *I Ching*, in its use as an oracle, is a gift from the Cosmos to communicate to us in words the feeling knowledge contained in our inner truth.

Once we learn about the abundance of the Cosmic possessions that make up our true nature, we realize the extent to which language has been misused to hide these possessions from us. Statements that make us believe we are born lacking and guilty, that life is a struggle, and that there is no help for us other than what we get from our families and society, are examples of the misleading language we grow up with. In the following, we will show how such language has deceived us about every aspect of our lives, simply through the invention of a few false words.

The False Words that Created the Collective Ego

We use the term 'collective ego' to refer to the body of mistaken ideas and beliefs of a given culture that have collected over centuries and been passed on to each new generation to create the individual ego in each of its members. These ideas and beliefs, which seem like a tree with many branches and leaves, have their origin in these few false seed words.

When we speak of *false words* we mean words that violate the Cosmic Principles of Harmony. We know this by the negative feeling they create in us. Words that create no deep inner resonance in us are inventions of a human mind that has turned away from inner truth, which is always expressed through feelings.

The word 'special'

As we learned from the Sage, the first step in separating our thinking from these feelings was made when the word 'special' was created to distinguish humans from the rest of Nature. Humans assumed this because they had the gift of verbal language, and the ability to think. The magnificence and arrogance that accompany the word special removed us from any further recognition of the gift-giver — the Cosmos, and from Nature. As we examine the other false words below, we will notice that this arrogant attitude created a delusional *parallel reality* that actually competes with the Cosmic reality. This parallel reality further separated humans from the Cosmos and the rest of Nature. Prior to this separation, humans were in a positive symbiosis with Nature and the invisible Cosmic Consciousness.

The word special violates the Cosmic Principles of Equality and Uniqueness of every aspect of the Cosmos. The difference between 'special' and 'unique' is one we can feel: while special creates a feeling of superiority, privilege, and 'being better than,' the word unique gives dignity to all things, and makes it clear that no thing is to be compared to another. The unique gifts that each thing possesses contribute to the myriad ways in which the Cosmic Consciousness expresses itself in the forms of Nature.

The word 'power'

The next false word, created as a result of humans separating themselves from the Cosmos and its myriad helping forces, was the word 'power.' The idea that power is needed to be success-ful in life needs to be seen as a coping mechanism for feelings of helplessness that resulted from this separation. The use of power then became connected with many other concepts such as hierarchy, security, dominance, and control, which serve as the mainstay principles behind conflict, which the collective ego uses as its main source of energy. The *I Ching* informs us that all use of power is contrary to the Cosmic Principles of Harmony, and therefore creates Fate. This fact is shown over and over in history. The Cosmic way of achieving things is solely through the principle of attraction. (See Hexagram 34, *Using Power.*)

The notions of special and power also became connected with the mind, making the mind the controller of the body.

The word 'evil'

The word 'evil' was invented to refer to anything that resisted being dominated. The word 'good' was then given a new mean-ing: it no longer referred to our true nature and to what is in harmony with the Cosmos, but to what is in conformity with the system of human domination and superiority.

The words 'guilt'/'culprit'

The word 'guilt' was invented by the collective ego to brand our animal nature so as to isolate our conscious mind from our true self. It did so because our true self, being connected with our inner truth, knows that the hierarchical order erected by the collective ego is untrue and pretentious, and that conforming to it suppresses our basic desire to fulfill our Cosmic destiny. By painting our animal nature in such terms, the collective ego has been able to hide itself as the cause of our deviating from our true nature.

As a result of these slanders and language tricks, we have developed the dread of becoming guilty, which is actually the dread of being merely who we are. This dread is caused by guilt being defined as an inextinguishable stain on our nature. This idea is the opposite of the Cosmic Principle of Blame: Cosmic blame is incurred when we go against our true nature. It is extinguished when we recognize our mistake and feel remorse. The Cosmos provides our true nature with the means to correct our thinking through learning from our mistakes. There is no need to be stuck forever, or at all, from making a mistake which is meant to be a learning experience.

The idea of being guilty for being who we truly are has proven to be extremely effective in suppressing our true nature. The threat of becoming guilty if we desire to return to our true nature maintains the collective ego's control over us. However, this threat is effective only as long as we accept these untruths. The pressure of the collective to negate what we feel to be true is reinforced by the threat of being abandoned by society if we do not conform to its values.

The word 'culprit' defines the person or thing onto which the guilt is projected. It is also combined with a number of threats: being permanently cast as the lowest in the hierarchy; being restricted in opportunities; being hounded by detractors; being watched by the keepers of the collective order, and being held in a state of permanent suspicion.

The Creation of a Hierarchical Social Order

It is a curious fact that once humans as a species had defined themselves as special, some humans defined themselves as more special than others. This led to the hierarchical structuring of society that is inextricably connected with dominance on the high end, and subservience on the low end. Because inequality created conflict, the control of some over the others became justified by the argument that this system created order and peace. As may be seen, the invention of the word special provided the basis for the development of a false social order, which then, with other false words and explanations added, became the autonomous, self-protecting, self-perpetuating mindset we see as the collective ego.

The prevalence of this mindset has made people assume that the collective ego is a natural ordering factor. However, the creation of hierarchical systems began relatively late in human history as the result of one clan seeking to dominate another. These systems eventually grew in number until they dominated the Earth. Although emperors and kings have decreased in numbers more recently, the structuring of today's oligarchies and democracies is nevertheless hierarchical. The titles have changed, but we see hierarchical structures all around us: in our schools, colleges, the judicial system, and corporations as well as in cultural, religious, scientific, and social institutions.

How These Four Words Affect the Individual

It is to be noted that words such as special automatically create their opposite — not special. This is highly relevant because the idea of being not special introduced the original doubt in the wholeness and goodness of our true nature. This self-doubt has been plaguing mankind ever since. It is so prevalent in the language that the psyche of every individual absorbs it at a very young age with the consequence that we all believe that "in and of ourselves, we are not special enough." As a result, we grow up with the idea that we are not smart or brilliant enough, not socially important or rich enough, etc. Our childhood conditioning causes us to look to the world to see whether we are seen as special, and to derive our worth from being recognized by others. Underneath is the constant anxiety that we may be a 'nobody' after all.

We are made to believe, through our conditioning, that the only way out of this negative view of ourselves is to turn over to the mind the job of finding something that would make us special. Lacking guidance from our inner truth, the mind is put to the task to realize a goal that never existed before the invention of the word special. Since that word has no substance, the goal is, in fact, an illusion. Pursuing an illusion inevitably leads to a failure of will to continue. This failure may manifest in illness, be it physical, mental, or emotional, or a combination of them. The failure may be expressed in a collapse of will, or in a rebellion against the system that promotes the idea that we need to become special. Because we are conditioned to believe in the superiority of the mind, we do not look to the misuse of language as the possible cause of this failure of will.

The failure is due to the mind's having been given the job of running our personality, a job it is unable to fulfill and was never meant to fulfill. Through being elevated over the body, the mind has been isolated from its greatest resources that lie in the body's knowledge; moreover, this arrogance causes a tremendous inner conflict and resistance in the body in the form of anger at the mind's domination. However, through our fear of being judged guilty by the collective ego, this anger energy is quickly repressed into a chamber in the psyche, where it becomes used by the ego to fuel its ambitions.

If we take a deeper look at the expression, 'not being special enough,' we notice that 'enough' is not quantified. How much is enough when we measure ourselves against an undefined standard of perfection? And, we must ask, "enough of what?" Because of its lack of definition, the abstract standard becomes a carrot on a stick that can never be reached. Indeed, these are the tricks the collective ego uses to keep us in a state of constant striving. Thus, we can never be a good enough parent, child, teacher, employee, etc.

Moreover, this lack of a defined measure leaves the body with a permanent anxiety, because the body hears words differently from the mind. The image of not being enough creates a hole in the center of our being that gives our body the feeling of hopelessness The mind, on hearing the same words, takes them as a challenge to imagine how we can become "special enough."

The 'hole of insufficiency' is felt either in the center of the chest or just under the navel. That hole reminds us constantly of our insufficiency and becomes the driving force to 'become something.' It drives some people to perfect their mind through obtaining knowledge; it drives others who have no hope of becoming special to engage in diversions, or to assuage their feelings of inadequacy by taking substances, such as prescription drugs, alcohol or other drugs. A fundamental cause of addiction is this hole of insufficiency, which can only be filled from within by the person's freeing himself from the false words that have created it: "In and of yourself you are not special/good enough." In order to supply the collective ego with the energy it needs to exist, a duplicate of its mindset is installed in the individual person through conditioning that begins at the earliest possible age. This mindset has the purpose to replace the individual's inner truth. We will be referring to this offshoot of the collective ego as the individual ego.

The Quest to Become Special

As the above shows, the mindset of the individual ego is one that demands our striving to be special enough. Circling around the question of who will be better, the striving to be special enough requires a constant measuring of our position in relation to others, and creates a mindset based on conflict and competition. On the surface it would seem that the collective ego has set rules and regulations that ensure that the competition is carried out fairly. However, this is a question of appearances only. Fairness is not in the nature of the collective ego.

To support and justify its incessant conflicts, the collective ego has created an encyclopedia of myths over many centuries concerning human nature, the nature of the Cosmos, and the human place in it. The first example is the myth of the 'hero.'

The hero is one who fights on the side of the good, with 'good' meaning what defends the collective ego. Since ancient times, the activity of fighting has been inextricably connected with the word hero and the glorious image that accompanies it. The notion of fighting also extends to sports contests, where the winner is considered 'superior.' In war, the fight is generally against whatever is defined as evil, be it another clan, race, religion, nation, or foreign culture. The highest honors for heroism are generally given to those who risk their lives to free the social structure from the perceived evil. People who seek glorification as a hero need to have something to fight. Thus they are constantly on the lookout for something they can call an enemy.

The paranoia created by this mindset leads directly to war. An example is the military buildup that occurs when potential enemies imagine each other to have gained a military advantage. The paranoia can be stoked by the desire to gain money from the business of war, or to force the beliefs of one culture on another by claiming them to be superior.

In the mind's quest to be the 'pure' hero, it has likewise demonized our human animal nature. The inner conflict this creates is so unbearable to our true nature that we feel compelled to throw off the supposed evil onto others whom we then are to fight. This fuels the drive to fight the evil 'out there.' This process is supported by the desire to be seen as 'good' in the eyes of the collective. The importance of being seen as special and good in the eyes of others causes us to adopt a self-image that reflects these qualities.

The Long Term Effect of the Four Words

Through the use of these four words, the collective ego has been able to maintain itself over the generations. This is because the words psychically intimidate each generation into passing its values onto the next. The words inspire fear in the parents that if they do not bring up their children 'right,' they will fail as parents, and their children will not succeed in life.

What most characterizes the mindset of the collective ego is its human-centered quality. To uphold the view that everything revolves around humans, the whole Cosmos, including our true nature has been redefined in words that deceive us about who we are, what our true place in the Cosmos is, and what it means

to live in harmony with the Cosmos. As noted, despite its appearance of being all-powerful, the collective ego has no energy
in and of itself. It gets all its energy from the belief people have
invested in its false words and concepts, and from the constant
conflicts it creates.

The fact that we experience peace and harmony when we are
in touch with our true nature makes us aware that none of the
claims of the collective ego are true. Renouncing the validity of
these four words and the false reality they have created, reconnects us with our true nature. Following this course keeps us in
touch with Cosmic help and protection, and causes the collective
ego to lose its control.

5. The Emperor and His Feudal Lords
The Development of the Individual Ego

We have seen that the collective ego owes its existence entirely to the invention of a few false words. With these words it has caused humans to create a social order that is not only outside the Cosmic order, it has set itself up in competition with it. Because the Cosmos does not entertain any relationship with what is harmful to its harmonious order, the collective ego is shut off from the Cosmic flow of energy. To succeed, it must get its energy supply from the individuals who invest in and uphold the ideas on which it is built.

How does the collective ego get people to invest in its ideas? It uses precisely the same false words and ideas that created its hierarchical system, to intimidate our true self while it is still too young to resist. This intimidation causes our true self to step aside and allow the collective ego's 'child,' to grow up in its place. This child is the individual ego.

The Installation of the Language Program of the Collective Ego in the Child

The takeover of our true nature by the collective ego begins when the *fundamental doubt in our intrinsic worth and wholeness* is installed in our psyche. This doubt is the result of the implied statement, "in and of yourself you are not special enough." This doubt is not achieved by an actual verbal repetition of these words; rather, it is a barely conscious conclusion the young child comes to after the sense has been created in him that he needs to 'become something,' to gain the love or approval of his parents. Only much later in life may he realize that for this time he has had this doubt of not being special enough to be loved for himself alone.

Once parents begin to *train* their children (at around four months), the giving and withholding of approval is generally used as the primary tool. So long as this training is directed to *things we do*, even as children we understand and cooperate. When, however, the approval/disapproval becomes mixed with *who we are* (as when we, rather than our acts are approved/disapproved of), doubt in our intrinsic worth and wholeness is established. Parents think they need to prepare their children to live in what they call "the real world." Usually, they are not aware that they are passing on to their children via language the mistaken ideas and false values they had themselves been brought up with. That the child simply be himself is not enough. He must *become* this or that kind of person, and for this goal to be successfully achieved, the child is given rules of conduct that tell him what he *should* or *must* think, do, and feel. Conflicted about whether to follow his true feelings or give in to the pressure put on him by parents and peers, he begins to suppress his true feelings in order to be accepted in the world.

The Pressure to Become Something Better than We Are

Because it is counter to the child's nature to develop self-images, he conforms at first by pretending that he is the image his parents and peers approve of. He behaves *as if* the image and he are one and the same. This pretending goes on for a long time while his parents and peers keep a close watch to make sure he does not depart from that image. Over time, he forgets he is pretending and begins to believe that he *is* what he has been pretending to be. On forgetting who he really is, his true nature becomes submerged in resignation; the self-image then takes over and begins to speak as "I" in the personality. This false self that has taken over, is the individual ego.

Alongside this training, the concepts of good, evil, and guilt are introduced. Good is introduced in a purified form as an ideal. But even as children acquiring experience of how good and evil are applied, we recognize that they sometimes contradict our natural morality. This leads to an inner confusion we are unable to resolve given our young age. The result is that we suppress the inner conflict in the attempt to conform to what is accepted by those we look up to. When we see some events connected with the words 'evil' and 'guilt' evoking harsh responses in our parents, teachers, and society, the fear of being evil or becoming guilty puts us on the lookout for anything in ourselves that could provoke such judgments. The use of these words makes us doubt the goodness of our nature and divides us within.

And when the king asked, "Colombin, what do you want to become?" Colombin replied, "I don't want to become anything. I am already something, I am Colombin."

Losing Our Sense of Who We Are

As we grow up in the world of the collective ego, we soon see that the ideals we were given as children in order to become good enough or special enough are not applied evenly. For example, we see how people around us praise as good and special others who have attained position, power, and wealth, while at the same time criticizing their lack of scruples, or envying them for getting away with behavior that does not fit those ideals. In such cases, we experience their ideals as contradictory. We also see how our mentors sometimes fault someone for too rigidly following the ideals they have preached, by saying that such a person is "being too good" or "too idealistic." They may even add, "You need to take some things (meaning the ideas they have preached) with a grain of salt." Confusion is the result. If this confusion is not processed in the light of our inner truth, we can start on the road to losing ourselves, either by following that fake morality, or by throwing morality (including our natural morality) out the window altogether. This can lead to the outright cynicism that is behind greed, lust, and totally selfish behavior.

The road that leads to the loss of self begins when that child of the collective ego is installed in us. It begins in two ways: by cultivating the idea in us that we are special and better than others, and by implying directly or indirectly that we are less special than others. Even though we may be told that we are special, doubts occur when we experience that some brothers, sisters, cousins, and neighbors are given privileges that make us feel they are more special than we are. Children who are born not as good looking as others, or with a physical characteristic that is irregular, get the feeling right away that they are not only not equal with others, they feel they can *never* be equal with them. The use of the word special creates psychological havoc because it has no Cosmic basis. No one is special. Everyone is unique.

The idea that we are not special enough or good enough negates the inner knowledge we possess from our Cosmic origin about the equality of all things in the Cosmos, and that our nature is intrinsically good. The word special not only creates endless fantasies either of superiority and privilege, or of inequality and insufficiency; these ideas in turn create a world of conflict. Many disturbances in human behavior arise from these primary doubts in our intrinsic goodness and wholeness.

The havoc created in the psyche when we take in a concept that has no Cosmic basis is this: the false concept contradicts and dumbfounds us in the face of our inner truth about that particular matter. The effect is to silence our inner truth out of the fear of being found guilty for not conforming. Through shutting off our inner truth by an increasing number of false concepts, the ego gains more and more control over our personality.

The doubts we develop about our intrinsic worth cause us to have the fear of being seen as a nobody, or as outside our cultural group. This leads to a drive to be validated by the collective ego that we are somebody. These self-doubts also propel us to want to be seen as free of guilt. During our teenage years, we are driven by these internalized self-doubts to fulfill the idealized image of the hero, either to leave the world a better place, or to save others, Nature, or the country, or our particular group, from an evil. All models of what defines the hero are given us by the collective to which we belong, which also ultimately approves of whether we have fulfilled that definition. As we enter adulthood, we adopt roles from our group's collection of accepted roles: the good father, mother, citizen, wife, etc. It escapes us, in all this striving, that all roles and self-images are fictions that have been planted in our imagination. It escapes us, as well, that by living simply, and in accord with our personal inner truth, all the virtues we possess would be expressed, not because we want to *be* someone, but because they are an expression of our true nature.

The Way the Ego Operates in the Psyche

The self-images that make up the individual ego are successful in dominating the psyche and suppressing the natural leader of our personality (our true self), so long as we heartily invest in them. This entails that we play the social games that the collective ego has tricked us into believing are necessary. The reward consists in being recognized by the others in the system as virtuous, good, selfless, dependable, responsible, and hard working. At all times, however, this reward is tenuous, and held like the carrot on a stick, just out of reach. The winning of the big rewards requires big effort (in the sense of suppressing our true nature), and holding onto the success is always on the condition that we keep up the self-image, regardless of circumstances. In the long run, the circumstances become untenable, because trying to keep up a fraud that is against our true nature exhausts our life energy. By contrast, our life energy is constantly renewed when we remain true to our nature.

When we begin to realize that trying to fulfill a self-image has led us on a wrong path, the same rationales that were used to get us to adopt the self-image begin to replay in our psyche. They reiterate all the reasons why we needed the self-image in the first place, why we are totally dependent on society for all our needs, and therefore why we must conform to its demands.

The Stealing of Our Cosmic Possessions

As part of the conditioning that develops the ego, every one of our Cosmic possessions gets stolen from our true nature.

For example, the collective ego turns our loyalty to our inner truth into loyalty to *its* values. It turns our natural caring into a command to be caring, regardless of whether it is appropriate. The collective ego declares we do not possess any virtues to start with. By telling us that we have to 'develop character' to overcome our supposed defects, we are made to cultivate abstract virtues that are based on rule and are therefore contrary to our true nature.

This stealing of our Cosmic possessions is carried out through the creation of untruths in the form of words, phrases, and images. The first untruth, as we mentioned, proclaims, "In and of yourself you are not special enough." Another tells us that "your nature is divided into good and evil," and that "to overcome your deficiency, you need to develop virtues." All these untruths establish the ego as the leader of our personality at the expense of our true self. The process begins with *doubts* that are thrust upon our true nature: (a) that it is whole, (b) that our existence is validated by the Cosmos, and (c) that our true self is capable of being the leader of our personality.

The creation of these self-doubts is accompanied by the threat that if we do not strive to become accepted by society, we run the risk of being abandoned by it. This threat obscures the fact that in following our inner truth we are supported by the entire Cosmos. The collective ego makes every effort to keep us from recognizing that Cosmic help and protection is available to us.

Our True Self

Our *true self* is that sense of self that gives expression to our *true nature* through our true feelings. Were it not for the ego's taking over the rule of the personality, the true self would be its natural leader and speak in the center of consciousness as "I." In this natural state, the center of consciousness is in the psyche, where it receives input equally from the feeling consciousness of the body and the thinking consciousness of the mind. In this state, the true self feels what is appropriate to do and what is not, and the mind carries it out. However, because the true self depends on our true feelings and holds to our inner truth, the ego does all it can to suppress it, in its effort to take over the center of consciousness. When it succeeds in its efforts, through flattering the mind that it is the correct leader of the personality, the center of consciousness is moved to the thinking mind, which the ego can more easily control.

Once as children we give up on the possibility of being able to express our true feelings, our true self, along with our feeling consciousness, becomes suppressed into a dungeon the ego creates in our psyche. This dungeon is called the "subconscious." Without the ego's repression of our true self, the subconscious would not exist. The memories of the punishments and rewards that were used to suppress our true self are stored there in demonic forms, where they act as guardians of the dungeon. The fears and traumas associated with the punishments are recalled in the back-of-the-mind whenever our true self seeks to leave the dungeon to express our true feelings. The purpose of the fears is to keep us in a state of hopelessness about ourselves.

This subconscious self-doubt and hopelessness constantly drain our life force, which the ego then uses to keep itself energized. To keep us unaware of our feelings of hopelessness, the ego keeps us engaged in diversions of all kinds that take on an addictive quality, whether the addiction be to our work, to fulfilling ego-inspired ambitions, or to substances.

The ultimate "problem," for the ego, is that it is made up of self-images. However much we strive to make these images real, they can never be more than mere images. All such striving, therefore, must fail. It is this final failure and the exhaustion of our life force that brings us to the state of burnout.

Burnout

The fact that self-images can never be real escapes our notice while we are investing our life energy in them. Our true self knows this, but its voice is not heard because the repeated rationales that accompany the self-images keep us believing we can fulfill them. The turning point comes when the promises accompanying the self-images turn out to be empty. Burnout occurs when our hopes are dashed, and the life energy we have dedicated to them is exhausted.

One reason we took the self-images to be real for so long is that those around us encouraged our investing in them by giving us recognition. Egos have a mutual interest in supporting each other. Mutual recognition makes the self-deception more believable. Hanna's burnout in doing this came when the energy she had invested in the self-image of the supportive wife was completely exhausted. Burnout came for Carol when the charade of unity she thought existed in her marriage suddenly evaporated. The image of herself as the one who could endure more than anyone else evaporated along with it.

The crash of these self-images, and the shock that accompanied it, is typical for those of us, who at mid-life, begin to see our lives as limited in years. Looming is the realization, even when we have made a lot of money or achieved fame, that we have not fulfilled the most important thing in ourselves. We begin to reassess what we have believed to be true. From the *I Ching* point of view, this is a very valuable time because it offers the opportunity to make a new beginning.

If, at this time, we allow ourselves to be led by the Sage, we gain the Cosmic help we need. We are shown that we, as humans, were not born with the fundamental faults and lacks we were told we had, that our true nature is not tainted with guilt, that our mind is not superior to our body, and that our body is not a vehicle for some abstract purpose. Furthermore, if we are open to it, we find a marvelous help that is available from the Cosmos that we previously did not recognize was there.

At this lowest point in the ego's control, the true self begins to emerge from its dungeon. However, we find that it has remained in the undeveloped state of a very small child. The reason for this is that our feeling sense of self has been discredited by the ego as having no worth, as being unreliable, and as dangerous to follow. Now, with every mistaken idea that we remove from our true nature, our true self gradually gains strength and trust in its natural abilities. In this process of freeing ourselves, we first need to remove any images of insufficiency of self before taking away the self-images that were adopted to "protect us" from our supposed insufficiencies. If we do not observe this order, there is the danger that psychologically, we will once again fall into the sense of feeling we are 'nobody.' Then we can hear the ego say, "life no longer has any purpose." In effect, the ego is the voice that tells us, "If I can't have it my way, life is not worth living." Thoughts of this kind are given weight because of the great investment we have made in trying to become something of worth.

Or, the ego can also take another tack and say, "having now failed in my purpose, I will flaunt society. To hell with it!" This would initiate a new self-image — that of the rebel. Although the rebel may believe he is placing himself outside the system, he actually fulfills a role *within* the system by giving it his energy. This is the case, whether his rebellion consists in a self-destructive withdrawal, or an outright fight against the system.

The ego can also attempt to regain control through putting all the blame for the "failures" it has created onto the true self. The self-chastisement in which the ego engages opens us up to other ego offers "to help" that have been waiting in the wings. They come in the form of new self-images and socially accepted "paths of self-development." They present us with an upgraded ego-program that gives us new hopes of success. One of the most popular and seductive self-images is that of the "spiritual person" who follows a well-trodden spiritual path. These paths, like all those offered by the collective ego, further delay our facing and conquering our self-doubt by giving us *group acceptance* and the promise of salvation and wholeness.

If we can avoid the temptations contained in these offers during this difficult time, we will draw the help of the Sage to make a new beginning: one that allows us to free our true self from the tyranny of the ego and its implicit demand that for whatever we do, we must have some kind of group approval.

The Emperor and His Feudal Lords

To put things in perspective, we can picture the collective ego as the emperor in a feudal system. The individual ego is its subservient feudal lord (or deputy) on whom the emperor relies to extract from the common people the tolls and taxes that go to the emperor. The collective ego is that body of established values, rules, and regulations that the individual ego applies to rule our personalities. The individual ego can speak in the psyche on behalf of the emperor and its system of values by using the royal "we," as in, "we must do things this way." Why do we make this distinction? In freeing ourselves from the false words, mistaken ideas, self-images, etc., we deconstruct the individual ego as the deputy of the collective ego. It is the inner oppressor. In order to carry out this deconstruction (through a method we call "deprogramming") we need to catch on to its strategies, which it has customized to fit our personal circumstances. By rejecting the acceptance we formerly gave to its words and phrases, we deconstruct the mindset, or mental program it has created to oppress us. In doing so, we also take away the control the collective ego has amassed over us.

6. The Wanderer's Journey
The Desire to Know Ourselves

Sooner or later the values we have adopted from the collective ego to make us successful in life lead to a burnout, because they have no substance. By this time, our true self has become "the stranger within." We no longer know who we are, but the shock of the fate has connected us with that which has substance inside us. We may now feel a strong desire to understand what went wrong, and what it is that would truly give us the sense of fulfillment that has been lacking in the past. This desire is the starting point for our inner journey.

The *I Ching* uses the metaphor of the "wanderer" to describe the inner journey our mind makes in search of our true self. This search is a journey into our own psyche, where every positive experience and every trauma has been stored, and from where every unprocessed event is still actively influencing our life.

On this journey, the mind revisits the events that have separated us from the three positive symbiotic relationships that make up our wholeness: our relationship with the Cosmos, with Nature around us, and that between our mind and body. In the following we will give a brief overview of the psyche, the inner realm in which our journey is to take place. Furthermore, we will introduce the reader to the Sage as the mind's guide on this journey, and discuss some of the myths that have been spun around it.

A Brief Description of the Psyche

The psyche, where this journey takes place, is the invisible side of our being, while the body is its visible side. Both are indivisible elements that together form our wholeness. The psyche has no specific location in the body.

As described in Chapter 3, under "Our Human Makeup," our psyche can be envisioned as the 'meeting place' for all the kinds of consciousness we possess. These include the thinking and imaging consciousnesses of our mind, and the feeling consciousness of every body cell.

The psyche can also be compared to the weft of a carpet into which all our positive and negative experiences, and the conclusions we have drawn from them, are woven. The carpet is a metaphor for the unique Cosmic destiny we are born to fulfill. That destiny is a kind of inner wish we possess from before birth, to express our inner truth, which is a combination of what we know from our DNA, and the talents and capabilities that want to be further developed in us. The carpet gets woven as we live our lives. When our lives are an expression of our Cosmic destiny, the carpet takes on a beautiful design. Although the psyche includes the consciousnesses of the mind, the psyche itself does not think. Rather, it acts as a sort of library in the background of awareness that contains all we have ever learned, all that we know intrinsically, and all we have ever experienced.

Unlike the mind, which relates to events in terms of *time*, the consciousness of the psyche is timeless. While the mind mostly concerns the present, it anticipates the future, and can become dominated by certain things in the past. Other thoughts and experiences fade gradually into oblivion. In the psyche, however, *everything* we have experienced and the conclusions we have drawn about events, remain present and active. If an event or thought has had a beneficial effect, that effect is sustained over our whole lifetime. If the event or thought has been destructive, that effect is likewise sustained. It remains like a splotch on the carpet, until we have brought it into our conscious mind and processed it with Cosmic help. (See Chapter 20: "Processing.")

Once created, these splotches interfere with the weaving. Unprocessed memories of negative events influence us subconsciously. They distort our natural responses to events, and even, at times, actively re-create versions of those original circumstances. We call these splotches "memory chips" because they contain the memory and emotions that accompanied the specific traumatic or shocking events, as well as conclusions such as, "I will never do such and such again," or "I will always do such and such if that occurs again." All conclusions are unprocessed reactions that generalize the event in order to shut it off from further consideration. Because the events are not processed in a Cosmic light, they remain stored in the psyche in a condensed form, where they constitute a "mini-program" that reacts automatically on cue. When the same event is also stored in the body cells, we speak of it as a "microchip." (See Chapter 18, "Harmful Microprocessors.")

We experienced an example of both these chips being the cause of a man's face flushing and his breaking out into sweat whenever he was in the company of people he regarded as socially superior. Behind his bodily reaction was the shame he felt as a child when his alcoholic father's behavior was mentioned in front of the whole class in school. These memory and microchips replayed when during his adult years he had contacts with people he regarded as socially higher. In effect, he was still afraid of being publicly shamed for something over which he had no control, even though he tried vigorously to rationalize the problem away. Deprogramming these chips freed him from these involuntary reactions.

When our negative childhood (or later) experiences are not processed in a healthy manner, they remain stored as these chips in the psyche and/or body. They inhibit our ability to grow and mature socially. Observers often attribute such aberrations to a defect in our nature. They will say, "you need to overcome that," without knowing that so long as these mini-programs exist, they operate mechanically and involuntarily. As a result, it is impossible for us to change our behavior by force of will.

The Main Functions of the Psyche

The primary function of the psyche is to help us fulfill our Cosmic destiny. The completion of this destiny is expressed in the carpet's beauty and unique Cosmic design. A number of functions of the psyche cooperate to serve this purpose. One of them is the transmitting function that perfectly illustrates how the psyche acts as a meeting place for the different kinds of consciousness. This function does the following:

- It transmits information coming from the body to the mind. This information comes in the form of bodily perceptions of events. These perceptions are *feelings* that are then translated by the Sage into words and insightful images. For the mind to benefit from them, however, it must be open and receptive.
- It transmits thoughts and images coming from the mind to the body. When these are harmonious, the body consciousness is helped to mature. When they are disharmonious (in conflict with the inner truth/DNA of the body cells), the body consciousness is injured, consequently the body becomes ill.
- It transmits the information coming from our inner truth to the mind so that we can fulfill our unique Cosmic destiny. This destiny is imprinted in seed-form in our inner truth and wants to unfold in our life. The question, "what are we here for?" or, "what is the meaning of my life?" indicates that we have lost connection with our inner knowledge that we have a Cosmic destiny to fulfill. We can regain this connection with the Sage's help.[1]

The Sage's Functions in the Psyche

When the Sage is engaged, it coordinates all the various functions of the psyche so that it operates as a harmonious whole. When this happens, we feel nourished and at peace due to the unimpeded flow of *chi* energy coming from our inner truth, which manifests in the psyche as *psychic energy*. The totality of our psychic energy is called our *will*. When our will is attuned to our inner truth, it is nourished and supported by this psychic energy, and can use that energy to move us forward on the path of our Cosmic destiny.

The Sage also uses the receptive function of the psyche to transmit messages from the Cosmos to our mind in the form of *insight-flashes*. This helpful function is activated only when we have a sincere desire to get to know ourselves and when we

---

1 The Sage is more directly connected with the psyche than with the mind because the Sage is a feeling consciousness.

wish to acquire Cosmic understanding.

(A more detailed description of the various functions of the psyche is given in Chapter 8.)

The Beginning Point of Our Inner Journey

Prior to beginning our inner journey as wanderers, our intellect has mainly been in the service of the ego. The beginning point of our inner journey is the dead end to which all ego-paths lead — the misfortune, or fate we are experiencing: our marriage or relationship has failed; an important goal has turned out to be an illusion; we are caught up in a catastrophe affecting the place where we live; we have lost our job, suffered a financial disaster, or someone on whom we were dependent has died or been killed, or we have had an accident or become seriously ill.

In these misfortunes we have hit the wall of Fate. The shock of Fate temporarily defeats the intransigence and super-confidence of the ego, making it possible for the Sage to communicate with our conscious mind. The shock has temporarily knocked the ego unconscious. Sometimes the shock also breaks the 'spell' that has led to the fate. What we mean by spell is a mistaken idea or belief that we have in one way or another agreed to, that contradicts our true nature, and has therefore blocked some function of our psyche. This blockage has led to the roadblock we are now facing. A self-image to which we have been attached, whether it is a grandiose or a self-deprecating one, can have the same effect of blocking a function of our psyche. This is because, through adopting self-images, we deny and put aside our true nature.

At the point of crisis, we do not yet know that the Sage exists; we only feel the deep need for help. The *I Ching* describes how the Sage comes to help: "A jug of wine, a bowl of rice with it; earthen vessels simply handed in through the window."[2] This help can come in many unexpected forms. Whether we take advantage of this help depends upon many factors, the most important being a deep sincerity in our desire to understand

---

2 Hexagram 29, *The Abyss*, Line 4.

our predicament.[3]

If we keep open, the Sage makes us aware that there is a life raft at hand, if we will only reach for it. This life raft can be a memory of having been helped in an unexpected way, or it can come in the form of the *I Ching*, as was the case for us, Carol and Hanna. The immediate effect was that we felt lifted out of the pit of hopelessness by *seeing possibility*. Our true self, at that moment, for the first time in a long while, was being made aware that it had the Cosmic support and help it needed to lead the personality.

Unfortunately, the ego does not remain unconscious for long. On regaining consciousness, it may be heard to say to the true self, which is now at the helm of consciousness, "You will be all alone on this path," and "You will become guilty for turning away from the time-honored values of society." Other objections coming from family and friends may imply: "Who are you to be different from the rest of us?" "That's a crazy path...It's uncharted, it's untried." "People get lost when they go alone." "How do you know you will get help?" "It'll never get you anywhere." "You ought to turn back." "Let your friends and family help you." "You need to make provisions for the future."

In the face of a fate, the ego makes the argument that we have only two choices: to either passively accept the fate or to actively fight it. The image it uses is that of a crossroad, where, it asserts, if we take the wrong road we will experience yet another shock. We scarcely notice that all these threats are based on falsehoods that hide *the third way* from our view, which is the Cosmic way.

With the Sage as our guide, there is no wrong path; furthermore, we are not all alone; as for guilt, that is a false concept invented by the collective ego to keep us within its domain. To further keep us from continuing on our path as wanderers, another guardian element of the ego suggests that our true path is "where everyone else has found it," pointing to the well-trodden paths followed by other 'seekers.' It replays the common doubt, "You are not equipped to go on such a journey alone."

---

3 It is interesting that the Chinese ideogram for misfortune has the second meaning of opportunity.

Even though we may decide to follow the path of our inner truth, the ego-mindset accompanies us for some time, attempting at every opportunity to pull us back into its world, either through flattery, intimidation, or through injecting a litany of doubts. Whenever we succumb to these attempts, the falseness of the ego's mistaken views is ultimately revealed through the fates they create. These new shocks give us further opportunities to correct our relationship with our true self, and thereby, with all the Cosmic help that is available to us. Over time, we become aware that the Cosmos, through its Helpers, sends us early warning signs that precede these fates. If we heed them in time and correct our thinking and our attitude, we avoid their consequences. In this way we learn that the ego-saying, "You can only learn the hard way," is a half-truth. It is a half-truth because while we can learn through difficulties, we can also learn in joyful and easy ways. Any conviction that learning must be 'hard' makes it so.

Carol experienced the beginning of her inner journey through a series of meditations. In the first, she felt herself falling into an endless abyss. This produced such a shock and fear that she ended the meditation. A second meditation having to do with this fall occurred some months later when she was more prepared through a dream to trust the process. In the meditation, she again experienced falling, only to discover that the fall ended quickly: she had fallen into a dry well only twenty-five feet deep. The only thing in the well was a lizard.[4] She could see the sun crossing the sky, and light entering the pit when the sun reached its peak above her. Thus the light came and went quickly. She wondered how she might ever get out, as the walls, which were lined with stone, appeared in the dim light to be slippery. Two or three months later in another meditation, she saw herself again in the well, but this time she was about half-way up with her feet braced against the walls. Several months later, she saw herself climbing out of the well. It was clear to her that this could have occurred only with the help of the Sage, speaking through

---

4 The lizard/chameleon, Carol later realized, was the early ideogram for the "I" in the name *I Ching,* representing transformation as a form of "easy changeability."

the I Ching. Looking about in the dawn glow, she could see the dark rims of hundreds of other pits into which she could have fallen. At the edge of the particular well into which she had fallen was a lantern that had not been lit. She suddenly realized that she had been crossing this plain of pitfalls without having lit the lantern. The lantern, she later learned, was an ability she possessed that could only be lit by the Sage. The dawn, which was just beginning, showed her that her path was leading out of this plain of pitfalls.

As mentioned, it is one of the tactics of the ego to make us believe that we are on this inner journey alone, without any guidance. This meditation made Carol aware that this is not true. She only needed to recognize the presence of the Sage for that lantern to be lit and available to her. The Sage, through such experiences, can reveal to us many other capabilities we have not realized we possess.

With the Sage as our companion on this journey, we are helped to free ourselves, step by step, from the numerous false beliefs that make up the ego. Among these is the mistaken belief in a higher power. The Cosmos does not want to be viewed as a higher power, nor does the Sage. We are made to realize that we are not meant to be subservient in our relationship with the Sage; the Sage wants us to see it as a consciousness, and a friend. We are not meant to pray, bow in craven obeisance, promise anything, or perform sacrifices and rituals in the hope of gaining the favors of a higher power. These acts of submission are carried over from our ancestors' experience of being subjugated to a human monarch. Within this hierarchical setup, they were trained to see themselves as insignificant, and even owned by their feudal masters. This long habit of compliance was passed on to us as the "natural order both on earth and in heaven."

The equality of every aspect of the Cosmos is one of the Cosmic Principles of Harmony. The Sage is assigned to each one of us in a personal way, to guide us through life. It relates to us as a friendly personal Helper that knows to what extent these fear-inspiring beliefs control us. The Sage patiently keeps us out of the reach of these fears by not confronting us directly with them. Instead, it helps us to see with clarity the falseness of the beliefs that have created the fears. The Sage brings up from the psyche into our consciousness only what we are able to process at one time.

When we consult the *I Ching* with an open mind, free of desire, prejudice, dread, or expectation, the Sage is freed to determine the way the coins fall, so that the text we receive is an answer to our inner need. It also answers questions we ask when we wish to clarify the meaning of the text received.[5] In this way we are able to hold a conversation with the Sage that makes our understanding come alive. The Sage always teaches us in the context of *present matters* with which we are concerned.

The Three-Headed Dog — The Fear of Going Within

A great number of myths have been circulated since the time of the ancient Greeks about the dangers of going into the "underworld." The underworld, called Hades, was said to be guarded by a three-headed dog called Cerberus, which had a mane of live serpents and a serpent's tail. Only a few heroes were able to get past this dog, and only then with the help of the goddess of wisdom, Athena, and Hermes, the messenger of the Gods.

Since no actual human being ever went to the 'land of the dead,' as Hades was represented to be, the underworld that was imagined clearly existed only in the human psyche. The Sage made us aware that the underworld imagined by the ancients was in reality the *subconscious* that is created in the human psyche when the true self is suppressed by the development of the individual ego.[6]

There are certain other truths in this myth that help us understand the subconscious, but we need to do some transposing to see what they are. First, the three-headed dog that guards the entrance to Hades corresponds to the demonic elements

---

5 The method used for asking these questions is called the retrospective-three-coin method (*rtcm*). It is described in Appendix 1.

6 Interestingly, in this regard, some myths describe Cerberus as having up to fifty heads, all of them fears. Another myth describes Hydra (the son of Cerberus that also guards the underworld) as a dragon that upon cutting off each of its heads, grows two back — an expression of the hopelessness the ancients felt in struggling against the inner demons.

guarding the subconscious where the true self is held prisoner.
Through the fears to look within that they create in the mind,
these demonic elements keep the mind unaware of the condition in which the true self is being held. Second, it is true that
we cannot simply enter the subconscious without help; this is
because the mind takes the terrors inspired by these demonic
elements to be real. In the myth, the goddess of wisdom, Athena,
makes this possible. Athena is a metaphor for the Sage.

Furthermore, because the collective ego is the creator of the
subconscious, the journey cannot be undertaken in the company
of the ego. As the *I Ching* puts it in Hexagram 41, *Decreasing*,
Line 3:

When three people journey together,
Their number decreases by one.
When one man journeys alone,
He finds a companion.

"Three people" here refers to the presence of the ego (which
has taken over the analytical mind) that makes sure we never
arrive at a true understanding. The reason for this is that the
ego has every interest in keeping us from learning the most important secret to which it owes its existence: that the demonic
elements guarding our true self are made of nothing more
than *papier mâché* images created by false concepts whose "life"
depends on our giving those concepts reality. When our mind
agrees to put aside its desire to take the lead on this journey and
to ask the Sage to be the guide, then indeed, the Sage can be the
mind's companion.

Through making this journey, the Sage restores the mind's
confidence in the true self's ability to lead the personality. The
Sage makes us aware that when we allow the ego to interfere
with this journey, our mind takes the fears as real and becomes
overwhelmed. This happens because our fear of the fears makes
us forget that we can say "No!" to them, and thereby reject their
claim to existence. This danger is mentioned in Hexagram 3,
Making a New Beginning, Line 3, which explicitly says, "Whoever hunts deer without the forester only loses his way in the
forest."

If we take a closer look at Cerberus' three heads, we see that they are formed by the three most prominent fears that created the subconscious: (1) the fear created by the doubt that we are special enough to make our way through life; (2) the fear of evil in our nature; and (3) the fear of becoming guilty. Each of these three fears is the result of giving validity to words invented by the collective ego: "special," "evil," and "guilt." Contemporary versions of these fears are contained in statements such as, "dwelling on yourself can make you insane," and, "spending time looking into yourself is selfish" (creating the fear of becoming guilty).

Another aspect of these three words is that they are vague; this makes them open-ended in their meanings, thereby giving them an ability to create a virtually endless realm of threats. Vague words create a psychic havoc that allows the imaging mind to go wild.

Other fears the wanderer will encounter on his inner journey:
- the fear of making a mistake
- the fear of being condemned and abandoned
- the fear of hell-fire
- the fear of the bogey-man

All these fears have taken on demonic forms in the psyche. We only see them in dreams and meditations, but they are behind ego-suggestions we hear in a barely conscious, back-of-the-mind way. Often, they create unconscious emotional responses and control our behaviors in ways we cannot explain.

In the following, we will give a brief description of these demonic elements as we first saw them in meditation. The reader will note that we were protected by Cosmic help.

Imps, Demons, and Dragons

The first demonic element that appeared to Carol in meditation was an *imp*. It showed itself fully at first, as if to say, "I am the boss here." The next time it showed only as a tiny figure that quickly darted past a doorway, saying something that sounded inappropriate as it passed. Immediately, Carol saw a 'Cosmic archer' shoot and kill it before it disappeared. This led her to realize that it was a dangerous element in her psyche. We later

confirmed with the Sage that imps are responsible for fleet
ing, back-of-the-mind suggestions that remind us of what we
"should" or "must do," and shaming thoughts that remind us
what we "should have done." Unlike the voice of the Sage, which
is firm and neutral, imps speak in a bossy and imperious tone.
They can appear as little human figures with sharp eyes or as
mechanical devices such as a crank being used to start a car.
(The crank represents the pressure to make something happen
without our first having acquired clarity.)

Demons were the next kind of demonic element to be recognized. They were behind voiced thoughts that repeated, in
a hounding way, the "musts" stated by the imp. They seem to
stand on the shoulder whispering into the ear. They can also
jump from one person's shoulder onto another's. Demons can
show up in dreams as a witch, a magician, and as demonized or
frightening animals, such as monster spiders, animals of prey,
snakes, and other reptiles.

Dragons appeared in our meditations as commanding figures
that included judges on a bench, a vindictive monarch surrounded
by warriors, and even a court of justice building, into which we
must go for judgment. They threatened us with capital punishments should we not obey their dictates. That showed us that
they represent the taboos and values of the collective ego that
are connected with punishments when not observed.

For a long time, these were the only demonic figures we experienced. We called them DDI's (demons, dragons, imps), for short.
Later, we experienced demonic elements that did not fit these
categories, which we labeled ODE's (other demonic elements).
Two of these were discovered to be even more important than
the DDI's, because they have the job of maintaining the ego's
control over us. The first is the ODE that creates the individual
ego; it is called the "doubter," because it creates the initial doubt
in our wholeness that causes us to adopt self-images.[7] Thereafter,
the doubter's job is to keep that initial self-doubt in place. This
doubt is based on the seed phrase we have already mentioned,
"In and of yourself you are not special enough." The second is

_____

7 See Chapter 11, Section, "The Doubter."

a group of other demonic elements called "changelings."[8]

An important fact emerged when we first discovered these demonic elements. We noticed that when we talked about them in ways that gave them a "real life," they grew in size and impressiveness. This happens, for example, when we call them "clever," "exciting," or "scary," or otherwise fantasize about them. This also happens when they are made the subject of movies, science fiction, and novels. We were helped by the Sage to see that they are entirely the product of a false use of language, and of the images that language can create. This is particularly true of a language that presents things as "matter devoid of feelings and consciousness," or otherwise reduces the way all things work to mechanical principles.

The first step in depriving demonic elements of their energy is to recognize the falseness of the words, phrases, and images to which they owe their existence. The second step consists in deprogramming these words, phrases, and images with Cosmic help. In this manner, the ego is gradually deconstructed, literally word by word. Deprogramming is a method of taking back the assent we have formerly (consciously or inadvertently) given to those words, phrases, and images. (See Appendix 3, "Deprogramming.")

We may not believe that we have given such an assent. However, we have accepted many mistaken ideas and beliefs by default through never actively saying No to them. For example, when someone tells us that he has swam across the Atlantic Ocean, we say, "No, that's absurd." We simply do not take that claim into our psyche. But, if someone in authority tells us the Cosmos is divided into good and evil, we do not know what to think; we thereby absorb that idea as 'possibly true,' taking it into our psyche by default. This is precisely the manner by which demonic elements are created in our psyche.

In addition to the fact that the above demonic elements can act singly in the psyche, DDI's and ODE's can combine into what we call 'ego-complexes.' (See Chapter 13.)

---

8 They are further described in Chapter 12.

Fears That Are Justified

As was shown above, the fear of going within to know ourselves is manufactured by the ego. All fears manufactured by the ego have the purpose of keeping our true self in the dungeon of the subconscious, and to keep the ego in control.

There are, however, legitimate fears we need to recognize. They come from the body consciousness, rather than the mind, and have to do with the mind's being cut off from the warnings that come from our bodily senses. The body, knowing that its warnings cannot get through to the mind, hammers on the closed door of the mind in an attempt to get it to wake up, and to open its ears. The only real cause for fear lies in not knowing ourselves.

Questions That Persist About the Sage's Identity

One question that presents itself to the wanderer upon beginning his journey is, "Who is the Sage?" This question arises from the preconceived ideas we have about the inner world. We are inclined by our conditioning to suspect that the Sage is either God or the devil.

During Carol's first two years of working with the Sage, the question of the Sage's identity persisted. In the only meditation in which the Sage appeared, the face was blank. Why had the Sage not identified itself? Finally, another experience in meditation resolved the question for her:

The meditation opened with her seeing a somewhat fat Chinese mandarin sitting in a yoga position. "Surely this is not the Sage," she thought, on seeing that everything about him looked plastic except his eyes, which were alive, as if a figure were looking through a mask. Then the image disappeared and was replaced by a blubbery-faced middle-aged Western man, who, as in the first image, looked plastic, except for the same alive eyes. This figure also produced the feeling, "Oh no, surely he is not the Sage!" Again, the image was replaced, this time with the famous picture of Jesus standing by a stream with his hand outstretched, saying, "Bring the little children unto me." On immediately moving to embrace his knees the image disappointingly proved to be nothing but thin air that disappeared. She wondered what was the meaning of the whole? Then a patient voice explained that people need images to understand, but these images were all incorrect. "If you want to understand what is closest to a correct description of the Sage," it continued, "it is this": immediately a ball of light filled her vision and then began receding upward into the sky until it became a bright star in the midst of billions of stars.

Many years later, after we learned how to ask the Sage directly about the meaning of this image, we were helped to understand that the billions of stars represented the invisible Cosmic Helpers, of which the Sage is but one.

For her part, Hanna had a different question about the Sage's identity: Should she view the Sage as a master, like an invisible guru, or as a servant like the genie in the story of Aladdin's lamp?

The Sage answered her in a dream: Hanna was in the pub at the train station in Heidelberg. It was a lively scene: on her right was the bartender's counter, where beer was being poured. The pub was populated with people sitting at tables, chatting and drinking their beer. She noticed a young man who was carrying beer glasses to the tables. Someone whispered into her ear: "By the way, he is the *bürgermeister* of Heidelberg." Hanna woke up in amazement. The dream had answered her question: was the Sage a master or a servant? The word *bürgermeister* means "mayor" (literally: "master of the citizens"). The fact that he was serving beer to the citizens lifted her out of thinking in terms of "either/or" — master *or* servant. She was shown how the Sage nourishes the wanderers on their journey, and teaches them about the falseness of either/or thinking.

Even though the Sage showed itself in this dream as a man, in other dreams the Sage showed itself as a woman. The Sage later clarified to us that it takes on the image of a human when that is the only way we can relate to it. We were eventually to learn that the Sage is beyond any human form or gender. That is why in referring to the Sage throughout this book, we have used the neutral pronoun, "it."

6. The Wanderer's Journey

As we mentioned earlier, the closest parallel to what we refer to as "the Sage" is what the ancient Greeks called a "tutelary spirit" that accompanies each person lifelong, to guide and teach him. The Sage resides in the psyche of every individual. There, it performs a number of functions, when asked to do so:
- it helps us come into harmony with our true nature, and thereby with the Cosmos
- it teaches us about the nature of the Cosmos
- it shows us the inner truth of situations
- it engages the other Helpers we need, to fulfill our tasks
- it helps to clear our psyche of ego-elements, in the most effective order, and without overwhelming us
- it makes us aware of when we are about to create a fate, or have already done so.

Despite all this wondrous help given only for the asking, the Sage, as Lao Tzu put it, "does not lord anything over us."[9] It neither considers itself as superior, nor allows itself to be treated as a servant. When the latter happens, the Sage retreats from all requests and remains disengaged until our attitude is once more modest and unassuming.

The retreat of the Sage is often mistaken as a punishment for having made a mistake. The idea of punishment is a carryover from the belief in an arbitrary higher power. As we have learned, there is no hierarchy in the Cosmic order, nor does the Cosmos operate through power. It operates only on Principles of Harmony, and thus ensures its own duration. All notions of hierarchy and power come from the collective ego, and are the very causes of disharmony and conflict in our lives. The Sage retreats when we allow the ego to dominate our behavior, because the Sage, as a Cosmic Helper, cannot join the ego.

The Sage is the first of many Helpers we meet on our inner journey. As long as we are in harmony with ourselves, the Sage resides within us. However, when the ego dominates, the Sage waits outside of us, in our presence. In this position, the Sage is not able to help us until we return to modesty.

---

9 Verse 34, *Tao Te Ching*, Lao Tzu, translated by Dr. H. C. Wu, St. John's University Press, 1961.

Building Trust

At various points on our path we meet the opportunity to restore the natural trust in the goodness of life we had at birth. This trust is evident in the child's taking of his first steps. None of his mistakes in learning to walk lead to a state of doubt. He simply keeps on making the effort. The state of trust to which we refer is similar. It is a passive state that is free of self-doubt and doubt in the total goodness of the Cosmos. This trust, unlike faith, is a state of knowing: knowing that help is there for us when we call for it. It is knowing that should we get lost, the help is there to find our way again. It is not a state of mind that can be achieved by resolving that "we are going to trust." It requires that we recognize and free ourselves of self-doubt, and doubt in the goodness of the Cosmos, through deprogramming them with Cosmic help.

7. The Path of the Wanderer

The Solitary Path

The path that leads to the fulfillment of our Cosmic destiny is necessarily solitary, and not trodden by anyone else because it is unique. We are tempted to look to others who have found their path and think they can provide us with the steps needed. While they can share their experiences, these experiences may or may not be relevant to us. The treading of our unique path is achieved through our developing an active relationship with the Sage and the other invisible Helpers.

The inner path of the wanderer is described in Hexagram 46, *Pushing Upward/Being Lifted Up by the Helpers*, as one that leads to "supreme success." The hexagram also states the conditions that create this success. The first paragraph of the hexagram defines the purpose of the path, and how it is to be accomplished:

> The Cosmic theme of this hexagram is how inner development leads to the fulfillment of one's life. Supreme success, in Cosmic terms, is achieved through freeing the true self by subtracting, phrase-by-phrase, and image-by-image, the false inner program of the collective ego. Each subtraction of a false seed phrase or image initiates a transformation that involves being lifted up by the Helpers of the invisible world.

Being lifted up by the Helpers refers to being lifted out of the difficulties that were created by the mistaken ideas we are now leaving behind.

The next paragraph describes two kinds of paths: the path of the wanderer who follows his inner truth, and the path trodden by those who follow rules written by humans in ancient books.

> Receiving this hexagram is counsel to make a decision between these two paths. Where he puts his wish, he puts his will: Is it the path of his unique destiny that he alone can tread by following his inner truth, or the one laid out by ancient wisdom that has been trodden by others?

The next paragraph describes the tricks and manipulations the ego uses to pull people back from embarking or continuing on their own unique path:

> With regard to the individual ego, this hexagram points to its ambition to remain in control of the personality. The thing the ego most dreads is the person's self-examination that would expose its [the ego's] tricks and manipulations; therefore, once a person has decided to undertake the liberation of his true self, the ego's first move is to join the effort with gusto. Just as it had once eagerly set itself goals of brilliance, power, and success in worldly attainments, it now renounces them, and puts up the values associated with self-development that will show the person as "modest," "true," "spiritual," and "devoted." It then proceeds, if not halted, to beat the person to death, to prove that he is devoted. It is the purpose of the many ascetic and complicated rituals and practices associated with self-development to divert the person from ever seeing that accessing the Sage is simple and direct. The lessons with the Sage always have a liberating effect, at every step, whereas self-development through the ego enslaves the person more and more. The ego is ever goal-oriented, and discovering its goal-orientation is one of the ways to catch on to its presence and trickery. Its means of 'pushing upward' is one of the upgrade features of the collective ego's program, which allows the ego to adapt to the shifts and turns the person makes as he tries to get free of it.

Many people, on beginning to work on recovering their true self, feel the desire to be in a group. However, the wanderer's path is one that has never been trodden before, because it is created as he walks it. This is necessarily so, because if he treads a path already formed by others, his experiences will be defined by them so that the path will never be truly his own. Moreover, it will be a path he has read about, not experienced for himself.

To give an example, Carol noticed that the method for meditating she had learned from the *I Ching* was unlike any of the other types of meditation she had heard about. Once, when she was describing something she experienced in meditation, the listener, before Carol had even gotten to the point, exclaimed, "Oh, that's a kundalini experience!" This left Carol feeling robbed of what she had experienced so uniquely. The listener had made it into something else. Carol also noticed that doing so gave the person a feeling of superiority because he already "knew" what the whole thing was about.

The Landscape of the Psyche

Through dreams and meditations the wanderer's path leads him through the landscape of his psyche. Thus we may dream of canoeing down a river that exposes us now to rapids where we need to avoid underwater objects, and then to peaceful scenes of real beauty; meditations, similarly, may present images that represent obstructions in our attitude, which, when we recognize that we need Cosmic help, suddenly disappear. We may be presented with a burned-out house that reflects a relationship that died. One dream showed Carol as a bird soaring around a mountain. As she flew, the Sage showed her that hidden within the mountain were numerous hidden treasures. This brought Hexagram 52, *Meditating*, to mind. It pictures a mountain as a state of inner quiet which is conducive to receiving experiences in meditation; the dream was telling her that through meditation she could find the answers to her many questions. Still other dreams and meditations made her aware of areas of her thinking that needed attention.

Such dreams and meditations come from the Sage, the wanderer's guide and companion on his inner journey. Hanna remembers dreams in which her path led straight through a house, where in a glance she saw a man who seemed to live there. She thought she was intruding in his space, and apologized. Much later, she learned that the man was a Helper of her psyche, who was waiting to give her directions; however, he had been unable to help her because she was under the spell, "There is no help for us from the Cosmos." (A "spell" is a phrase or image that has created a program in the psyche so that we either act or react unconsciously in a fixed pattern; see Chapter 10 for a more detailed description.)

A typical kind of dream may show the wanderer on a steep mountain road ready to give up. The dream wants to show him that he misunderstands the Cosmic way through thinking that the path to finding his true self is one of striving upward, as described above in the quote from Hexagram 46. Generally speaking, whenever the wanderer has dreams that are frustrating, or cause him to become angry, or show him in some kind of difficulty from which he does not know how to extract himself, he needs to take them as hints to look for a spell he has either put on himself, or one someone else has put on him. (Also see the descriptions under "The slough of mud" below.)

When in a dream the wanderer comes to a bombed-out city, or a complex of buildings that have burned down, the Sage is showing him that an ego-complex (see Chapter 13) has either burned out, or has been removed from his psyche through the shock of a fate.

Sometimes, the Sage gives us a panoramic vision over a beautiful valley, a breathtaking view over a land that seems to be out of reach. It is a view of the true landscape of our psyche where we meet our Cosmic family, which is made up of the Helpers of the Nature around us and the Cosmic Helpers, all of which are there to further us on the path of our unique Cosmic destiny.

The Slough of Mud

Mud, in the *I Ching*, as a metaphor, has a number of meanings; all point to interference by the ego that makes progress difficult or impossible. Thus, mud commonly refers to self-doubt, guilt, fear, or spells. Mud can also refer to unrecognized guilt for having followed our inner truth, rather than being loyal to a higher power, a parent, a mate, or the values of the collective around us. All pacts and promises are spells that create guilt when we do not live up to them.

Wading through mud can also be a metaphor for the guilt we may feel for having turned our backs on the beliefs of our forefathers.

Mud can also refer to the guilt we have taken on for all the mistakes we have made in our lives, especially those that we have regarded as sins.

All the above kinds of guilt keep us from making progress, despite our sincerity. For example, a friend in her late forties, seeking help from the *I Ching*, described her situation in these words: "I find that I want to do things that would fulfill me, but as soon as I want to make the first step, something pulls me back." The *I Ching* pointed to guilt as the cause of her problem. The guilt had started piling up when at a young age she was made to feel that following her own path meant going against her parents' wishes. Once on her own, she did more things for herself, but continued to accumulate guilt, because in her parents' view, to do things for herself was selfish. By the time she sought help from the *I Ching*, the pile of guilt had become so huge that it completely blocked her from even making a first step toward self-fulfillment.

Mud can also stand for the paralyzing fear of making a major mistake. This fear haunts the back-of-the-mind with the thought "What, if after all my efforts, I am wrong in the end? Then I will be stuck." When this fear is not recognized and deprogrammed, it causes many people to give up on their journey.

Once, in a dream, Carol saw herself trudging laboriously through mud that came up to her knees. Looking back over her path, she saw that she had come miles and miles in this way. Just to the side, she saw an encampment of people laughing as they sat around a table sharing the joys of their experiences. The ground within the encampment was solid, free of mud. She realized that the mud represented all the guilt she had taken on for the mistakes she had made throughout her life. She had carried these feelings with her, mile after mile, year after year. The Sage was making her aware through the dream that we are not meant to feel guilty for our mistakes, because, in the hands of the Sage, mistakes become the material of our learning.

In an earlier meditation, during the time when Carol was consulting the *I Ching* to help repair her marriage, she saw herself as having crossed a deep ravine on a bridge newly built by the Sage. She had reached a place that was light and sunny. Looking back, she saw that the other side was dark and gloomy, and that the road leading up to the bridge was knee-deep in mud. She saw her husband stuck there, and called to him to come over. He replied that he could not because his shoes (a pair he had recently bought at a bargain, costing only $8) were stuck in the mud. She called again to say, "Why don't you leave your shoes behind so that you can come over?" He replied, "I can't because I like my shoes too much." The shoes, as Carol understood from the Sage, stood both for his self-image (here, of being clever for buying $8 shoes), and for his dependence on cleverness to make progress in his life.

Being stuck in mud can also refer to being under the spell created by the phrase, "I can never change," which fixes the psyche. Such a spell can also be put on us by someone else.

The Wanderer's Need to Free Himself from Self-Created Prisons

The Cosmos creates justice through the Principle of Fate. At the beginning of his journey, the wanderer finds himself in the inner prison of his fate. The fate incurred fits the crime precisely, and comes at the correct time to make the wanderer aware of the mistaken ideas and/or attitudes that have caused it; thus, his fate provides the opportunity he needs for self-correction. The fate is able to heal all the effects of the crime because it incorporates the Cosmic Principles of Harmony.

The Ego's Concept of Justice

The ego's concept of justice differs from Cosmic justice in that it circles around the false concepts of evil, blame, guilt, punishment, and forgiveness.

Its concept of evil divides the world into those we consider good and those we consider evil. Because evil is defined differently from culture to culture, one culture ends in regarding the other as evil. Such differences also occur within a culture in terms of 'classes.' The values of each class differ so that there is a saying, "the uppermost and lowest classes of society have no morality; it is middle class morality that holds the society together." Thus, evil is defined differently for each class.

The ego's concept of blame makes the individual believe he is empowered to act on behalf of a higher power in assigning blame to others. It is his duty to observe things from the viewpoint of his god.

The ego's concept of guilt is accompanied by the image of a guilty person's having an inextinguishable stain on his nature. It also is connected with the word 'unforgivable.'

Its concept of punishment is based on the perceived need of a society to act while the 'guilty' person is alive on behalf of the higher power, which will continue the punishment after death.

Its concept of forgiving and non-forgiving causes us to incorrectly believe that we have this option. Behind it is the image of sitting in judgment over others, as if one were God. It has various expressions such as "this can never be made good," and "this offense can never be forgiven." Forgiving thus is thought of as an act of great-heartedness, while not forgiving is considered to be a correct application of power. The *I Ching* makes us aware that both forgiving and not forgiving create "magnificent" self-images that are compared to "the finest clothes." The text in Hexagram 63, *After Completion*, Line 4, describes the consequences of taking on such self-images:

> The finest clothes turn to rags can be a metaphor for a magnificent attitude by which a person magnanimously 'plays God' by taking it upon himself to forgive or admonish or condemn others. While he condemns one person by telling him, "you have really failed this time," he lets another off the hook of his fate by telling him that what he has done is "okay," or that he forgives him…. Such pretensions of possessing power come only from the ego, and bring about the fate referred to above, as "rags."

Also part of the ego's concept of justice is the holding on to anger at misdeeds until such time as the other has apologized, or the victim has been vindicated, or been 'paid back.'

This mindset is based on the idea that the collective ego is legitimated by heaven, or a higher power. It therefore assumes that it has the mandate to take justice into its hands, and to use power to protect its false values. Because of the nature of these values, it keeps a perpetual conflict going between factions. Conflict is then regarded as an 'inescapable fact of life'. As the above indicates, the system is human-centered and negates the existence of the Cosmic Principles of Harmony that, when acknowledged, create a harmonious order.

The Cosmic Principle of Justice

This principle is described in the *I Ching* in Hexagram 56, *The Wanderer*. It specifies that participating in outer conflicts creates a fate, whereas saying the inner No to their causes, and No to participating in them, and then turning the conflicts over to the Cosmos, leads to the end of the fate. What keeps conflicts going are the various ego concepts described above, such as guilt, and the mistaken concept of justice.

Not only do outer conflicts create a fate, inner conflicts do as well. In the latter case, the person punishes himself unconsciously. An example came to us in an *I Ching* session with a woman who learned that she had created a fate. The fate was experienced as both guilt for having betrayed her inner truth and the constant fear that she would have to pay for this self-betrayal with a fate.

The *I Ching* made her aware that the ego had buried this betrayal out of sight by justifying it as necessary to the successful outcome of the goal she had wanted to achieve. However, her true self knew better. It also knew that if she did not square with herself, Fate would undo the success. This fear of Fate became her punishment.

The *I Ching* clarified that the mistake was not irrevocable. The woman needed first to apologize to the Cosmos for her self-betrayal. Next, she needed to forgive herself. The *I Ching* informed her that she had misread the Cosmic way in believing that her misdeed was unforgivable. Her true regret, combined with deprogramming the guilt connected with her self-betrayal, was all that was needed to erase her misdeed.

We also found that the woman's fear of losing what she had attained through false means had falsely caused her to form an attachment to what she had attained. As demonstrated above, attaining anything through false means creates a fate. The attachment was the ego's attempt to save her from experiencing that fate. However, as the example shows, even though she achieved something through false means, she did not necessarily have to pay with a fate. The Cosmic Principle of Justice is directed at allowing us to learn from our mistakes.

During the session, the *I Ching* also made the woman aware of the cause of her self-betrayal; it was the mistaken belief that "no help is available from the Cosmos for just causes." This belief had made her think, "I have to take matters into my own hands if I want to have success."

In the Cosmic order, corrections are neither made through punishments nor forgiveness. They occur on the individual level through the *natural self-correcting function* of the psyche, when it has not been distorted by the ego.[1] The working of this function can be described as follows: our conscience, which is part of the reflecting function of the psyche, sparks images in our mind of our misdeed, causing us to feel shame and embarrassment; these feelings, in turn, lead to remorse. Remorse switches off the gnawings of our conscience and reunites our mind with the Cosmos.

When a person has willfully harmed another, or betrayed his true self, his crime is actually between his mind and the Cosmos. He can undo his blame through feeling remorse over his deed, and through freeing himself from the ego concept of guilt and from the ideas and beliefs that led him to do what he did. Then the Cosmos can harmonize the situation. It needs to be noted that if those harmed hold fast to a grudge, the Cosmos will be limited in harmonizing the situation on their behalf. The answer, in both cases, is for each to square their relationship with the Cosmos in regard to what happened. For the victim, the sooner he turns the need for correction, together with his anger, and any other negative attachment he has to the event over to the Cosmos and lets go of it, the sooner Cosmic justice takes place; then, what might be seen as restitution happens of itself.

Anger plays an important part in any injustice done, as well as in its restitution. However, for it to have the correct effect, it needs to be correctly understood: when a person is the victim of an injustice, anger energy flows to him from the Cosmos. The anger is meant to make him aware that he needs to say an inner No to the aggressor for committing the deed; he then turns his anger over to the Cosmos. His releasing his anger allows the

---

1 See Chapter 8 for a detailed description of this function.

Cosmos to transform the anger energy and use it for two purposes: (1) to alleviate the victim's needs, and (2) to correct the aggressor at the precisely appropriate time, and in the precisely appropriate measure.

Before a victim can let go of an injustice done to him, he may need to deprogram a demonic element called the "ODE of the Unforgivable."[2] It can express itself in the phrase, "I can never forgive…my mother, myself, society, etc." This ODE is present in all grievances and feuds and it is one of the causes of progressive alienation. (See Chapter 16, for a discussion of ODE's.)

This ODE can also be present in the aggressor. People who harm others have themselves often been the victim of an injustice in childhood. This has, in turn, led to their unconscious desire to "pay back" others by doing harm to them. Such a person needs to identify the original event that created his desire to pay back others with harm, and free himself from the traumatic memory of that event. (See Chapter 18, "Harmful Microprocessors," and Chapter 20, "Processing.")

Common Ideas and Beliefs that Need to Be Deprogrammed at the Beginning

As wanderers at the beginning of our journey, we are usually not aware of how the conditioning we have undergone blocks our making a new beginning.

The ego's definition of self-development creates the first obstacle. This definition is based on the following false premises about our true nature:

- Human nature is divided into a good/higher/spiritual and an evil/lower/animal nature
- We do not possess natural virtues
- We are born guilty for having an animal nature
- There is no such thing as help from the Cosmos

The following are the actions proposed by the collective ego to remedy the above-mentioned supposed faults:

- We must strive toward the good

---

2 The expression, "ODE" refers to "Other Demonic Elements" in the psyche than the original imps, demons, and dragons found there.

- We must develop virtues
- We must develop our spiritual nature
- To free us from guilt, we must renounce/overcome our animal nature by sacrificing it, and its needs
- There is nobody but you to do it

When we look at the premises on which the ego's self-development program is based, we see that they are the very same premises that have been used to suppress our true nature. This is why they are the first that need to be deprogrammed. (See Appendix 3, "Deprogramming.")

Waiting

There are times when we need to be patient while transformations are in the process of unfolding. During such times, such as when the new job has not appeared, the ego enters with doubt and accusations such as, "you are foolish to think things are going to happen this way." It holds the Cosmos up as "lying," and as "not producing the miracle" we are waiting for. Such expectations come from the mistaken belief that the Cosmos works through miracles. The ego further describes our situation as "endlessly waiting at a crossroads without doing anything!" Samuel Beckett has described this situation masterfully in his play "Waiting for Godot."

The *I Ching* makes us aware that these ego demands for proof seek to make us succumb to impatience, and give way to its demand that *action be taken, even though no clear path of action is seen.* The ego would have us act for the sole purpose of taking action. According to the ego's logic, we must choose between two alternatives. As in Hanna's experience described in Chapter 1, the ego made her think that she was faced with only two choices: either to take the job that promised security and social success, although the job did not feel right to her, or to have no work, no money, no security. As is typical when we work with the Cosmos, the solution came on a different plane altogether. At her therapist's suggestion she redefined the negative images; no work became "time for myself in a place of my dreams"; no money became an opportunity to sell things she no longer needed; no security became the prospect of finding something that would truly fulfill her.

Waiting, we need to mention, does not mean that when we have no job in sight, we simply sit back and do nothing. The inner action that needs to be taken is to ask the Cosmos to help. Secondly, we keep our minds open to the new opportunities the Helpers want to bring to our attention. These opportunities often do not fit at all into the categories in which we have envisioned our future job; however, they are the perfect fit for our present needs and circumstances. We block these opportunities if we have already a too precise image of our future job in mind.

Ego-Attitudes that Obstruct Our Relationship with the Sage

Since the Sage is our guide and companion on this journey, it is important to become aware of ego-attitudes that keep the Sage from being able to help us. Due to our ignorance of the Cosmic Way we tend to carry the following ego-attitudes that create these problems into our relationship with the Sage:

- We think the Sage requires us to make deals in order to be helped; as when we think, "if I turn my life over to the Sage, the Sage will see how devoted I am and help me." However, the Sage cannot respond to any deal-making; it responds only to modesty and sincerity, and gives its help freely.
- We share our experience of Cosmic help with people who are not receptive and thus throw our Cosmic gifts away. This habit causes the Sage and the Helpers to retreat.
- After receiving insights from the Sage we think we are special in some way. This is what the *I Ching* refers to as a false enthusiasm in Hexagram 16, *Enthusiasm*. Seeing ourselves as special violates the Cosmic Principle of Modesty.
- We proselytize and want to save the world. This occurs when as wanderers we experience how easily the Helpers come to help and how much they achieve. This brings a rush of enthusiasm from the ego, which causes us to see ourselves either as 'someone in the know,' or as called to 'save the world,' or as one of the few who have access to the Cosmos.

- We have the commonplace belief that defines self-development as a spiritual search for "the truth." Our path as a wanderer is to search for the *untruths* that have imprisoned our true self, and that keep us from accessing our inner truth. We search for these untruths in order to deprogram them.
- We congratulate ourselves for achievements that were made possible only with the aid of the Helpers.
- Because we are working on freeing our true self, we view ourselves as better than others. This view is often coupled with criticizing others who are still dependent on the collective ego. Self-flattery is the most direct way the ego regains control over our personality. Self-flattery leads to a false self-confidence that makes us overlook dangers that trip us up.
- Taking shortcuts. The ego tempts us constantly in our everyday situations to skip taking the time to find out the inner truth of a situation, and instead to take the shortcut of relying on its outer appearance for our judgments. This habit also leads to taking as true others' beliefs without subjecting them to reflection.

The Belief in Changes

At each point where we fall into any one of the above traps, we create a fate. We may not realize that the cause of our misfortune is the result of an ego attitude. Therefore, we have readily accepted the superficial view that "changes are the rule of life," and that "life is a series of ups and downs, with good fortune followed by misfortune." The belief in changes constantly recreates the pattern of ups and downs. The *I Ching* makes us aware that *duration*, not *change*, is the rule when we live in accord with the Cosmic Principles of Harmony. Duration is assured through *transformations* that take place in the atomic realm. Transformations are the result of thoughts and actions that are in harmony with the Cosmos. One such action is to inwardly reject what feels disharmonious by saying an inner No to it.

The belief in changes can easily lead to a depressed view of life, although such a view was not characteristic of ancient China.

Of the 64 hexagrams in the *I Ching,* 62 show a way to overcome adversity.[3] The belief that "life is suffering," and similar dark views of life, however, have characterized the belief systems of the rest of the world from India westward to the Americas.

Other Myths About Life that Challenge the Wanderer

Mistaken views about life have been the stuff of myths since ancient times. We are reminded of the myth of the Sphinx, a demon that put a riddle to the passerby. If he was unable to solve it, he got strangled and devoured by the Sphinx. This myth is the origin of other myths that have become commonplace in our language such as, "Life is a riddle (implying that you need to solve it in order to master it)," or, "Life is a challenge."

Indeed, life remains a riddle and a challenge to the mind as long as the mind is separated from our feelings, and from what we know through our deepest inner truth. The riddle has the purpose of engaging the mind in trying to solve a problem that has been invented solely to titillate and busy the mind, so that the untruths of the above slanders on life are never recognized. The real answer is to free our psyche from these mistaken beliefs, and thereby take away the fear-demon's control over us.

The same can be said about the way we are to deal with obstructions. Upon meeting with a seemingly insuperable set of obstructions in her life, Carol received Hexagram 39, *Meeting with Obstructions.* It pictures a mountain path that on one side is a sheer cliff, and on the other a steep abyss. The path itself has become blocked. The counsel given in the hexagram is to retreat from struggling with the obstruction. "How then is one to deal with it?" she asked herself. Meditating, she once more saw this image and the blocked passage. It was clear there was no way around it. Then, clarity came in the word "acceptance," meaning to her to accept the fact that she was blocked, and *needed help.* Immediately, on recognizing that she needed help, the blockage disappeared. It had simply been taken away by Cosmic Helpers. Indeed, this is what happened very quickly

---

3 The exceptions are Hexagram 12, *Being Halted,* and Hexagram 47, *Oppressing/Exhausting.*

in her external situation. Help came from unexpected sources, so that the obstruction simply disappeared. She later realized that the obstruction was created by the idea, "I have to do it all myself," thus ruling out the Sage and other Helpers.

Questions about *the meaning of life* are so abundant as to plague the mind of the wanderer as long as he busies himself with them. Indeed, it is the very purpose of speculation to busy our mind on such theoretical questions. Because such questions cannot be answered by the mind, and are outside of experience, the tendency is to draw cynical conclusions such as, "Life has no meaning," "Life is a bad joke God played on humans," and "Life plays dirty tricks on us."

The Sage made it clear to us that the meaning of life is not to be found outside ourselves. Indeed, the idea that life has a purpose that we must find, is false. To give expression to our uniqueness, which is an inner directive that needs no further definition, can be translated into the simple words, "it is enough to simply be neither more nor less than what we are."

As the honored stuff of literature, the idea that life is a hero's journey leaves us with the feeling that we are 'little beings' in the greater scheme of things, lost in the mysteries of life without a guide. We feel belittled by these feelings until we realize that we are only humbly and simply seeking to find our lost true self. The meaning of our lives begins to reveal itself as soon as we free ourselves from these myths.

8. The Functions of the Psyche

Our life in a body gives us the unique opportunity to experience the Cosmos both in its invisible aspect as the Cosmic Consciousness, and in its myriad expressions in form known as Nature. Both aspects *interpenetrate* to create the indivisible whole we call the Cosmos. The Cosmic Consciousness supports everything that exists in form through a multitude of invisible Helpers that provide us with everything we need to fulfill our Cosmic destiny.

The human mind, being the youngest function in the development of the animal consciousnesses, needs the most support from the Cosmos due to its inexperience. As the previous chapters have shown, its inexperience has led it to create a false reality that not only threatens the continuation of the human species, but that of other parts of Nature as well. Fortunately, the mind has not been pushed out on the stage of life helpless and alone. The Sage, as our Cosmic Teacher, uses the psyche to help the mind understand and correct its mistakes. The psyche has many functions that are directed toward helping the mind understand the meaning of our life in a body. It is also "the well" referred to in Hexagram 48, that contains the chi energy, or "clear, pure water" that is capable of nourishing the mind.[1]

To accomplish its tasks, the psyche possesses certain active and passive functions. We have described some in Chapter 6.

The following descriptions show the various functions of the psyche and their capabilities when they are not blocked or otherwise interfered with by the ego. We will show in Chapter 13 how complexes created by the ego block these functions, or otherwise interfere with and distort them.

Passive Functions of the Psyche

The Storing and Reflecting Functions
To understand these two functions, we need to remember

1 See Hexagram 48, *The Well.*

that each of us is manifested from an image that is stored in the Cosmic Consciousness. This original image is also stored in our psyche. Its primary function is to provide our DNA with the information needed to create our body as a perfect expression of our original image. Although the images the ego creates of us are plastered over this original image, this image remains consistently true and whole; the ego cannot destroy or damage it. It remains like a homing beacon throughout our lives that flashes warning messages to us in times when the mind has lost contact with our true nature. The Sage protects that image so that it can serve as a shelter and refuge for the true self when the ego tries to reassert its domination after the true self has been freed from its imprisonment.[2]

Also part of the storing and reflecting functions of the psyche is the *dream function*. It is used by the Sage to bring things to the attention of the conscious mind while the ego is asleep. (A detailed description of what things are brought to mind is given in Chapter 21.) It can happen that the ego seizes the dream function to intimidate us. Such dreams need to be clearly distinguished from dreams that are messages coming from the Sage.

The *reflecting function* of the psyche enables the Sage to transmit insight-flashes coming from the Cosmic Consciousness. The mind needs to be modest in attitude for this to be possible. By modest, we mean liquid and still, like the still surface of a lake. Liquidity means not fixed in its views, while stillness is the absence of ego-emotions and preconceived ideas that would rile the surface of the lake. Liquidity and stillness make us receptive to the liquid light that enables instant communication with the Sage through insight-flashes. Such a flash occurs when the liquid light transforms Cosmic Consciousness (which exists as a feeling) into words or images that express the Cosmic truth needed in the moment. Insight-flashes are but one of the myriad ways in which the Sage is able to communicate. The insights we have received remain stored in the psyche. The psyche also stores and reflects to the conscious mind memories of good experiences: of helpful coincidences and of blessings received. This storehouse

---

2 See Hexagram 56, *The Wanderer*, Line 4.

of positive assets is available to the mind in situations of need. Drawing on these insights and memories keeps us from falling into hopelessness and helplessness.

The Psyche as Facilitator for the Sage

We have mentioned in Chapter 5 that the Sage translates sensations coming from the body into words and images that the mind can understand. The Sage also coordinates the various functions of the psyche so that it operates as a harmonious whole.

In addition, the Sage assembles Helpers of our nature to aid the mind in accomplishing given tasks. An example is learning a language. The Helpers needed are the Memorizing Helper and the Helper of the language to be learned. This latter Helper is created in us the moment we have the desire to learn a language.

The psyche is the source of most of our dreams. At times the Sage uses dreams to communicate with the conscious mind. This is particularly the case when other ways of communicating, such as through meditation, have become blocked.

The *I Ching* has shown us that when we free our mind of our preconceptions about the specific subject we would like to learn about, and keep our mind receptive, the Sage can communicate directly with us through meditation.

The Involuntary Response Function

This passive function of the psyche used by the Sage is brought into play in situations where someone is physically, emotionally, or otherwise threatening us. The response comes from our body consciousness and causes us to do something that has exactly the correct effect. This innocent action, which is free of both forethought and intention, is directed by the Sage.

In an actual example, a man on his way home at night was approached by three men intent on robbing him, one of whom brandished a knife. Suddenly, the man found himself enacting brisk karate-like movements toward the aggressors, while screaming like a tiger. The aggressors, taken aback in shock, did not know what to do. At this moment, the man found himself reaching out his hand to shake the hand of the lead robber, and laughing. When the robbers responded with laughter themselves, the man walked away from them in peace. In relating the event the next morning, he described his response as a complete surprise to himself. (In Chapter 13, we discuss how this particular function is frequently blocked by certain ego-complexes.)

The Receiving Function

One of the functions of the psyche is to receive love from the Cosmos. Thus, we are supplied with love energy regardless of whether we have a love partner or not. When a love relationship is appropriate for us, the Cosmic love comes through the partners and is received by the psyche, which shares the nourishment of the love with our whole being. The energy then returns to the Cosmos in the form of gratitude for this gift.

Another passive function of the psyche is to receive and register every event of our lives, along with the impressions we have had of those events. As mentioned before, the psyche is the storehouse of positive memories and the impressions they have made on us. It also stores our negative experiences and traumas, and the conclusions we have drawn from them. When these negative experiences have not been processed, the ego is able to use them to keep us in doubt about the goodness of life, and to accuse the Cosmos of being indifferent and punishing.

The psyche also receives disharmonious thoughts such as spells, whether they come from us or from others. However, this can occur only when the protective function of the psyche has been made dysfunctional.

The Remitter Function

This function serves to remit requests for help coming from one body part to another body part, and to the mind. This function is used when a particular organ or bodily system is overloaded or in some other difficulty. (See Chapter 21, "Dreams.")

The Protective Function

The psyche, in its healthy state, wards off disharmonious/harmful consciousness coming either from our own mind or from outside sources — other people (dead or alive), the media, or literature. Lao Tzu described this function as an inner neutrality that makes negative thoughts bounce off, and that keeps us from becoming embroiled in conflict. In meditation, Carol saw this function in the form of an opaque mirror. It reflected negative thoughts back to their source in the ego, thus preventing them from being taken into the psyche. Many forms of Eastern martial arts build their exercises around inner neutrality in order to strengthen this protective function. Modesty, combined with inner neutrality, act both as a shield and sword.

The Passive Transforming Function

This function has a passive and an active aspect. In its passive aspect it can be engaged to transform certain ego-emotions such as grief, hopelessness, self-blame, fears, doubt of the Cosmos, resistance, hatred, arrogance, reverence, ego-enthusiasm, depression, boredom, envy, and feelings of possessiveness. The *I Ching* refers to this function as "a big wagon for loading,"[3] which we can picture as a dumpster truck that frees us from the burden of these ego-emotions. When we are plagued by any of the above ego-emotions, we say an inner No to them, and picture ourselves putting them on this wagon. What is important is our conscious consent in letting them go.

Active Functions of the Psyche

The Organizing Function

The working out of our Cosmic destiny is something that occurs mostly outside the direction of our mind, but which nevertheless needs the mind's assent. The organizing function puts together the seemingly unrelated paths we have taken, in such a way as to make mind aware, in retrospect, of how they have all contributed to a learning process, the goal of which is the fulfilling of our Cosmic destiny. In terms of the metaphor of the weaving of the carpet of our Cosmic destiny, the psyche provides the weft onto which the material provided by the thinking consciousness gets woven, while the color of the material

3 See Hexagram 14, *Possession in Great Measure*, Line 2.

comes from our feeling consciousness. Our feeling consciousness must guide each movement in making the carpet. In this
weaving process no experience is wasted, provided that we later
make the effort to process any negative experiences.

The carpet in our psyche gets woven when we work on
something creative. The psyche finds the pieces we need that
explain something of Cosmic significance to us. It also draws
us to see how one thing is related to another in a way that is
unconscious to the mind. Thus, it is as if we are on a treasure
hunt that combines skill and surprise. It is the psyche that possesses the skill in finding and putting the pieces together, while
the mind, by staying open, delights in the surprise. In the end,
as every person who has ever engaged in an art form or creative
project knows, the psyche is the lead element and the completer
of the project.

The Processing Function

We naturally have this function in us, which helps the mind
to give negative events a *sense of proportion*. This sense of proportion prevents the emotional shock that would otherwise be
created by slanders such as "you're bad, you're guilty," "it's all
your fault," etc., by reflecting to the mind that the harmful words
and phrases have no Cosmic basis.

The processing function also feeds input to the mind in such
a way as to temper its conditioned responses. This input draws
on remembered positive experiences, and can also draw on
meditations and dreams. The *input function* does this through
the psyche's ability to draw on Cosmic knowledge that comes
through our inner truth.

Once children become conditioned, their processing function
is rendered dysfunctional. A parent who seeks to help a child
process a traumatic experience needs to put the event in its
correct proportion. In doing this the child's *processing function*
is re-activated. We can picture this function as a switch that
directly connects the child's mind with his inner truth, so that
his memory of the event becomes harmonized.

Once, when Carol's oldest son was age four, and the family was new in a small village, her son, along with three older children, taunted a boy who was age two. When the group was chastised by the parents, the older children claimed that Carol's son had proposed the taunting. They said he was the "bad boy." The next morning, another child in the village stood outside their cottage and yelled over and over, "J... is a bad boy." When her son cried inconsolably, Carol realized that he might get psychologically damaged. For the next hour she took him aside and repeatedly explained in different ways that the words "bad boy" were words that existed only in that boy's head, and that those words were not true. It was true that what he did was bad, but that did not mean he himself was bad. He had only made a mistake, and mistakes can be corrected. Through these different approaches to separate him from the idea that he was a bad boy, and to make him aware that the boy's judgment of him was only his judgment, not everyone's, a separation was made between himself and the word "bad." Although it took an hour to get this message across to him, he finally understood the message, and was no longer affected by the event. Seeing the situation in the Cosmic light erased his excessive emotional response to it, and his incorrect conclusions about it.

The Active Transforming Function

This function is related to completing things. Hexagram 64, *Before Completion*, makes it clear that in any undertaking, we can go only so far in our conscious effort. Before the completion can take place, we need to recognize our limits and turn its completion over to the Cosmos. By this we mean to completely let go of the matter. This humility automatically engages the Helper of Transformation, also known as the Helper of Completion. The poet Robert Frost described the process as similar to sledding down a hill in the snow: at the top, where the snow is worn off, you have to push the sled a little; then you connect with the snow and fly down the hill.[4]

Hexagram 63, *After Completion*, makes us aware of the consequences of not having included the Helper of Transformation:

4 Frost gave this description in a speech given at John F. Kennedy's inauguration.

the success either does not occur, as when a performer does not perform well, or the success becomes obstructed or erodes, as when someone else claims the achievement, or the person himself claims the success as "all his doing."

The Transmitting Function

The first task of the transmitting function of the psyche is to transmit the feelings of inner truth to the mind. These feelings are a basic Yes to go with what feels harmonious, and a basic No that causes us to hesitate, or to withdraw because the matter feels disharmonious. Our inner truth makes this assessment on the basis of the perceptions of our commonsense, which is a consensus of all our senses. (See Chapter 3.) The psyche transmits this consensus to the mind.

Another aspect of this function is to transmit to the mind fears coming from the Helper of our Commonsense and the Helper of our Inner Truth. They attempt to warn our mind that by blotting them out of our awareness, we are endangered because they are unable to function. Because these Helpers are necessary for making sound decisions, it is essential that they be consciously recognized.

The psyche also sparks images in the mind to get its attention and warn it of the danger that comes from disharmonious thoughts and actions that would lead to a fate.

Another active function of the psyche is to send warning messages to the mind when it is not listening to the body's warnings. These messages sometimes come as a loud inner voice.

The psyche also transmits to the mind real opportunities offered by the Cosmos. These opportunities suit us because they fulfill a legitimate need, and because we are ready and capable of carrying them through. An opportunity can be of a business nature, or an inspiration to write a book, or a love relationship offered when we are ready for it. The psyche is the first to become aware of the opportunity and how it matches our need; it then transmits to the mind a strong feeling that there is a real opportunity before us. This feeling, and the image accompanying it, having originated in the Cosmic Consciousness, is so clear that one is totally free of doubt about it. Upon perceiving this real opportunity, the Cosmic energy that has been waiting, breaks through. This energy represents the Cosmic Helpers that are all lined up, waiting for that moment to help the event manifest.

The Focusing Function

When an opportunity like the one described above arises, the psyche then acts as a focusing agent by concentrating all our physical energy on the creative event while it is manifesting.

The Linking/Harmonizing Function

Also part of the creative process described above is the psyche's linking/harmonizing function. It links our physical energies to the Cosmic energy by harmonizing the two. It does this by keeping us focused on the initial image of what wants to manifest, so that we are not diverted by the ego (in us or others) that would shift our focus to an ego-goal and spoil the opportunity. The ego, in its search for the energy it needs to sustain itself, often attempts to redefine the goal to suit its purposes.

Another part of the linking/harmonizing function is the *human conscience*. It connects the Cosmic Consciousness with the mind when the mind needs to be reminded that its decisions can isolate us from Cosmic help and protection. It also reminds the mind that its first responsibility is to the Cosmos, which it fulfills by clinging to our inner truth in all situations.

The Remorse Function

The remorse function becomes active when we realize that we have gone down a wrong path. Feeling remorse over having followed a mistaken idea or belief turns a switch in our psyche that allows us to return to the path of our Cosmic destiny.

Our Natural Self-Correcting Function

It is little known that we possess a self-correcting function that allows us to return to harmony with the Cosmos after we have acted against our true nature. The process of self-correction is set in motion by the Sage's retreat. This retreat gives us a feeling of utter loneliness. The support we usually feel from the Earth, the sunshine, the trees, is also suddenly gone. The loneliness reflects the barrenness of depending on the ego.[5]

The absence of the Sage, with all the above consequences, produces *true shame*, which gradually pushes upward into our conscious awareness. This process can be supported by dreams, in which we feel embarrassed. When we become consciously aware of the shame, we feel *remorse* for having been untrue to ourselves. Even if we may not be able to put into words what has caused us to betray our true nature, our remorse switches off the gnawing feelings of our conscience. At the same time, the Cosmic blame we had created becomes extinguished.

It becomes clear from the above description that we have the ability to return to harmony with ourselves and with the Cosmos *without necessarily* becoming aware that our false use of language had been the cause of our mistake. Some humans have self-corrected for millennia in this way. However, the Sage informs us that humankind, now poised on the brink of self-destruction, can no longer remain ignorant about the role that language has played in creating this dilemma. We humans need to recognize the destructive effect of words, phrases, and images that violate Cosmic truths. When we identify those words and images and free ourselves from them, that act penetrates to the inner truth of all humans, even though it may take years before that truth emerges into their conscious minds. When we as individuals recognize the destructiveness of our false use of language, our mind will have learned the basic lesson that allows it to return to unity with the Cosmos.[6]

In order to decrease the mind's ignorance, humans need to

---

5 Hexagram 33, *Retreating*, Line 6: "Cheerful retreat. Everything serves to further. This line refers to the Sage that, in retreating from the ego in a person, never does so in anger or vindictiveness, or to punish him. It retreats cheerfully, knowing how that person will ultimately feel relief when he turns away from the ego in himself to reunite with the Sage. The Sage's retreat to support the person's true self is the meaning of 'everything serves to further.'"

6 The *I Ching* refers to the end of our separation from the Cosmos in Hexagram 38, *Separating/Opposition*, Line 6: "Isolated through separating, through seeing one's companion as a pig covered with dirt, and as a wagon full of devils. First one has drawn a bow against him, then one has laid the bow aside. He is not a robber; he will woo at the right time. As one goes, rain falls; good fortune."

learn things they are usually not taught in school. For example, they need to learn about their natural self-correcting function. When this function is correctly understood, the role that punishments play in correcting people, can be seen as counterproductive in that they create the fear of making the mistakes that would teach us things.

When we know about this self-correcting function, we have a better understanding of the role of Fate. Through its boomerang action, Fate not only returns to the originator the negative energy created by his disharmonious ideas, it brings to his mind the very words, phrases, or images that created the fate. These ideas are brought to mind by the psyche's self-correcting function to give him an opportunity to recognize how he has violated a Cosmic Principle of Harmony, and to regret these thoughts.

The shock that accompanies Fate also brings us back to our inner senses and to our commonsense. This fact increases the possibility that the mind will stop to reconsider the words or phrases that created the fate. If this opportunity was missed, then at any time later we can ask the Helper of Our Commonsense to bring those words or phrases to mind. We are never helpless when it comes to understanding and ridding ourselves of the cause of a fate we have created. The Sage and the Helpers of our nature immediately join any sincere effort we make in this direction.

The Categorizing and Searching Functions of the Psyche[7]

These functions store all ideas and images that are contrary to our inner truth, in a separate place. When we seek to know the source of a particular disturbance, these functions find and bring the particular idea/image causing the disturbance into our conscious mind. These functions also seek out such ideas and images when asked by the Sage, or when, with our conscious mind, we ask the "Finding Helper" to bring them to mind.

The psyche keeps a record of all our experiences, which it

---

7 This function is referred to in Hexagram 11, *Harmony, Peace, Prosperity,* Line 1, as "pulling up ribbon grass…each according to its kind." Ribbon grass is a metaphor for the mistaken ideas and beliefs a person needs to dispose of in order to return to harmony with the Cosmos.

categorizes according to the Cosmic Principles of Harmony. For example, they are categorized according to their usefulness in the short or long term, which determines whether they are stored in our short or long term memory. This is different from how the ego mentally categorizes them as pleasant/unpleasant, gain/loss, good/evil, useful/not useful according to *its* standard.

The Premonition Function

This function warns us of an imminent danger, usually one or more days before it is to happen. Some people whose premonition function is very keen have falsely believed that they were to blame for actually *creating* the accident or adversity they "saw" in advance, and that this function was "a curse" rather than a gift. This is a complete misunderstanding. The premonition function, in this case, wants to give the person an opportunity to say an inner No to the adverse event that is being announced. His "No" engages the Helper of Cosmic Protection to prevent the event. The inner No needs to be said in all cases of a threatening danger, whether the danger is to the person himself or to another, or to a larger group of people.

This function can also make a person aware of an opportunity, a challenging event about to happen, or of a strong emotional event taking place in someone close to him. The function is to make the person act to come to that person's aid, without an external knowledge of what is taking place.

Premonitions are different from fears the ego can project before our inner eyes. Fears have an emotional charge connected with them, while premonitions do not. The premonition function removes the person emotionally from the event that is about to happen.

The Mind's Cooperation with the Psyche

As the above descriptions show, the healthy psyche has an abundance of functions that help the thinking and imaging minds to respond harmoniously to situations. These functions also allow the mind to cooperate in bringing to expression our Cosmic destiny, which is simply to be who we truly are.

The mind's cooperation with the psyche depends on its willingness to be receptive to the feelings that come from within us. These feelings tell us whether something is harmonious or not. The mind's receptivity also enables the Sage to keep our psyche connected with the Cosmic Consciousness.

What Causes Dysfunctions of the Psyche

Here, we can only cite briefly the causes of dysfunctions of the psyche. They will be discussed in detail in other chapters. Dysfunctions include mental, emotional, behavioral, and learning impediments. They also include so-called personality disorders, depression, lack of inner peace, persistent anxiety, phobias, codependency, obsessive/compulsive behaviors, addictions, and drives.

These dysfunctions are caused by disharmonious influences coming from the collective ego through its influence on the mind. *Ultimately all enter the mind through the opening made by the self-doubt that creates the individual ego.* None of the harmful influences listed below would be able to injure the psyche if it were not for the splitting of our wholeness caused by the false assertion that "in and of ourselves we are not special enough."

All these influences have come from our cultural and social environment. They are, as a rule, passed on to us by our parents, teachers, books, media, and playmates. These influences also come from the false names that slander the true nature of things. An example is calling our animal nature "inferior," and seeing a part of our nature as evil.

Other disharmonious influences that create dysfunctions in the psyche come from the use of words that have no Cosmic basis, such as 'guilt.'[8]

Additional influences come from negative thoughts other people have or have had about us, whether spoken or unspoken; they may have occurred as early as when we were *in utero*. For example, a mother may have had the thought during pregnancy, "this child will take care of me during my old age." The conse-

8 See Glossary entry: *Guilt.*

91

quence is that the person feels bound to the mother lifelong, and feels guilty when he ventures to follow his inner truth. Another example is that of a father who sees his wife's pregnancy as an unwanted responsibility. Such thoughts create the feeling in the child of "being a burden."

Dysfunctions can also be caused by traumatic events that are not processed in a healthy way. Their memory and the confusion they cause are stored in the psyche. Unprocessed traumatic events disarrange the natural harmonious cooperation between our psychic functions. They can result in tics, stuttering, heart palpitations, and other physical manifestations.

In our modern society, many influences coming from images and thoughts conveyed by the media (TV, books, games, etc.), and various commercial techniques used to sell goods and services, also damage the psyche.

A List of Harmful Influences of the Mind Upon the Psyche

Among them are ideas and beliefs that:
- make us see ourselves as superior or inferior
- make us deny, openly or by implication, our connection with the Cosmos
- elevate the mind over the rest of the body
- see humans as the centerpiece of creation
- disregard the dignity that is inherent in all things
- slander Nature, or any part of our personal nature
- divide our wholeness
- slander life

The above kinds of ideas and beliefs provide the basis for the ego and the types of self-images we develop. Once the ego becomes dominant in the psyche, the psyche's ability to connect with our inner truth is damaged.

Harmful Influences Caused by Traumatic Events

These traumatic events include:
- acts that violate our essential dignity and uniqueness
- acts of encroachment into our intrinsic space
- acts that violate our deepest feelings

• unjust accusations and acts
• involvement in violent events (hate acts, imprisonment)
All traumatic events leave a memory in the psyche in the form of a memory chip that distorts the way the psyche functions from that point on. To use the metaphor of the carpet, they cause a variety of problems ranging from rips in the weft to creating unwanted knots, holes, and splotches. Some of these do sufficient damage to prevent further growth in one area or another of our lives; others distort the design, or even create an entirely new design that is not in harmony with our Cosmic destiny.

Harmful Effects on the Psyche Caused by the Media
The media is often the means by which the harmful ideas and beliefs mentioned above are spread. The effect is to:
• cause us to doubt our intrinsic goodness
• make us forget the innate resources we are born with to express our uniqueness
• cultivate false needs in us (as through advertising)
• cultivate the development of self-images
• cultivate violence and conflict
• cause terror in us
• cultivate dominance and inferiority
• cultivate helplessness and hopelessness
• cultivate the idea that we are by nature weak, defenseless, and vulnerable to illness
• cultivate insensitivity to the value of life
• cultivate disregard for the dignity inherent in Nature
• cultivate bravado
By overruling what we know through our inner truth, all these influences contribute to the collective ego's control over our lives. As a result, the psyche is made the slave of the ego, which causes its beneficial functions either to be damaged or negated altogether. The consequence is to make us sub-human, meaning devoid of feelings and sensitivity.

Summary
All the above-mentioned negative influences that are often

unconscious to the mind are demonstrated in a number of mental and/or emotional disorders, and in so-called personality disorders that people falsely believe to be inborn negative character traits. When these events cause a complete separation of the mind from the psyche, they cause insanity.

The causes for dysfunctions of the psyche are only partially described here. Further causes will be shown in Chapters 13, 18, and 19.

The Sage has made us aware that all these negative effects can be repaired with Cosmic help. This help begins with our willingness to be guided by the Sage.

9. Who Is the Fairest?
The Self-Image Aspect of the Ego

Without images, the ego is nothing, because it is a composite of images that pretend to be the self.

Due to the self-doubt created by the statement, "in and of yourself you are not special enough," the true self has been halted in its growth often as soon as in its first year. The true self possesses something the ego needs if it is to take a commanding place in the personality: *the reservoir of life energy the true self comes with at birth.* As quickly as possible the collective ego establishes a "pipeline" to this energy source. It does so by proposing a mafia-like deal: "You will be protected from being seen as deficient if you make me your protector." Taking a seductive tone, it adds: "There is an unrecognized greatness in you that the world needs to see. I will help you, if you turn matters over to me. However, you must conform to what I expect of you." Under the influence of self-doubt, the true self accepts the collective ego's deal.

To fulfill this expectation, the first self-image we take on is that of "the good child." Goodness, in the definition of the ego, means subservience and obedience to the collective ego's authority, and conformity to its values. These values have the sole purpose of securing the collective ego's control over us. As mentioned above, this control has been defined as "protection." Thus, the reservoir of life energy that belongs to the true self is given over to the individual ego, which turns it over to the collective ego.

All virtuous self-images are defined by the collective ego's standard of goodness. This standard is defined by external rules of behavior that specify what we must *be* and *do* to fulfill the self-image. Failing to comply automatically means that we have fallen into a *vice*. The notion of a vice originates in the collective ego's logic, which defines all things in terms of opposites.

Following external moral rules of behavior conflicts with our inborn natural guidance system and morality that is based on our inner truth. Every person possesses this inner truth/DNA, which contains all the Cosmic virtues we need to live in accord with the Cosmic Principles of Harmony. Among our Cosmic virtues are our total goodness, our loyalty to our inner truth, and our natural kindness and love toward others when they are sensitive to us. Our Cosmic virtues are exercised with a clear distinction between what is harmonious and what is not. They cause us to be reticent, or to withdraw when the ego in another is present. Through the virtue of reticence, we maintain our dignity. We protect our energy from being stolen by the ego by holding to the Cosmic virtue of loyalty to our inner truth.

However, with the adoption of a virtuous self-image, we shift our loyalty to the moral rules of behavior dictated by the collective ego. Through this shift, we lose our natural ability to distinguish between what is harmonious and what is disharmonious. Now, the distinction is based on a mental judgment that defines things in the categories of good and evil/bad, and virtues and vices. The *I Ching* speaks of the harsh white light of judgment that comes from the intellect when it relies on absolute standards. This white light is contrasted with the yellow light of inner truth, which discerns things in a relativistic and moderate way. This is the way our commonsense discerns the truth of things. Because the clarity produced is in harmony with the Cosmos, it leads to what the *I Ching* calls "supreme success."[1] Success, here, means that we draw all the blessings and help from the Cosmos.

When our loyalty has been shifted to the moral rules set up by the collective ego, our commonsense becomes blocked and gets replaced with 'faith.' The word faith is surrounded with high honor: The stronger our faith, the better person we supposedly are. In reality, the investment in faith is the willingness to put aside all commonsense — about the meaning of words and the meaning of things in general, in favor of beliefs that can be based on the most absurd statements.

The ego knows that it, the ego, is not real. Nevertheless, it

---

[1] See Hexagram 30, *Clarity*, Line 2.

believes that it will become real if it tries hard enough to *appear* real. This "reality" is always betrayed by the fact that it is only bravado. In this effort to be seen as real, the ego makes us frequently look in a mirror to see whether the image we present to the outer world is convincing. *The problem for the ego is that it can never really exist. It is doomed forever to be an image.* Therefore, when we are dependent on such an image, there is the need to constantly work at perfecting it, to prove it to be real. This effort, and the energy it takes from our life force, is what gives the ego its "life" and keeps it alive. The price is a constant base level of anxiety.

Furthermore, the self-doubt that fuels this effort can never be erased by the self-image that has been adopted.

It needs to be noted that the ego not only lives on positive recognition, it can also live on negative recognition when we have failed to gain recognition for a "good" self-image; it then makes us adopt a negative self-image such as that of "the rebel," "the outcast," or "the non-conformist."

The Consequences of Taking on a Self-Image

Adopting a self-image causes the mind to become *fixed* on fulfilling the requirements that suit the image. Visual proof becomes the focus: how we look, dress, hold our body and take care of it, what careers we choose, and what we do as activities; it likewise influences the habits we adopt in regard to eating, drinking, smoking, what we say and how we say it, which people we associate with and choose for our mates, which products we choose (house, car, etc.), and what we want from people. In short, every aspect of our life comes under the command of the main self-image we adopt, without our having noticed that we are under the influence of an illusion that, in turn, is based on our self-doubt.

All the self-images presented to us are taken from models present in the society in which we grow up. Many factors determine which image we choose for ourselves. The significant fact is that in one way or another, it makes us feel special, in order to compensate for the feelings of inferiority based on self-doubt. Depending on our family background, being special can be defined by any of the following: intellectual abilities, popularity, physical prowess, titles, temperament (gentle, bullying, great-hearted, etc.), religion, race, economic position, or family history.

Because self-images are masks that have no Cosmic reality, they need to be supported by a number of rationales that give reasons why they make us special. While aspects of the ego are obvious in the person who, through bravado, asserts himself as a leader, they are less obvious in the person who meets none of the criteria for good looks, bravery, or heroism, but who finds his superiority in a self-denying, humble self-image.

To maintain the self-image of being special, the ego keeps renewing our self-doubt through maintaining an inner dialog. This dialog takes place in our psyche without our conscious awareness. In it the ego reminds us, on the one hand, that "we will never be good enough, no matter how hard we try," and on the other, it plays on hope by urging us to strive ever harder to bring the self-image to perfection. We become conscious of this dialog only when the image of being special has failed to bring us the promised recognition. Even when it has brought us the promised recognition, the recognition never resolves the self-doubt.

Building a self-image directly affects our relationships with others in several ways. It causes us to seek their recognition and approval at the expense of our self-worth. It can cause us to form a codependency with another solely to gain that recognition. We become attracted to partners who will do that for us and we define our partner's loyalty in those terms. Pursuing this recognition leads us to make deals with others that imply, "I will support and tolerate your self-image (ego) if you support mine." Friends and our relationships with fellow workers, family, and the groups we join, can similarly serve this purpose. We may even view our children as adjuncts of ourselves whose duty it is to reflect well on us. We let them know our disappointment when they make the mistake of failing this expectation.

Self-images wreak havoc on our commonsense, as when a

grandiose self-image causes us to take out loans we cannot afford in order to buy houses and fill them with furniture that tell our neighbors, "we are successful." We similarly indulge in buying clothing that reflects the self-image we want to project. Self-images govern the weddings in which we show off our daughters, the cars we drive, the toys, games, and computers we buy for our children, and the multitude of other products and services we use that enhance our self-image and announce our "life style."

Addictions of various sorts are often the consequence of attempts to project a self-image. An example is the daredevil who drinks too much or drives too fast, and who takes thoughtless risks of his life to prove himself to be "a man." The same can be said of a woman who, during middle age, wants to have a child at all cost, because she has been told that she is not a woman until she has had a child.

Self-images are likewise built into the way a person holds his cigarette or in the kind of wine or mixed drink he buys, to show himself either as "sophisticated," or as "one of the guys." These addictions constantly whisper in the psyche, "I must have this to prove myself." The voice behind such words is the self-image, preying upon our self-doubt. The more we allow it to take over our personality, the more our true self is repressed into the subconscious.

The Ego's Ascent to the Throne

The ego takes control of the psyche only gradually. At first it speaks in terms of "we," "you," and "one," as it internalizes the various ways in which the collective ego speaks. These voices say, "We do things this way," "You ought to know better," and "One never says such things." By conforming to this we-thinking, the individual who is full of self-doubt feels safe. Around the age of fourteen or fifteen, the individual ego has formed to the point where it attains control and speaks in the psyche as "I." By this time the true self has become so repressed by self-doubt that it has ceded the rule over the personality to the ego. The blotting out of Cosmic help and protection gives the ego total control over the personality. Once the ego has arrived at this point, the confusion in the psyche is complete.

The individual ego now appears within our psyche to be an entity comparable to a feudal lord — with his court, guards, an army, a court of law, a central prison, and all the other institutions that characterize a tyrannical regime. It fosters this impression to make the true self believe it is insuperable. Under this disguise, the ego appears to be an entity, whereas in reality it is a conglomeration of words, phrases, and images invented by the human mind, once that mind has lost its connection with the person's true feelings.

How the Self-Image Blots Out Our Original Image

We have mentioned in the previous chapter that the original image of a person is stored both in the Cosmic Consciousness and also in the psyche. This Cosmic image is like a blueprint the psyche uses to guide us on the path of fulfilling our Cosmic destiny. The psyche does this by drawing our attention to choices that lead toward this fulfillment. We have mentioned the weaving of a carpet as a metaphor for the way the psyche goes about this task.

The development of a self-image, with its focus on fulfilling ego-goals causes the fulfillment of our original image to be bypassed. We are turned in an entirely different direction that leads only to disappointment. The burnout that we, Carol and Hanna, experienced, is a typical example. However, when we realize that the point of burnout is the point of opportunity to return to our original image, we become aware of the self-correcting function that is built into our nature. When we make the choice to correct ourselves, the life energy that went into creating the ego begins to accrue back to our true self.

Unfortunately, not all burnout leads to self-correction. A person may allow his true self to be 'executed' by the ego. This happens when, after he has been made aware by the Sage through a dream that his true self is on the verge of extinction, he consciously gives his consent for the execution to happen. At this point he becomes what the Sage calls a 'walking dead person.'

That is someone who has lost his ability to care. This is not to say that this person is 'forever lost.' Someone else can ask for Cosmic help for him, and deprogram his decision on his behalf. Then the Sage temporarily returns to him, giving him an opportunity to rescue his true self. (We always need to ask the Sage whether we are meant to give this kind of help to such a person.)

Freeing Ourselves from the Individual Ego

The first step is to recognize that the ego is a fictional entity that owes its sole existence to the fact that we have accepted certain false words, phrases, and images as true. By accepting them we have implicitly agreed to give them our life force. We can free ourselves from this fictional entity by withdrawing our consent to those false words, phrases, and images, and by making sure that we do not give them any energy. In this manner we deconstruct the ego phrase-by-phrase and image-by-image. We also say No to all ego-emotions. As one of our readers put it, we "starve the ego with a steady diet of inner No's"!

10. It All Comes Down to Language

Language has the potential to either allow us to live our life joyfully and happily or to make it into an experience of pain and suffering. In this chapter we will share what we have learned about how language affects the body and psyche. We will also explore the kind of language that harms.

In recent years, scientists studying the atom have made the startling discovery that *consciousness affects matter*. This principle is at the heart of quantum theory. It is also at the heart of the way the *I Ching* addresses our problems: it makes us aware how our thoughts create our reality. More specifically, it comes down to words and phrases, and the images that accompany them. It is a matter of how we describe things, and whether our words reflect their essence, or merely their outer appearance.

Language that has harmful effects uses words and a logic that is in conflict with our inner truth/DNA. Alfred Korzybski, in studying the effects of language on people in the 1930's, described the harmful effects of using what he called the "*is* of identity."[1] By this he meant that telling a child he *is* bad, creates a trauma in the psyche because it impugns his nature as bad, rather than saying his deed was bad. The *I Ching* made us aware that such a use of language has a fixing and distorting effect on the child's psyche. As such, it is a *spell* that causes him to automatically associate his view of himself with the word "bad." All slanders put on a child's nature create spells that make him doubt his true nature. He thereafter suffers one or another form of self-condemnation that depends on the words used, until these spells, lodged in his psyche, are brought into consciousness, processed, and deprogrammed.

We have also learned from the Sage that negative consciousness affects not only humans, it affects the consciousness of every

---

1 Korzybski, Alfred, *Science and Sanity*, An Introduction to Non-Aristotelian Systems and General Semantics, 1st. Ed. 1933, The Non-Aristotelian Library Publishing Co., Lancaster, PA; S. I. Hawakawa, *Language in Action*, 1st Ed.,1939, Harcourt, Brace and Co., NY.

thing in the outer world toward which it is directed. It can have a harmful effect on the way plants and animals behave, on the Earth, and even on the weather. Because all living organisms on the Earth are an expression of the Cosmic Consciousness, our giving them names that misrepresent their true nature causes disturbances in them, and ultimately creates fates for us. In the following, we will focus on the effect of harmful consciousness on humans.

The Mind Hears Words Differently from the Body

The Sage made us aware that the mind hears words differently from the body. To give an example, the mind makes little or no distinction between the expressions "to let go of something" and "to give up on something." The body, however hears "letting go of something" as detaching from it, whereas it hears "giving up on something" as meaning, "there is nothing we can do about it." This gives rise to hopelessness. It is important to notice this distinction when we want to turn a matter that we ourselves cannot solve, over to the Helpers for resolution.

Another example is found in writings that dwell on melancholy. Melancholy is frequently encountered in poetry, novels, and the stories of operas. In fact, poetry is often read in a dramatic and sing-song melancholic style, while in operas, music fills the role of amplifying the melancholy. While the mind enjoys the relating of such emotions when they are expressed in such dazzling ways, the body falls under the sway of the melancholy, and the hopelessness it implies. The body cells, which are sensitive to statements that pose life as hopeless, can lose their will to live.[2]

Spells

The most basic spells are those put on a person's nature by the

---

2 Carol was reminded of a book she had read by Stefan Zweig in which he detailed how the famous German writers, *Hölderlin, Kleist, and Nietzsche* were plagued by inner demons that "pursued them lifelong". Zweig openly believed that the greatness of these writers was actually due to these demons. This fact must have influenced Zweig because he later committed suicide. See Stefan Zweig, *Der Kampf mit dem Dämon: Hölderlin, Kleist, Nietzsche.* Insel Verlag, Leipzig, 1925.

verbs of Identity, *to be* or *to have*, as in "you have a bad temper." They are also created by the words *always* and *never*, as in "you always do this" or "you are never on time." Once such phrases are taken into the psyche, the person thus described finds himself involuntarily behaving in those ways, and is unable to correct the behavior through force of will. He can, however, become free of those faults through deprogramming the spells.

The further effect of such spells is to inhibit the maturation of a person's true self. It is as if a knot has been put into the carpet of his psyche, preventing its further weaving in that place.

In terms of the functions of the psyche, identity spells negatively affect its reflecting, storing, and transmitting functions. The *reflecting function*, instead of reflecting and strengthening the goodness of the true self, reflects to the person the soiled image that has been put on him. This image has now covered over his original image. As to the *storing function*, all his good experiences of Cosmic help get trashed by an ego-element that keeps him focused on the negative image put on him, and on the mistakes he has made. Normally, the *transmitting function* would make the mind aware of the danger created by the spell; however, a demon, created by the identity spell, has taken over the transmitting function and now uses it to repeat, over and over to the mind, the same spell and false description of him.

To make things worse, the self-doubt created by identity spells dismisses the help available from the Helpers of our body that would protect us from invading negative thoughts. This lack of protection creates a constant back-of-the-mind anxiety and defensiveness. The mind deals with this anxiety in a number of ways: by rationalizing away the dangers, by seeking diversions, by developing addictions to forget them, or by covering them up through acquiring titles, or by transferring the same spells onto others. None of these tactics frees the person from the spell's harmful effects.

Projections

Another type of phrase that has a fixing effect on the psyche is the *projection*. Phrases of this type project a behavior that will take place in the future, as in "I knew you were going to say (or do) that."

We experience the effect of such projections coming from others when we find ourselves saying something we do not believe, or when we find ourselves doing something that is inexplicable to us.

Projections are based on false conclusions drawn from earlier events. These false conclusions usually are the first premise in a logical sequence that leads to yet other conclusions. Because the basic conclusion is false, the conclusions drawn from it are necessarily false. However, so long as the first premise is unreflectingly accepted, we take the whole sequence to be true. The following shows this string of logic when a boy has told a lie:

"He *is* a liar" (A false conclusion and spell)

"Once a liar, *always* a liar" (A projection and spell)

"He will grow up to be a no-good" (Another projection and spell)

All these conclusions fix the boy in this behavior and thus become self-fulfilling prophesies.

Hexagram 25, *Innocence*, emphasizes the importance of keeping the mind innocent by "not expecting, not projecting." Both the acts of expecting and projecting have negative consequences, since they set up, in image form, a situation that then manifests into reality. Both expecting and projecting reflect the planning and contriving activity of the ego. Behind these activities is the ego's desire to control the future.

We are also made aware in this hexagram that the ego is behind all intention, and that intention is a form of projection. It is thought to be helpful to "have good intentions," however, our true nature needs *no* intentions. It responds appropriately to the need of the moment without forethought.

Through the influence of the collective ego, people tend, on the one hand, to deride the idea that thoughts can either help or harm others, while on the other they proclaim the power of positive thinking and the power of intention. When thoughts (words and images), even those that supposedly promote a good message, are used as instruments of power (that is to say, they are pushed forward through mental focusing), the ultimate consequences are negative, i.e., the success achieved comes with a fate. This is because the intention projects desires that are inappropriate for the true self.

Negative predictions by "authorities" about future events such as climate change and earthquakes are *projections* that can make those events happen. These predictions are based on conclusions drawn from analyses of patterns collected in the past. They are not based on a correct understanding of the causes of these past events, which are not outwardly visible to the observer. These causes lie under the same kind of spells put on the climate and the Earth that were put on the boy who once told a lie.

In all these situations, the ego is active in constructing a logic based on a "circular reference," where a false conclusion is used as the premise from which further conclusions are drawn. (The term "circular reference" is taken from a computerized mathematical operation in which we have mistakenly included the sum-to-be in the numbers to be added. If the computer program would not make us aware of this mistake, the sum would continue to add itself in, *ad infinitum*.) The ego, having based its first false conclusion on external observations only, then acts as the all-knowing "predictor of the future."

The ego neither includes the invisible Helpers of the Cosmos nor those of Nature, nor those of our own nature in its logic. Consequently, its explanations of cause and effect are invariably faulty and mechanical. Neither does the ego take into account the Cosmic Principle of Fate, which brings back to humans the negative energy they create through their incorrect thoughts and actions. So-called negative events, as a rule, are such fates.

Poison Arrows

Yet another kind of spell is what we call "poison arrows." They, too, fix certain functions in the psyche by inserting a poisonous energy into them. They also affect the body, creating a poisonous reaction that is felt in some part of the body, such as a sharp pain, a crick in the back, or sting in the heart. When not removed by deprogramming, they cause physical illness at

some point in the person's life. Poison arrows include the following kinds of thoughts:
- envious thoughts
- thoughts that put guilt on oneself or another
- comparisons of all kinds, such as a strong wish to become or not to become like someone else
- mechanical descriptions of the body or of the nature of a thing (example: speaking of the body as a machine or the heart as a pump)
- attributing a disability to one's nature
- wishing harm on another
- viewing the mind or body as one's enemy
- slanders on certain food and drink (causing allergic reactions to them)
- fears and hopes that imply there is no help available from the invisible world

All poison arrows contain ego-emotions that constitute the poison at the tip of the arrow. An example of an ego-emotion is envy that is behind the thought, "She is getting away with murder!"

Poison arrows can be put on us as early as *in utero*. This happens often with unwanted children. Fortunately, the Cosmos does not leave the child without help. Various events are constellated by Cosmic Helpers on his behalf that aim at breaking the fixing effect of the poison arrow. They come in the form of shocks that are experienced positively or negatively, such as an unexpected gift in the form of a helping friend or relative, or in the form of an illness that has the purpose of breaking the poison arrow and removing the poison that has been inserted into the child's psyche and body.

Cosmic help also comes to us when we have put spells or poison arrows on ourselves, on life in general, or on our relationship with the Cosmos. This help comes in the guise of Fate, the shock of which breaks the spell or poison arrow. (See the discussion in Chapter 2 of the effect of this kind of shock.)

All this help is offered to teach us about the harmful effect of the misuse of language, and to give us the opportunity to correct uur thinking. The *I Ching*, when consulted to find out the cause of a misfortune, helps us identify the kind of projection, spell, or poison arrow that needs to be removed from our psyche. Once deprogrammed with Cosmic help, the fate connected with it is quickly ended.

The reader may ask, for example, how can we avoid putting poison arrows on people who have made us angry? If we allow the ego to seize our anger, it will castigate the person with language that contains poison arrows. Indignant language such as "How dare you" is an example. Other phrases can be, "He/she is impossible," or "a threat." We need to realize that the other person is under the control of the ego, and that his behavior is not coming from his true self. We say a firm inner No to his insensitive behavior, turn the matter over to the Cosmos, and ask for Cosmic help for the situation. Outwardly, we withdraw without making a demonstration of it. We also avoid any temptation to use power, be it in thought, speech, or action.

The Harmful Effects of Poison Arrows on the Body

To fully understand the harmful effect of poison arrows on the body, we need to know that the body, under healthy conditions, receives nourishment and information from our original image, which is stored in the psyche. This image includes every part of our body. When an individual body part is injured by a poison arrow, its original image and the body's connection with it gets obscured; then the cells that make up that body part no longer receive the nourishment and information they need for the cells to replicate, grow healthily, and maintain themselves.

Being deprived of this nourishment and information makes those body cells susceptible to becoming ill. The poison arrow remains there until it has either manifested as an illness (with the possibility that the illness will break it), or we remove it through deprogramming. Poison arrows may remain relatively inactive for years, and manifest as illness in connection with events that cause a weakening of the will to live.

A further consequence of poison arrows is that the body cells degenerate as a result of their impeded ability to renew themselves. One consequence is premature aging. Another can be the formation of unnatural growths due to the cells' loss of their knowledge of how to grow themselves. Depending on the kind of poison arrow, another result can be conditions of ill health ranging from infections, to life-threatening conditions such as auto- immune disorders, leukemia, and HIV/AIDS.

The strong emotions that accompany poison arrows continue seething in the person who receives them. They affect his good will. An example is a person who during youth received a poison arrow of impatience from a teacher; thereafter, he found himself unable to be patient and understanding with others who are learning. The poison arrow had damaged his good will to be patient in like circumstances. The teacher, likewise, had received such a poison arrow during his youth.

"Seeing the Great Man"

The *I Ching* frequently counsels us, "to see the great man." By this it refers to the transforming effect of seeing the possibility that a person's true self can emerge temporarily from its prison to correct a given situation. Merely seeing the possibility of greatness in another can temporarily transform the most hardened person, or bring harmony where before, a longstanding feud has ruled; or, it can open up the possibility of making progress in stalled negotiations.

Although we may have experienced this phenomenon more than once, it may have eluded our notice that until we have consciously made this effort, we have harbored the opinion that such a person, relationship, or situation "is impossible" or "hopeless," without noticing that this judgment is a poison arrow that holds the situation in that state of hopelessness.

The Sage pointed out to us that the same opportunity is there to see the potential in people we view as too rigid, harmful to the environment, indifferent toward inequities in the law, or otherwise incorrigible. We need only to see the "great man potential" in them to free them from the poison arrows we have put on them. Practicing this view, which holds open the *possibility* of their evolving through transformation, enables them to permanently return to their true nature. In part, it achieves this result through removing our view of them as hopeless.

Applied to the way we view our body, we "see the great man" when we hold our view of it open to being repaired through correcting our thoughts about it. This means removing the mechanical view of it that permeates our culture, as when we see heart murmurs as caused by defective valves, and high blood pressure as due to plaque in the arteries and veins. Mechanical relationships in the body are on the secondary level of causes; the primary cause is on the level of consciousness. A fallen bladder, for example, can result from the common assumption that the bladder is a mechanism that has no ability to adapt and learn. That may sound absurd until we allow for this possibility. That possibility is what has allowed for the evolution of all organisms. For example, seeing the possibility that the bladder can learn, automatically takes away the poison arrow that it is merely a mechanism, and speeds up the time required for its transformation. Seeing possibility acts as a positive shock that breaks the poison arrow.

Failure to see possibility in all aspects of our lives keeps us stuck in negative situations; our negative view wards off the helpful coincidences that otherwise come repeatedly into our lives. Seeing possibility is not the same as focusing on what we desire. Rather, it is to open ourselves up to what the Cosmos offers in terms of help.

The Propagation of Harmful Language

Harmful language that has been put on a person in childhood (or even before birth) is so unbearable to his nature that he will develop the coping mechanism of throwing it off onto others. We call this *propagation,* since it is the main means by which the collective ego spreads its control over people. As a consequence, the person constantly repeats his attempt to pass the harmful language off onto ever more people. Through this mechanism, a whole population can become infected with disharmonious thoughts and the destructive ego-emotions they generate. The demonic element that carries out this process is the "dragon of propagation." It needs to be noted that passing off these thoughts does not free the person of them.

Propagation occurs in the following ways:
- through judgments
- through idle speech and gossip that contains judgments
- through blaming
- through ego-fears
- through guilt
- through doubt
- through denial
- through humor (as used in sitcoms) that laughs at people who, like the viewer, have received similar poison arrows

Judgments are thoughts that are critical, hypercritical, condemnatory, or disapproving of the conduct of others. Particularly harmful is the practice of mentally 'executing' people, which happens when we give up on them as hopeless. All judgments come from self-righteousness, which is a means of passing off onto others judgments that have been made about us. Self-righteousness gives us the feeling that we have redeemed ourselves.

The propagation of spells, projections, and poison arrows *through idle gossip* is obvious. Because these spells and poison arrows occur behind someone's back, the effect is that they hit him in the back (meaning outside his direct awareness). The demonic elements contained in the spells and poison arrows then influence that person's behavior in ways that are unconscious to him.

Blaming another shows the denial aspect of propagation, because it throws off onto another blame that was formerly put on us. It is also used to shift Cosmic blame we have incurred by going against our true nature, onto others. It can also be an attempt to cleanse ourselves of blame.

Fears coming from the ego are also unbearable to the psyche, and want to be passed on whenever possible, so that the person does not feel alone in his fear. Paradoxical as it may sound, he is comforted by knowing that other people share it. This is one of the reasons bad news gets so much coverage in the media. Another reason is the misguided idea that knowing about something bad enables one to protect oneself from it. Quite the opposite results when bad news, such as warnings of a pandemic, is spread broadly. The fear is usually accompanied by a barrage of negative images. Once the fear is accepted in the mind, the body cells adopt it; their fear makes them susceptible to the disease. Through propagating the fear, the susceptibility is spread broadly to others.

What Allows Propagation?

Propagation can occur either through an inner channel between two people, or through 'holes' in a person's natural protective system. An inner channel exists between parents and their children. It is meant to facilitate helpful inner communication from the parent to the child. For example, when the parent has learned a Cosmic truth, this truth is automatically communicated to the child without its needing to be stated aloud. An inner channel is also created between two people who open themselves to each other. The inner channel can become polluted by the ego when it uses it to pass blame or judgment onto the other in the form of a barrage of poison arrows and spells.

In all other relationships between people, holes in their natural protective system allow the harmful thoughts to enter. Such holes are created by self-doubt, guilt, fears, bragging, making ego-judgments, and by any kind of self-image. These holes get closed when we make the inner effort to free ourselves from the respective ego-aspects.

Stopping Propagation by Saying the Inner No

Stopping propagation is essential to protecting the boundaries of our personality and to restoring and maintaining our wholeness. When someone directs harmful thoughts at us, it is like an invasion of our inner space that we are able to stop by saying a firm inner No to all ego-thoughts that are being expressed. Saying the inner No engages the Helper of Transformation, which then dissipates the negative energy.

The *I Ching* is clear about our relationship with the ego. It says simply, "No relationship with what is harmful."[3] The inner

---

3 See Hexagram 14, *Possession in Great Measure*, Line 1. This statement makes clear how we protect our Cosmic possessions.

No needs to be said to all aspects of the ego with the firmness of a rock.[4] That means we do not allow, within ourselves, even the slightest tolerance of its false statements. With every inner No we say to the ego's temptations to compromise our integrity and dignity, we are lifted out of our servitude to the collective ego, and out of the helplessness, hopelessness, and depression it creates in us.

Saying the inner No is combined with an inner retreat from engagement with persons whose egos seek to engage us in their harmful thinking. The inner No communicates on the inner plane, outside the notice of the ego. It is said matter-of-factly, without the judgment or admonishment that occurs when the ego says No. In saying it inwardly, we simply refuse to join the ego-attitude; afterward, we remain inwardly neutral.

To understand the effectiveness of saying the inner No we need to know that the ego's awareness is limited to what is seen and heard. The true self, by contrast, perceives through our inner senses. It perceives, for example, what the ego in another thinks, plots, and plans, and it perceives the false logic that dominates a person's thinking. Our common language tells us how the true self knows this when we hear expressions such as "that idea stinks."

Saying an inner No not only stops the ego from propagating itself in us, it engages and strengthens the true self in the other. The activated true self then resists the ego's going further. The fact that the inner No is so effective in stopping the ego in its tracks has caused the collective ego to do all it can to disable our ability to say No. One of its rationales is that saying No is "being negative." The disablement of our ability to say No is an important part of the collective ego's childhood conditioning. It is carried out through the use of rewards and punishments: the good child who does not say No to parents or teachers is rewarded, while the one who says it is punished. People with this disablement are unable to successfully deprogram ego-aspects by saying the inner No, because of the guilt connected with saying it. (See "Restoring the ability to say No" in Chapter 19.)

4 See Hexagram 16, *Enthusiasm/Motivating the Helper of Transformation*, Line 2: "Firm as a rock."

113

Summary

Looking at the subject of spells, projections, and poison arrows, and how they are passed on, we understand many of the causes for inexplicable outbursts in ourselves and others, as well as other behavioral disturbances. The Sage made us aware that propagation is the main cause of behavioral disturbances.

The original cause for being open to receiving poison arrows lies in the primary doubt inserted in us at an early age, "in and of yourself you are not special enough." Deprogramming this phrase is essential in the process of reclaiming our wholeness.

Through deprogramming spells, projections, and poison arrows, we become more aware of when someone puts them on us. Thus, we have the opportunity to free ourselves from them immediately. We also find that once we have set out on the path of getting to know ourselves, the old poison arrows that are lodged in our system are gradually brought to our attention for deprogramming.

We give methods for deprogramming that do not require this ability, in Appendix 3.

11. The Darkening of the Light
Through Self-Doubt and Fear

In Chapter 5 we described how our wholeness becomes divided by the introduction of self-doubt into the psyche. This was accomplished by the statement, "In and of yourself you are not special enough." The effect of this event on us is described in the *I Ching* as the "darkening of the light."[1] This refers to the crowding out of the light in both our psyche and our body cells by this one phrase.

When self-doubt is not halted through deprogramming, it can lead, in its extreme form, to a type of mental illness that allows the person to feel safe only when his actions are confirmed as safe by some outer authority.

The most common consequence of the introduction of self-doubt is that we become separated from our inner senses and commonsense; then, insecurity rules our lives, causing us to look to outside authorities to tell us what to think and do that will keep us secure. Through this subtle process we shift our reliance on the Cosmos for our protection, to the institutions of society (the government to keep order, the banks for the protection of our money, and so on). While these institutions have legitimate functions, they are not our true source of protection and help. When we forget that the Cosmos is that source, then indeed we are in jeopardy.

The Sage helps us view our situation from the broader (Cosmic) perspective when we are willing to take off the blinders that self-doubt creates. We take them off by acknowledging the existence of the Helpers. When we do this, they will bring us the help we need at the exact time we need it.

We understand the meaning of "the darkening of the light" when we realize that the life force (chi energy) that exists in every body cell and in the psyche, is made up of two forces, the light and the dark, both of which are Cosmic in origin. Their

---

1 See Hexagram 36, *Darkening of the Light.*

115

interaction with each other makes possible the transformation of consciousness into form. It also makes possible the renewal of the form.

However, when the light in a body cell gets crowded out by self-doubt, the effect is to split the consciousness of the cell into two parts, with one part still able to create transformations, while the other part cannot. The ability of the cell to create transformations has this importance: we mentioned in the previous chapter that the body cells receive their information of how to grow, regenerate, and maintain themselves from the original image of us stored in our psyche. This information is normally transformed into form in the cells; the presence of the original image insures that the cells manifest into the form that corresponds to our original image. When the ability to create transformations is reduced to only one part of the cell, the transformations become incomplete; then, what is manifested does not follow the original design. Unfortunately, as self-doubt eats away the light, the voice of the ego becomes stronger, while the voice of our inner truth becomes dimmer and dimmer. When self-doubt becomes dominant, the dark in the cell becomes demonic, causing us to see the world as through dark glasses.

These dark glasses constitute a limited frame of reference into which all our experiences thereafter get squeezed. For example, self-doubt interferes with our ability to draw help from the Cosmos. It also interferes with many of our natural talents and abilities. Even those most developed come under the shadow of doubt when self-doubt dominates. These effects make clear that self-doubt is a fully active rather than a passive force. Once initiated, self-doubt tends to spread into all corners of our being, damaging our wholeness. The slightest entertaining of phrases that create self-doubt invites the predatory ego in ourselves and others to take over, and to pull us into its dark thinking.[2]

The *I Ching*, in its ability to confirm to us our inner truth, first helps us to go around the self-doubt; this is necessary while

---

2 The *I Ching* describes this in Hexagram 44, *Coming to Meet*. The inner No needs to be immediately said to the doubt, which is the meaning of the oft-repeated words in the *I Ching*, "It furthers to be firm and correct."

we still lack the ability to deal with it. As our trust in our inner truth grows, the *I Ching* helps to free us from the source of our self-doubt.

When our wholeness is not divided by doubt, we receive inner guidance and clarity from our inner senses (commonsense). This guidance is based on the Cosmic Principles of Harmony. Reliance on our inner senses draws all the help from the Cosmos we need to make sound decisions.

Self-doubt also makes us doubt that we possess Cosmic virtues. This doubt opens us to accepting the moral rules of the collective ego that protect us from the supposed evil in our nature. The idea that there is evil in our nature is responsible for many addictions. The addictions attempt to fill the dark hole that self-doubt has created in our self-worth, by diverting us temporarily from being aware of it.

Reliance, either on substances, or on outer social structures never releases us from our deeper feelings of insecurity. This is because these outer measures cannot replace the only true security we attain from the Cosmos through following our inner truth.

The Doubter in the Psyche

When as children self-doubt has turned us to looking outside ourselves for support and protection, a demonic element called the "doubter" is created in our psyche. It is the consequence of the dark having become demonic. The doubter tells us, "Only the eyes can see the truth." Through this false statement, our sense of outer seeing is given the role of determining what is true and what is false. Thereafter, the doubter puts into doubt everything we feel to be true, by saying things such as, "I will only believe it if you prove it," "Maybe it is true, maybe it isn't," "What, if you are wrong?" "How can you be sure if it is not proven by science?" "Your feelings are only subjective."

Depending only on what we can see with our eyes as a measure of what is true results in *a purely mechanical approach to life.* Because this approach excludes the invisible Helpers, fears and doubts are the result. For example, the mechanical view makes us believe that our protection lies in keeping our doors locked, or through having an alarm system. The doubter seeks to make us believe that the mechanical view is the only acceptable view of the way things work. Inducing us to doubt our Cosmic protection, the doubter introduces fear as the basis for our actions.

The effect of the doubter on our heart, body, and our feeling of being at home within ourselves

When as children we were made to depend only on what we could see with our eyes, all our other senses of perception became blocked. These other senses are the very ones that connect us with the Cosmos and its Helpers, and thereby give us an absolute feeling of inner security.

Being blocked from the Cosmos and its invisible Helpers creates a deep sadness in the child's heart and body. He is then told that his parents and the social fabric are the only sources for his needs. This creates a conflict between the child's true needs and the parents' ability to fulfill them, because no humans can fulfill the kind of love or supply the kind of needs that only the Helpers can supply. As a consequence, the parents begin to see the child as "too demanding," and to dismiss the needs they cannot fulfill as "superfluous." At the same time, they may feel guilty for not being able to fulfill these needs; they then may attempt to placate the child with compensating goodies. In this process, the true self is gradually imprisoned and a *false self,* the spoiled child, is created. The newly created spoiled child learns that he can play on the parents' feelings of guilt while his sad true self is suppressed into the dungeon of the subconscious.

The combination of presumed insufficiency, blame, and guilt put on the child's true self leads him to feel he cannot fit comfortably in the world as it is. Nevertheless, he keeps trying to fit into that world by developing the self-images that bring him recognition. Simultaneously, he loses contact with the original image of himself that is stored in his psyche. With that, he loses his inner peace, and the feeling of being at home within himself. The longer he continues on this path of self-alienation, the more his original sadness about losing his connection with the Cosmos changes into a cynical view of life. He then becomes consumed with the challenge to play the ego's games better than others. The true self, stuck hopelessly in its dungeon, is condemned to being sucked dry of its life force, with that life force going to build the individual ego.

Fear as a Device of the Collective Ego

Like guilt, fear is actively promoted and used by the collective ego to keep people under its control and to supply it with the energy it needs for its existence.

Fear is the result of being taught to doubt those things that would normally give us inner strength. Thus we are taught to doubt our wholeness, to doubt the protection we gain from following our inner truth, to doubt the harmony and beauty of the Cosmos, and to doubt the care and love it has for all the things that have manifested from it.

Fear is strong in us because it has been taught in our homes and schools for thousands of years. Fear also is inculcated in us by the collective ego's falsely portraying the Cosmos as an invisible hierarchy that is remote, arbitrary, indifferent, cruel, and to be "naturally feared."

To justify the existence of fear, the collective ego has invented the idea that fear is useful as a protective mechanism. However, the doubt in our wholeness that creates fear shuts us off from the very bodily senses that enable our quick and unthinking responses to danger. Unlike our natural response to danger, fear causes us to freeze, thus making us even more vulnerable to harm. (See Chapter 13, on the harmful interferences of Complexes of Conflict on the *involuntary response function* of the psyche.)

Self-doubt and fear are inseparable components of the collective ego. Once we see this with clarity, we can begin to free ourselves from them, and draw to us all the Helpers we need.

12. The Guardians of Untruth
The Effect of False Rationales on the Psyche

One of the functions of our thinking mind is to phrase in verbal language, explanations of the inner truth of things. These explanations are true rationales. They can be received as insight-flashes in meditation, or come as the result of experiencing the harmonious nature of the Cosmos and its workings.

The *I Ching* uses true rationales to show how a metaphor fits a certain situation. For example, the meaning of the metaphor, "graceful and moist" is revealed in the commentary to Line 3 of Hexagram 22, *Grace,* by the rationale: "'Graceful and moist' can refer to a person who indulges in the pleasures of life in a purely egotistical way."

Another metaphor is in the following text from Line 4: "Grace or simplicity? A white horse comes as if on wings. He is not a robber, he will woo at the right time." This metaphor is explained by the following true rationales:

> "This line contrasts two different kinds of logic. In the Cosmic logic, grace and simplicity are one and the same thing. In the logic of the collective ego, grace is identified with complexity, brilliance, and contradiction. In terms of thinking, it employs half-truths and falsehoods, giving them [false] rationales upon rationales to support their contentions. The more cleverly it makes these half-truths and falsehoods believable, the more brilliant it considers itself."

In order for the ego to take over the personality it needs to replace our inner truth with 'ego-truths.' The first of these is the idea that "in and of ourselves we are not special enough." However, since this idea is an untruth and cannot hold its ground, it needs to be supported by false rationales, the first of which is the rationale that "only the eyes can see the truth." This one rationale excludes the invisible world of the Helpers, along with all our inner senses of perception that would keep us connected with our inner truth. Because the idea that only the eyes can see the truth, produces any number of mistaken ideas, the ego needs a constant procession of rationales to support its claim.

120

It turns to the mind that has the ability to produce rationales to provide this support. The mind, on being flattered as capable of brilliance, cleverness, and complexity, takes on this challenge, without noticing that it has been tricked into fooling itself.

False Rationales as Changelings

Once created, the false rationales provided by the mind become demonic elements in the psyche that *change* Cosmic truths into ego truths. The name "changeling" is taken from the European folktales about a demonic element of that name. These tales also happen to describe how changelings operate in the psyche.

The tales warn of leaving a newborn child unattended outside the house, because a "changeling" may come and take that child and substitute its own defective child. This defective child, also called a changeling, is described as crying incessantly, as requiring constant attention, and as driving its parents to despair. Furthermore, it does not grow and mature.

This description illuminates the mechanism by which false rationales are introduced into the psyche, and by which the true self is gradually replaced by the spoiled child — the individual ego created by the collective ego. The fact that the changeling's child is also called a changeling tells us how the changeling multiplies itself into the endless number of false rationales that are needed to support the collective ego's false logic.

Changelings *change the Cosmic truths that want to emerge into our conscious mind into ego truths.* They do this through a number of devices that include language tricks. One of these devices is the creation of *frames of reference* that stand like doorways through which all experience is to be interpreted. It is as if we are in a room full of windows through which we could see the panorama around us, but we are permitted to look only through these doorways. The frames of reference instituted by the changeling limit us to giving validity only to (1) what we can see with our outer eyes, (2) what has been instituted as true by the given culture, and (3) what custom and law have defined as true. These frames of reference exclude and negate what we are able to perceive through our five inner senses and our metaphorical senses, all of which are necessary to tell us the inner truth of a matter.

Among the language tricks are false comparisons, the omitting of words that would correctly qualify meanings, the tailoring of the meaning of words, the use of false associations, the invention of new words that have no basis in Cosmic logic, the appending of false names to things or situations, the use of implication to create suspicion, the instigating of fear and doubt, and the making of open-ended statements such as, "in and of yourself you are not special enough," and "you never know."

The changeling attempts to prevent true introspection by calling introspection "selfish," and by suggesting that introspection is "dangerous," implying that it can lead to insanity. When we have unique insights, it dismisses them either as "something everyone already knows," or as needing scientific validation.

We have mentioned above that the changeling has numerous progeny, which are also called "changelings." Each changeling is a different rationale that accompanies a given ego-emotion, attitude, self-image, or mistaken idea or belief, in order to keep those aspects of the ego in place. For example, by calling the ego-emotion of hate "natural," we are deceived about the fact that hatred is not true to our nature. Changelings employ numerous language tricks of this sort. We distinguish them by the specific language tricks they use.

The ego claims that we are free to think for ourselves. However, as we describe the various changelings below, the reader will see how the ego restricts our thoughts to its galling set of limits in every area of our lives.

The Changelings as the Suppliers of the Ego's Need for Energy

The function the changelings serve in justifying the mistaken ideas and beliefs of the collective ego cannot be separated from their function of supplying the individual ego with energy robbed from our inner truth.

An example is the interaction between two changelings called the "reasoner" and the "devil's advocate" that engage in a debate. The debate can occur entirely within the mind of one person, or be carried out with others. As in this case, it will become clear from the following descriptions of the various changelings, what kinds of language tricks they use to gain that energy.

The Names of Changelings

The names we have given the changelings are taken from the role that each plays. For example, the name given to the changeling that drives us to obsessively listen to, or read about bad news, and to then report that bad news to others, has the name, "The Spreader of Bad News." This changeling stands for the rationale, "the more you know about bad things out there, the better you can protect yourself." This rationale belongs to the ego's view that "we are thrust into this life all alone and must depend on our own resources." On the basis of this rationale it gives the mind the job of protecting us.

What is not apparent in this scenario is the fact that bad news, if not processed through attaining a Cosmic understanding of the situation, has a harmful effect on the body. This is because the body cells hear things differently from the mind. For example, a new statistic that shows a notable increase in breast cancer among women in a certain age group can create the fear in women of that age group that they may be among the next to get the cancer. Their fear puts a poison arrow on that part of their body, creating the possibility that they might get breast cancer. Comparing ourselves with others, or with a statistic, not only ignores the fact that every person is unique, it introduces fears that, as poison arrows, injure the consciousness of the part of the body pointed to. Whatever self-doubt we possess then becomes magnified, further weakening the will of the body cells, causing them to succumb to that threat.

The Main Kinds of Changelings

We describe here only a sampling of changelings. It needs to be said that no list of changelings can be complete, since new false rationales are constantly created by the ego as needed, so long as it dominates our psyche. To take away the basis for their existence, the original doubt in our wholeness needs to be deprogrammed, along with the three basic changelings mentioned in Appendix 3, "Deprogramming."

Looking at these rationales, it becomes clear that none of them are actually "rational" — they only pretend to be. They influence us simply because they have been stated in words that have been accepted by others before us, without reflection. They are taken as true in much the same way we may believe advertising hype to be truth, or because, like most advertising, they contain a half-truth; we also take them in because they have cleverly used words that are vague, or have double meanings, or, while totally false, have been said with great authority.

It may seem exaggerated that we can be influenced on such a flimsy basis, but we ask the reader to reflect on how the great swindles of recent times have resulted in the collapse of the entire world's economies. These swindles depended on clever schemes, the misuse of words, the hiding of key information, the greed of investors, or on the weakness, fear, and collaboration of regulators. Similar false rationales have fooled generations of people around the world into waging wars.

A brief study of the techniques of deception in any of these situations reveals not so much the cleverness of those who carried out the deceptions, but the unreflecting acceptance by those they deceived.

It may interest the reader to note that the changelings often appear as stereotyped characters in comedies such as sit-coms.

The Inventor of Rationales and Counter-Rationales

The original changeling is "the Inventor of Rationales." Described in metaphorical terms, it acts as the "Speaker of the House" that keeps order when a spectator in the gallery shouts out a serious objection. Such an objection might be made to the obvious illogic of a common conventional belief. To keep order, the speaker orders the spectator to be removed through the rationale, "disorder is dangerous."

The spectator gallery, in this "house of rationales," is the place where the true feelings reside after being pushed out of any official status in the governance of the psyche. There, they are generally forbidden to make any noise, but in extreme situations they may forget themselves and cry out.

Phrases that have created the changeling called the Inventor of Rationales are: "There is a reason for everything," "We have nothing other than the rational mind to give us answers," and "Things have to make sense" (meaning that they have to fit the collective ego's logic).

Since ego logic automatically creates opposites, there is also "the Inventor of Counter-Rationales." In this way, a new rationale is created every time a rationale is recognized as false.

The Guardian of Ancient Wisdom

This changeling calls up old rationales by playing on the reverence that is given to ancient wisdom. Its substantiating phrase is "You can't disregard the wisdom of the past" (also falsely referred to by the ego as "commonsense" or "conventional wisdom"). An example of this "wisdom" is the phrase, "Go with the flow." Subliminally, this phrase has a good ring to it because it suggests going with our true feelings. However, the meaning intended is to the contrary: "Accept things as they are," and "don't make waves."

This changeling, together with the Inventor of Rationales, highlights the fact that *the entire function of changelings is to keep us in a frame of accepting ego rationales as true, and thereby preventing us from using our sound judgment and ability to reflect.*

The Public

This changeling addresses us as "you," as in, "You must do things this way," "You will never succeed if you don't make compromises," etc. The word "one," is also used, as in, "One never knows what is true and what isn't." This changeling also makes us worry about what the anonymous "they" are thinking about us, or what they will think if we do a certain thing. In this role it acts as the inner judge and upholder of correct conduct. It also speaks on behalf of others, as if it knows what they need. It can also use the so-called royal we, as when the nurse enters the patient's room and says patronizingly, "Have we taken our medicine this morning?"

125

All these types of statements have a hypnotizing effect through suppressing our own authority. This confusion brings us under the umbrella of the collective ego, which pretends to protect us from the evil in ourselves.

"You have to be open-minded"

This changeling voices an inner directive that always begins with the words, "You have to be…." It seeks through these words to draw us away from our feelings as the first determiner of what to take as true. The words "have to be" (or "must") are the telling element. They cause us to put aside any hesitation we feel coming from our inner truth, so that we believe as true what we are told. If we pay attention to our inner hesitations, we realize that something being said is not complete, and that we need further clarity and the guidance of the Sage before we alter our current viewpoint.

"You Never Know…"

This phrase is used by the changeling to promote doubt in what we know through our inner truth. It also uses it to open us up to any number of other changelings by implying that we can never know the truth. It rules out the trust we would naturally have in our inner truth.

The phrase is often said by a person who has been trained to keep his mind half-open to doubts, even when he knows a thing to be true or untrue. He doubts everything that is being said, including his inner truth.

The changeling also uses this phrase to introduce and create acceptance of ideas that are not in harmony with our inner truth. It is said in order to lure us into entertaining these proposed ideas, giving them the chance that they might be true ("you never know"). Even if we do not fully agree with what is being said or read at the time, the mistaken idea is taken into the psyche by default through allowing that it might be credible.

The Reframer, or Shifter of Meaning

This changeling shifts the meaning of a word by applying it incorrectly. For example, it uses the term "self-development" when it is referring to developing an ego-self-image such as the image of "being virtuous." The development of this image actually oppresses our true self. In its Cosmic meaning, self-development refers to bringing the true self to maturity through ridding ourselves of values and ideas that are foreign to our nature.

In another example, this changeling shifts the word "self" to "selfish" by implying that any concern about the self is "selfish." Introspection and acquiring self-knowledge are thereby seen as being "self-indulgent" and as an egotistical pursuit.

The reframer, or shifter of meaning, acts always to block us from attaining a true understanding.

The Seeker for a Culprit

This changeling keeps us seeking to pin blame on someone or something instead of seeking to understand the true cause of a misdeed, which invariably lies in the ego. Its relish for the word "culprit" has the purpose of engaging us emotionally so that we are diverted from understanding the way the ego works. In this subtle way the changeling protects the ego.

The Shifter of Attention

This changeling shifts our attention away from our real concerns to those on which we can have no direct effect. Its partner is *The Diverter* changeling. Their sole purpose is to distract us from coming to an understanding of our true concerns.

When this changeling makes us focus on world affairs, it is accompanied by the "imp, demon, and dragon of world affairs." They change our naturally modest view to a grandiose one in which we see our paying attention to these affairs as important to saving the world.

The Diverter

This changeling uses all kinds of diversions to keep us from seeking the inner truth of a matter. One such means is to make us fall asleep when we attempt to find that inner truth. Another is to keep us focused only on complaining and pitying ourselves. Another tactic is to ward us off from seeking this truth on grounds that we may find out something terrible, either about ourselves or the other person.

The Generalizer

This changeling takes one or two experiences and makes them the rule, as by saying, "everybody does it," or, "it always (or never) happens." Examples: (1) Two neighbors mow their lawns on a Sunday. The generalizer causes the observer to comment, "everyone around here mows his lawn on Sundays." (2) After it has been raining two weekends in a row, the generalizer comments, "It always rains on weekends." Generalizations put poison arrows on people and things and fix them in self-fulfilling ways.

The Creator of Contradictions

This changeling describes things in contradictory terms by keeping us focused on their mere appearance. For example, it would claim that the individual human being is "all alone in the world." Ruled out in this view is the fact that every person is part of the Cosmic family. The Cosmic family is the name for the totality of invisible Helpers and all aspects of Nature. Our Cosmic family supports us in everything we need to fulfill our Cosmic destiny. By keeping us held to descriptions that are based only on what we see, the creator of contradictions is one of the major distorters of our perception.

The Reasoner and the Devil's Advocate

These two changelings operate as a team that engages us in debate. The debate does not have the goal to find the inner truth of a matter, but is carried out for the mere sake of argument, and of proving who is "right." As is obvious, the ego in the person who wins congratulates itself to be superior, and compliments the mind for its brilliance.

This debate, as mentioned earlier, can also take place within the mind of the same person. The purpose of the devil's advocate, in this game, is to keep doubt alive. Because of the self-congratulatory nature of this game, the person is kept from searching for the inner truth of matters. Through believing that the person has arrived at the absolute truth of the matter, this game leads to a self-righteous and rigid attitude.

The Intruder

The intruder changeling causes a person to intrude into our

inner space by asking invasive questions such as, "how do you feel about me?" This question steps far over the border of what people have a right to know about us, and therefore is immediately intimidating. If we accept this intimidation, we give the ego in this person control over us and in doing so, decrease our inner strength.

A person under the rule of this changeling constantly subordinates others to his will. Napoleon's humiliating his subordinates by pulling their ears is an example of this changeling.[1] Because intruding questions and actions catch us by surprise, they confuse us about how to respond.

A person under the influence of this changeling believes that "success is dependent on networking with others." He can be seen working hard at creating networks of "contacts," — people he sees only in the light of how he might use or control them. Many politicians, fund-raisers, professional organizers and holders of public office are under the influence of this changeling.

Parents who ask their children, "Don't you love your mommy?" are also under this influence, as are teachers who demand loyalty to a school, a religion, or to the country. Such invasiveness inhibits the child's, student's, or adult's loyalty to his inner truth, and destroys his sovereignty.

The Appropriator

Appropriation is the main way the collective ego deprives people of their Cosmic possessions and gifts. The appropriator changeling uses certain rationales to accomplish this task, such as the following: "All wisdom comes from the same source, and no one owns the copyright." This rationale is used to justify the stealing of Cosmic gifts given to an individual. This changeling is also active when an individual or institution embraces insights given to others, and then turns those insights to a use that is contrary to their original purpose.

The appropriator changeling becomes active when we are about to reach inner clarity; it then appropriates the unique-

1 This habit of Napoleon's was described by Alfred DeVigny in his short novel, "The Malacca Cane." See: Great French Short Novels, The Dial Press, NY, 1952, pp. 146-158.

ness of what we are about to learn from the Sage by saying, "At the bottom, all truths are the same." This reduces and dismisses the insight to "nothing of consequence." Another phrase it uses to achieve the same result is, "This is not different from what I believe," although in reality it is. Another activity of the appropriator is to credit our insights to the brilliance of our mind, thus denying the Sage as their source.

The Negative Mirror

In the role of a "negative mirror," the changeling changes positive facts into negative ones by finding at least one fault that diminishes every positive thing.

The Labeler

The labeler changeling also gives wrong descriptions to our experiences. For example, it calls inner work "hard," harmony "boring," and working with the *I Ching* "a crazy path." It trashes good experiences by saying, "that's nothing."

The Guardian of the Ego Conscience

The guardian changeling pretends to represent our conscience by reminding us of the rules of conduct that are to be applied to all the situations of our lives. The 'shoulds' and 'musts' contained in these rules create a tribunal in the psyche that prohibits us from listening to our true conscience.

The Substitute

This changeling puts ego-emotions in the place of our true feelings: it replaces anger with hate and vindictiveness; it makes love into a token of the ego, sadness into grief, joy into an exaggerated enthusiasm, and kindness into compassion. It thus injects ego pride into every innocent private feeling. By turning sadness into grief, it demonstrates to others the depth of our loss; by turning kindness into compassion it demonstrates our "kind nature"; by turning true enthusiasm into exaggerated enthusiasm it shows us as "being positive"; by turning anger into hate and vengeance, it demonstrates our righteousness; by turning love into possessiveness it controls the relationship. The main rationale used by this changeling is, "Nobody would notice your true feelings."

The Makeshift

Here the changeling acts to trash good experiences either through denigrating them, or by introducing doubt of their worth through the word "but." Example: When we have experienced the trustworthiness of the Cosmos, this changeling says, "but you still don't know what the future will bring," implying that the experience could turn out to be bad after all.

The Changeling as Stop-Gap

This changeling seizes gaps in conversations to insert negative or hopeless observations that destroy an otherwise positive conversation. It does this by activating a demonic element of self-importance in the person seizing the gap.

The Deputy

This changeling is evident when the ego causes a person to assume the role of bringing divine justice and order to Earth. Such people, Napoleon, for example, authorize themselves to do this. Anyone who acts from self-righteousness sees himself as a deputy of God. However, in seeking to punish or ban those whom he thinks are offenders, he creates a fate. Cosmic justice eliminates disharmony by correcting a person's thinking.

"You Need a Belief System"

This changeling causes us to assume that the *I Ching* is a new belief system we can adopt after we have turned our backs on the one we previously held. This causes us to look at the *I Ching* as presenting us with rules and maxims on which we are to base our life. Taking this view prevents us from seeing that the only purpose of the *I Ching* is to mirror back to us our inner truth so that we rely on it for guidance.

The Changeling of "Deserving"

The idea of "deserving" is this changeling's rationale; it credits the success we have achieved with Cosmic help as something we have deserved. The entire idea of deserving is not in accord with the Cosmos.

The Changeling of Defensiveness

This changeling is behind the rationale that asserts, "it is natural to defend yourself." However, when we take our defense into our hands, we lose our Cosmic protection. The Cosmic way is to say an inner No to wrongdoings, then turn them over to the Cosmos and let go of them.

The Pacifier

The pacifier changeling argues that we need to create a balance between opposite forces in order to create peace. The result is that we are put in a constant balancing act that tires us out without solving the problem. It also puts forth the argument that peace is created through meeting the other halfway through accommodating his incorrect attitudes.

The Operator of Fearful Projections

The operator changeling flashes a millisecond image of a threat into the mind whenever we want to free ourselves of an aspect of the collective ego's program. An example is the image of hell fire, or some other eternal punishment; such threats are put forward subliminally just when we are ready to free ourselves of the ego concept of guilt.

The Enlightener

The enlightener changeling pretends, in meditation, to "disperse illusion" by projecting a bright white light on a single aspect of a greater truth that wants to emerge from our inner truth. As a result, we become consumed by that single aspect, which then produces the "enlightened" thought, "now I understand things." This intervention shuts the door to a true understanding. The enlightener shuts down the Helper of Mind-Flashes.

The Spoiler of the Pleasure of Bodily Love

This spoiler changeling points the finger of shame at us, saying, "It is sinful to combine love with sex." The shame causes hot flashes and nightly sweats.

The Depriver of the Senses

This changeling causes us to dismiss those senses that are the foundation of sensitive behavior. Its rationale is that paying attention to those senses makes us weak, helpless, and ineffective. It is the cause of insensitive behavior and the subsequent denial that we have been insensitive.

The Employer

This changeling gives us one task after another to do. When we want to relax or meditate, it can be heard to say, "What about this unfinished business, and what about that…?" This changeling is coupled with another changeling called "the blamer" that then starts blaming us for the things we have not finished.

The Predictor

By predicting evil situations yet to come, this changeling gives itself the air of being "wise." It says: "As soon as one thing (ailment or bad thing) is gone, another comes." When something has been deprogrammed, it says, "It will come back." In speaking about the world, it says, "Evil is always lurking somewhere."

The Changeling of Mechanical Thinking

This changeling says, "Everything has a mechanical explanation." It insists that the reason why something worked out successfully is due to a mechanical action, such as a pressure being exerted, or by replacing one part with another, or due to a change in the chemicals.

This changeling also insists on relying strictly on plans that have been made. It says, "You must have structure or you are lost," and "things work best when your plans have covered all contingencies." While it is necessary in many activities to have a plan, as in building a house, designing machinery to make a product, or coordinating efforts to make travel efficient and safe, these activities work best when Helpers are asked to be a part of the project, and are thereby given space to deal with the unexpected that occurs in every activity.

The Changeling of Right and Wrong

This changeling replaces Cosmic judgment that is based on whether a thing is harmonious or disharmonious, with an ego judgment that judges things as either "right or wrong." Discerning something as harmonious or disharmonious is based on our true feelings, whereas right and wrong are mental judgments that vary with the values that different cultures put on things.

The Spoiler

This changeling distracts us from enjoying the good things of the moment by introducing an unpleasant subject. For example, the changeling may intrude while we are enjoying a good wine. Someone then points out what he has read about the danger to our health of sulfites in the wine. In another instance, while we are beginning to enjoy a delicious and carefully prepared meal, someone introduces the memory of an unpleasant meal they had. The harmony between the body and the food, and the gratitude we would feel toward the host and Nature are thus spoiled.

The Projector of Worst-Case Scenarios

This changeling interjects itself in times of difficulty when the road ahead is not clear; it projects the worst things that can happen while at the same time it reviews our inability to respond adequately. This kind of thinking creates a downward vortex that drives us toward imagining ever worsening consequences. The cloud of hopelessness and impossibility gets ever darker, ruling out all the possibilities that are available when the Helpers are brought into the situation. Behind this activity is the belief that events are driven by predestination.

The Changeling of "You-Need-to-Be-in-Control"

The rationale represented by this changeling is, "You need to know, otherwise..." behind which is the thought, "you might miss out on an opportunity, or you might not be aware of something that threatens your future."

The Changeling of "The-Attraction-of–that-which-is-For-bidden"

This changeling exerts an irresistible attraction to go against a prohibition, once we have accepted that the prohibition is correct. We can see this changeling as a generator of guilt on which the ego then feeds.

The Obsessive Thinker

This changeling can be unconsciously present during the whole day, but then becomes conscious when we are physically passive, as when we are lying in bed. It is accompanied by a demon that can be called "the engine of thoughts left running" and a "demon of obsessive thinking." (See Chapter 16 for an explanation of demons in the psyche.)

The Undoer of Deprogramming

This changeling puts forward doubts in the effectiveness of our deprogramming, thus undoes it. It says, "How can you be sure that this will work?" This changeling is more frequently found with people who are new to this approach.

Free-Floating Changelings

Free-floating changelings are rationales that have remained undetected in the deprogramming process. They have become detached from the idea or image that has been deprogrammed and now become another problem, as described below.

How free-floating changelings act in the body as free-floating radicals

The name "free radical" is commonly used in chemistry to describe an electron that has been separated from its atom, molecule, or ion. To understand the functioning of free radicals we need to realize that neither they nor atoms are "chemicals" (which term implies that they are devoid of consciousness and operate mechanically), but are aspects of our nature that have a feeling consciousness. Atoms are part of the Helpers of our nature, among which are functions involved with the digestion of food, with our respiratory processes, and with healing.

In a healthy process, because free-floating electrons are highly reactive, they can attract and pair with unpaired electrons that are attached to other atoms, and thereby change the nature of those atoms. These "changes" are what the *I Ching* refers to as *transformations*.

When changelings, as false rationales composed of words and images, remain in the psyche after the main ideas to which they have been attached have been deprogrammed, they become free-floating radicals. In this state, they seek something to become attached to. This something can be an unpaired electron in other atoms in the body. Being harmful, they capture unpaired electrons, and use their *radical property* to block transformations. Thus, they can create serious consequences for the body. For example, free-floating changelings can cause sudden pains that shift from one place in the body to another. When such symptoms occur, it is wise to ask if any free-floating changelings are the cause, then find out how many there are and deprogram them. (See Appendix 3, "Deprogramming.")

Since many mistaken ideas, beliefs and self-images have one or more changelings connected with them, we need to pay attention to the possibility that changelings may be present when we are deprogramming a mistaken idea, belief, or self-image.

13. The Maze Exposed
Ego-Complexes

We have described the changelings at work in the psyche as providing the false rationales that support the ego. Another role played by the changelings is to assemble untrue statements about human nature, about Nature in general, about life, and about every aspect of the Cosmos. These statements are rationales that are used to explain the nature of things and how they work from the view of the collective ego. They are assembled into *ego-complexes* that create rigid structures in the psyche. Usually, these complexes combine two or more spells that lock a person into self-defeating behavior patterns. In dreams, ego-complexes are often seen in the form of buildings, or complexes of buildings.

The *Inferiority Complex* and the *Superiority Complex* illustrate how combinations of false rationales create typical behaviors. While the true self is unique, and does not display anything that could be called "typical," ego-complexes are behind the typical, or typecast behaviors that are often described in plays. We sense in advance the types of drama these typecast characters are going to create, and are fascinated by the way they march straight to that dramatic outcome. In comedy they become "the ones fooled"; in tragedy, they are the ones whose fate we sense as "inevitable." Their roles are drawn from the script of false rationales that are contained in the ego-complexes they represent. The true self, by contrast, does not live life from a script.

When an ego-complex has burned out, we may have a dream in which we see ourselves on a stage practicing for a play, but without a script. We fear the embarrassment of being publicly exposed for not having anything to say. This makes us aware how conditioned we had been made by the ego-complex that has burned out. The true self has no need to fear that it will not know what to say, because it follows our inner truth; our inner truth guides us to say the right things at the right time. Then, what we say has substance and appropriately fits the needs of the situation.

The Inferiority Complex

This ego-complex is based on spells that falsely assert that "human nature is flawed," and that "evil comes from the animal aspect of human nature." Another spell making up this complex is, "No matter how hard you try, you cannot overcome the deficiency of your nature." To these basic spells are added personal experiences that reinforce our feeling inferior due to differences of class, rank, race, education, wealth, etc.

The conclusions drawn from these experiences, in combination with the basic spells, create a negative image of the self that feels like a hole in the center of our being. The hole produces an empty, gnawing feeling that drives us to find some way to ameliorate it. The feeling is unbearable because the spells totally contradict our true nature. Some people attempt to fill the hole with a compensatory positive self-image, as by developing the Superiority Complex. Others sink into a lifelong depression. Still others temporarily numb the gnawing feelings through diversions. These negative feelings about ourselves are like an open wound in the psyche that needs constant attention.

The Superiority Complex

The Superiority Complex is based on the spell: "Humans are superior/special." Rationales supporting this view include the Western religious view of man as created "in the image of God" and the scientific theory that humans are "the pinnacle of evolution."[1] This complex finds further justification in spells that cast one's clan, nationality, and/or culture as superior.

The above two ego-complexes are illustrations of having taken the words, phrases, and images used by the collective ego as "the truth." The statement, "human nature is flawed," is an

---

1 The notion of being special violates the Cosmic Principle of the Equality of every aspect of the Cosmos. There is no hierarchy in the Cosmic Order. Everything that exists in form exists first as an image in the Cosmic Consciousness, and each form that manifests is a unique expression of the Cosmic Consciousness.

example. Behind this statement is the implication that we humans do not measure up to an imaginary perfection. From the Cosmic standpoint, we are whole by nature and have no need to match up with anything. The Inferiority and Superiority Complexes create a totally needless struggle within the psyche of most people.

How Ego-Complexes Enslave Our Natural Psychic Functions

The "order" created by the collective ego in the psyche by the complexes is a purely *mental* order superimposed on the psyche. It is maintained at the expense of the person's natural order. Through this false order, the ego is able to draw all the energy it needs from the reservoir of life energy with which we were endowed at birth.

The ego's purely mental order is in conflict with our true nature in all respects. It is also in conflict with our inner truth that would normally guide us through life in accord with the harmonious order of the Cosmos.

Since the ego does not possess anything in and of itself, it must appropriate our Cosmic possessions and turn them to its service. Each of our Cosmic possessions has a specific function in maintaining and furthering our whole being and keeping us healthy. We have described the various functions of the healthy psyche in Chapters 7 and 8. In establishing its rule over the personality, the ego enslaves all the functions of the psyche by putting *spells* on them. This causes the functions to become organized in new ways: while before, each function held an *equal* place in the natural order, they now become ordered *hierarchically,* with the thinking mind taking over the role that each function served. This new ordering takes the shape of a feudal order in which the mind becomes the feudal lord that is in the service of the king, represented by the collective ego. Just as the feudal lords had to make sure that the common people worked hard to support the feudal system, the mind now has the job to make sure our energy is spent feeding the collective ego.

The ego-complexes have strategic importance. They are constructed in such a way as to prevent the mind from catching on that it has been turned into a servant of the collective ego. They achieve this through flattering the mind into seeing itself as the master of the personality, and important in maintaining the various human hierarchies: lord and master of all the species, and of other humans who are "lesser." To achieve this purpose, each complex gives the mind the necessary justifications for its dominance. Thus, the complexes not only determine how the individual relates to himself, they determine how he relates to everything else. This enables the collective ego's dominion to spread through propagation from culture to culture.

The large number of ego-complexes described in this chapter may give the impression that the collective ego has securely established itself. This, in fact, is what it would like us to think, so that we see no point in following our inner truth. Neither does it want us to realize that its thinking and actions contradict the Cosmic order, and therefore lead only to fates and dead-ends.

On the personal level, the division of our wholeness, created by these complexes, inevitably leads to illness, whether it is mental, emotional, and/or physical. Illness, as a fate, offers us a window of opportunity to throw off an aspect of the oppressing ego. A fate can indicate that an ego-complex has burned out, or has only very little energy left. Its weakened state gives us the opportunity to free ourselves from it. With the Sage as our guide we can safely deprogram the burned-out complex.[2] In this process, the *I Ching* can be of great help by giving us the necessary background understanding.

The following ego-complexes have been grouped in categories, each of which negatively affects a particular function of our psyche.

Inferiority Complexes

Complexes in this category enslave the *receiving function* of the psyche, causing us to draw negative conclusions so that we experience life as though seen through dark glasses. They also block the love energy we would otherwise receive from

---

2 "Deprogramming a complex safely," means we avoid upsetting the precarious balance that exists between two complexes that complement each other.

the Cosmos. The Inferiority Complex itself has already been described above.

The Self-Doubt or Oppression Complex

This complex is the first that gets installed in our psyche. It is based on our accepting the following statements, which are poison arrows: "Human nature is divided into good and evil," and "You need to learn what is good and what is evil." Sometimes another poison arrow is included: "You have to be good to avoid evil." Because these words imply that evil is part of our nature, they divide our nature against itself.

The first poison arrow, i.e., that human nature is divided into good and evil, divides our heart from the rest of our body; it also divides each body cell into two conflicting sides. Through this division of our original wholeness, and through the introduction of the notion of evil, an inner conflict is installed in the psyche that pits us against all that we know through our feelings. The fundamental self-doubt that is thus instilled in us opens us up to any number of other doubts. One such doubt leads us to believe that our life is not authorized, and that our worth needs to be validated by the collective ego. We also doubt that what we feel is true.

Phrases characteristic of this complex may be heard in the psyche in the form of an inner monologue: "You can't trust your feelings," "What you say has not been authorized," "Who are you to say this?" (This is said even when what we say comes from our true feelings.) "You need to be able to substantiate yourself" (meaning, in such a way that others, outside, will agree); "How do you know that the Cosmos will come to your aid when you follow your inner truth" or, "How do you know that the Cosmos will come to your aid in time?"

The imp and demon of forgetfulness are also active in the Self-Doubt Complex.[3] They make us forget the Cosmic gifts we have received and the good experiences we have had in the past, by drawing a veil of forgetfulness over our stored good memories of Cosmic help that came when we needed it. The *I Ching* refers to Cosmic help that comes in emergencies in the words, "A jug

---

3 See Chapter 16 for an explanation of imps and demons in the psyche.

of wine, a bowl of rice with it; earthen vessels simply handed in through the window."[4]

The Self-Doubt Complex produces two self-images: that of the "decision-maker" and that of the "unsure person"; the self-image of the decision-maker causes a person to mentally prepare what he is going to answer when asked, although often the situation for which he prepares does not occur. Busying his mind uses a lot of energy — energy on which the ego thrives. When the Self-Doubt Complex is deprogrammed, the connection between the person's feelings and his mind is freed up. His mind is then able to make decisions that are based on what feels right and appropriate in each situation as it presents itself, and what he says is no longer a pre-written script.

The Self-Sabotage and Self-Deprecation Complex

This complex consists of one or more self-deprecating self-images and the projection, "Things will never get better." It may also consist of a negative phrase that contains the word "always." At the root of this complex is the Inferiority Complex. An example of such a self-image is expressed as, "I'm dumb, I was never able to do those things."

The I-Am-Not-Lovable Complex

This complex is based on the projection, spell, and poison arrow, "I am not lovable." A person with this complex is driven to find every conceivable reason to support this view of himself.

The Self-Pity Complex

This complex is based on the spell, "No one is as bad off as I am." It is often accompanied by the "I-Am-More-Deserving Complex." (See below.)

Superiority Complexes

These complexes block the protective function of the psyche by making us believe we are even above the laws of physics.

The Hero Complex

This complex is a derivative of the Superiority Complex described above. It is handed down from ancient beliefs in the

---

4 Hexagram 29, *The Abyss/Danger*, Line 5.

hero as having the purpose of fighting evil in the world, even though doing so may require the sacrifice of his life. His life's sacrifice is often connected to the image of the hero. The catch in this idea is that for there to be a hero, there also must be something to fight (as, for example, the mythical dragon). Therefore, the hero looks constantly about for his counterpart to fight, often if only in some form of competition: personal, sports, business, cultural, or religious competition; it is always a battle against an adversary. Wherever the words "battle," or "fight" are used to describe a situation, a hero motive is behind it. Either the person speaking wants to be a hero, or someone seeks to encourage another person to become one, through evoking the nostalgia in him that he will never "be enough" until he proves his valor. This nostalgia is carried forward in honoring people as heroes even when they have acted from their true nature, without any intention to be a hero.

That the ego depends on conflict to maintain its dominance over people and to obtain their energy is revealed in the Hero Complex. Not only does the collective ego depend on conflict to maintain its hold on people, either through touting the glory or the fear of it, this complex shows that conflict is one of the easiest ways it can gain the energy it needs to keep itself alive.

The God or Spirituality Complex

This complex is meant to answer a person's question about what is good and what is evil. He is informed that "God knows what is good and evil," and that if he learns this, "he can become immortal like God." Next, he is told how this goal can be achieved: "To become like God you have to develop your higher nature and repress, or conquer your lower/animal nature." The image that accompanies this statement — that of humans in the image of God, is a spell. It only includes the mind, which is equated with good; it excludes and demonizes our human animal nature by equating it with evil.

The habit of judging others and ourselves has its roots in the God Complex and the Guilt Complex (see below). Under the influence of the God Complex, a person unconsciously takes on the role of God as judge, in the belief that he is working on behalf of God (i.e., the biblical God, and not the Cosmos). Phrases that press a person to take up this role are: "You are either on the side of God or you are not," and, "If you don't judge others, you yourself will be among the guilty ones."

A further manifestation of this complex is the proselytizing that goes with it. It includes the phrases: "I am important to the process of correcting what is wrong in the world," and, "I must watch over the situation, or else the truth will be kept from the people." The person's distrust that Cosmic truth finds its own way to manifest, and needs neither to be defended nor promoted, prevents him from seeing that indeed, truth *is* always manifesting. It may not be manifesting as he envisions it, but in the fates people create. All the phrases and images mentioned above are projections, spells, and poison arrows.

The God Complex also contains the dragon of moral authority that rules through the Self-Punishment Complex and the Punishment Complex. It appropriates our moderate innate inner sense of morality, changing it into a harsh inner judge.

The God Complex exists in relation to every religion and its individual adherents, for invariably, each religion poses its beliefs in competition with all the others to be the "right one" to follow. Each contains the threat of being in the wrong, and the promise to be emancipated from the guilt of "being wrong." The vehemence of the idea of right and wrong shows itself in the intense competition for the mind that characterizes religions.

Also part of the God Complex is the belief in hierarchy; therefore, those most versed in the texts and traditions are believed to be the most fit to lead.

The belief in the community of the believers is another part of this complex. It contains the hidden threat that leaving that community will make the individual guilty.

The Self-Punishment Complex

This complex is a consequence of the God Complex and the Guilt Complex. It can be described in the image of the "supreme court of justice." It is composed of several collaborating demonic elements within the psyche: a supreme judge before which our case is being presented, a prosecutor, a defender/excuser (whose excuses are lame and ineffective), a torturer (a demonic element called a "grabber" that tortures the mind) that presents us with the various forms of punishment that will be inflicted on us, a jury that judges us according to ego-thinking, and eye-witnesses that say, "your guilt is obvious." Our true self that is being subjected to this inner court has been declared guilty before it has ever entered the court.

The Punishment Complex

This complex is based on the poison arrows: "Humans have sinned before God," and, "They therefore deserve to be punished by God." "Humans have to take on that responsibility of punishing others."

The Survival Complex

This complex is based on two spells put on life that are based on the doctrine of the survival of the fittest: "The fittest are the superior ones; that is why only the fittest survive," and, "It is a dog-eat-dog-world, therefore you have to be superior and fit."

Complexes of Evil

These complexes distort the *organizing function* of the psyche, which would normally give us a healthy perspective of our unique Cosmic Destiny as the road to true happiness. Through them we are led to call this road to happiness an illusion, and to call "real" the illusion that the road to happiness is through conformity. Complexes in this group also block the *natural self-correcting function* of the psyche.

The Complex of Evil

This is a compendium of phrases that slander Nature, including human nature. They describe all the "evils" the hero sets out to fight. The existence of the Hero Complex not only makes the Complex of Evil necessary, it is what keeps evil alive.

The Resistance Complex

This complex is based on the spell, "I have to resist what I feel and what is." At the root of the Resistance Complex is *denial*, regardless of whether the reality is positive or negative. The denial is due to a conflict between the reality that is lived, and the words that are said about it. For example, the reality can be a dysfunctional family that describes itself as a "happy family." The "happy family" is an image the family members cling to in the hope that it will one day become true. The denial of *what is*, is inserted by the changeling to protect the happy-family-image. The child who grows up in such a family develops a mechanism that splits his mind off from what he feels about the reality around him. In order to protect himself from the ongoing inner conflict this split creates, he resists his feelings. The image prevails because the family command is to believe in the happy-family-image; it is accompanied by the threat of not being part of the happy-family-image.

The same split from reality occurs in the "we-thinking" that is promoted in nationalism. The collective ego encourages us to view ourselves as part of the national family and therefore to be loyal to it, regardless of what it does. We are likewise encouraged to think we are guilty if we do not agree with its policies.

In a seemingly reverse situation, the reality is positive, but is constantly defeated by observations to the contrary. In this situation, a team of demonic elements is active that may be called "the inner observer and defeater." The inner observer makes flattering comments about the person's intellectual, artistic, or other creative abilities, such as "you are a genius," but these are immediately followed by defeating comments, such as "don't fool yourself," "you are not good enough," "you are just a small number," "nobody would believe that you did that," etc.

The resistance can also come in the form of a "defeater," or demon of denial of *what is*. It says, "don't fool yourself, things aren't going well" when they really are going well. The defeater does not allow us to acknowledge anything as good. A typical remark of a person with such a complex is, "this is too confusing for me to figure out, but I must keep trying, because I need to get away from this mess." This remark describes the subtle way the Resistance Complex works to defeat the person.

Complexes of Conflict

These complexes interfere with the *involuntary response func-*

tion of the psyche that allows us to respond spontaneously to conflict. Conflict is the *modus operandi* of the ego that consumes us with thoughts about how we should act. Such deliberations make it impossible for us to act from innocence.

The False-Cosmos Complex

This complex is based on the following projections and spells: "The Cosmos is divided into good and evil," "The Cosmos is all-powerful," "The Cosmos is indifferent to human suffering," "The Cosmos is indifferent to all the created things," "The Cosmos has abandoned humans," and "The Cosmos holds us guilty."

This complex is a major cause of our splitting from the path of reclaiming our true self. This splitting occurs at crucial points in our development, particularly when we are near to successfully expelling the ego. At this point, the ego claims "there is no point in turning away from the collective ego because the Cosmos, too, is hierarchical, is divided into good and evil, and will hold us guilty." On this basis it re-inserts into our minds the fundamental doubts in our wholeness, the fundamental doubts in the total goodness of the Cosmos, and the claim that "no matter how hard or sincerely you try, you will never succeed."

The Lack Complex

This complex is based on ideas that cast the Cosmos as stingy and poor. Accordingly, it associates virtue and spirituality with poverty, and wealth with a-spirituality. Associated ideas cast the Cosmos as unable to help us, and as devoid of Helpers. They also cast the Earth as needing human intervention to bring about abundance. This complex falsely equates modesty with poverty, subservience, and the acceptance of unjust conditions.

The Abandonment Complex

This complex is based on the following false conclusions humans have drawn after having separated from their unity with the Cosmos due to seeing themselves as special: "God has expelled us from paradise"; "We are all alone in the world"; "There is no one to help us but ourselves," and, "We are guilty for our sexuality." (The Abandonment Complex can also be a conclusions drawn during a childhood experience of being ᴜexually or psychologically encroached upon by a parent or other caretaker. "My parents (and God) have abandoned me. I am without help, I am all by myself.")

Children who have been caught handling their genitals, or who have experienced that they cannot please their parents, may also develop this complex.

The "I-Am-More-Deserving" Complex

This complex is based on the following phrase accepted as true early in life, "I deserve more than others, because of the way I was born." Implied is a disadvantage the person must ever endure. He may describe his disadvantage in words such as, "Nobody knows the trouble I've seen." He may go from therapy to therapy as a demonstration to other people: "See, I am doing everything I can, but no one can help me." Bouts of self-pity accompany this complex. To keep from feeling isolated (because this belief isolates him), he may seek to network with others with whom he competes for "who is more deserving," or "whose cross is bigger and more painful." Two changelings are attached to this complex: the "No-One-Understands-Me" changeling, and the Changeling of Networking.

The Disbeliever Complex

This complex is based on the spell: "You must not believe what you feel." Although it is similar to the Resistance Complex, it is restricted to not believing in anything harmonious. It allows a changeling to discount harmonious feelings as "worthless" and "meaningless." It is made up of several demonic elements that include an "observer," which makes a comment based on hope, and a "defeater" that puts it down. For example, when a person is beginning to have some success, the observer says, "I hope this success will continue, upon which the defeater says, "Don't fool yourself, you never have success." The person is then led to conclude, "No matter what I do, things don't improve." Another demonic element in this complex is the demon of denial. It denies the reality of the person's successes by calling them a "fantasy."

The Devil, or Job Complex

This complex is taken from the story of Job, in the Old Testament, and is based on the following poison arrows: "The devil is God's counterpart"; "The devil is the opposite of God"; "The devil is the ruler of hell"; and, "If you don't obey God, you will go to hell." God and the devil are presented as equals in power, and as sharing the invisible realm as lords and masters. People with this complex suspect that their trials and tribulations are put before them by the devil to test their adherence to God. The story of Job reveals the following projections and poison arrows: "God is testing me," "We are cursed by God, although we have done nothing wrong," and, "God is unjust, but we must not argue with God." (This complex is always accompanied by a Ball-of-Conflict. See below.)

The Ball-of-Conflict Complex

At the basis of a ball-of-conflict is the idea that a person, thing, or the Cosmos can be to blame for an experience that is being viewed as negative. Whatever, or whoever is blamed, then becomes the "culprit." In the Cosmic order, the word culprit has no basis. In all cases of negative experiences, a ball-of-conflict is created when Cosmic help is left out of the picture, and the person looks for someone or something to blame. Blaming back and forth usually involves relying only on what can be seen. It ignores the inner truth of situations, which can only be understood with the Sage's help. So long as the conflict endures on this level, the round of misunderstandings continues. This is a ball-of-conflict.

Because a person under the influence of the Ball-of-Conflict Complex insists on seeing the components of the conflict in terms of "what is visible and evident," the conflict cannot be resolved. The same holds true of a person who possesses an inner ball-of-conflict about an issue. He is always looking for a culprit outside himself, in spite of finding no beginning or end to the issue. The only solution is to say No to the idea that there is a culprit, to drop looking for one, and to ask the Helper of Dissolution to dissolve the whole ball-of-conflict.

149

The Not-Trusting-Life Complex

This complex is based on slanders put on life as an entity. Such slanders imply that life is a personality that has opinions, puts requirements on people, can be hostile, and has a power of its own. All of these views of life are slander that can create a hostile reality for those who hold them. Each person under the influence of this complex needs to find out which of the phrases listed below apply to him, and add others, if necessary, before deprogramming this complex:

• Life is a series of ups and downs, good times followed by bad times. Sometimes you get what you need, sometimes you don't. (Upon learning of the Helpers, the person extends his distrust to them and to the Cosmos.)

• Life is suffering (Life is a vale of tears)

• Life cannot be trusted

• Life requires a lot of you (patience, continuous effort, and that you face and conquer your fears without knowing how)

• Life is difficult; the qualities and capabilities we come with at birth are not enough to deal with it

• Life is a maze meant to puzzle, confuse, and trick you: it has dead-ends, dark corners and pitfalls; your life depends on your figuring it out; you have to be constantly on guard

• Life is unforgiving (you must keep your heart constantly steady, otherwise there will be retribution)

• Life is unjust (you could have been born poor, in a famine stricken country, in a rich family, etc.)

• Life is all about waiting

• Life is ruled by changes ("changes" are falsely presented by the ego as "the way of Nature.")

Note: In putting all these false ideas onto life itself, we blot out of our awareness the fact that we are surrounded by Helpers that, when asked, do everything to help us root out our fears, worries, demonic elements, and other ego aspects. Through transformation, they make every aspect of our lives easy. By casting these negative views on life, we imprison the helpful forces that would otherwise carry us through life.

The Life Complex (also the Death Complex)

This complex is based on mistaken ideas about life and death, such as "Life has a beginning and an end," "Death is the end of life," and "Death is the opposite of life."

In the Cosmic order, life is an ongoing experience. Death is the name for the transformation that takes place when life in a body has completed itself; it then continues in the invisible realm. However, when a person believes that life ends in death as a final extinction of the self, it can take a long time before the transformation that occurs after death takes place; meanwhile, until he develops a perspective that is more in harmony with the Cosmos, he is held in an intermediary place.

The Competition Complex

This complex is made up of these and like phrases: "Competition is fighting with other means," "Competition is good," "Competition brings out the best in people," "Competition shows who is the best," "You have to be competitive," and, "If you aren't competitive you can't win." This complex extends itself into science: "Evolution/natural selection is a brutal competition of species and their genetic material." The complex is often accompanied by the demon of jealousy, and the imp of competing.

Guilt Complexes

These complexes are based on the false concept of guilt invented by the collective ego, and the image of an inextinguishable stain that guilt supposedly puts on our nature. The guilt complexes threaten, "If you dare to follow your inner truth, you will be guilty." Through pretending to protect us from making mistakes that would render us guilty, these complexes inhibit (1) the *remorse function* of the psyche (which is part of the *self-correcting function*) that would normally return us to the path of our Cosmic Destiny, when we realize that we have gone down a wrong path, and (2) the *active transforming function* of the psyche that normally would complete our return to harmony through transformation.

151

The Guilt Complex

This complex is based on the spells: "Humans are born guilty," and "Humans are guilty because they have an animal nature." It is accompanied by the image of guilt as an inextinguishable stain put on our nature. As long as the Guilt Complex dominates a person, he feels guilty whenever he allows his true nature to surface. For a person with this complex, the fear of becoming guilty is so strong that he generally would 'walk miles' rather than even appear to be guilty.

Before we can free ourselves from the Guilt Complex, we first need to free ourselves from the false concept of guilt, otherwise we will feel guilty for having deprogrammed the Guilt Complex. Possible other components of the Guilt Complex are: "What I feel is wrong," and the poison arrow, "To free yourself of your guilt, you have to redeem yourself in the eyes of God."

Another component is the self-image of a sinner who must suffer for his sins (as by carrying the cross). Other poison arrows related to guilt are, "My existence harms others, angers them, makes them crazy, makes them hate me, makes them hurt me."

The Guilt-Toward-Self Complex

This complex is made up of the following spells: "Humans are guilty because they have an animal nature," Humans need to redeem themselves by sacrificing their animal nature," and "Humans need to transcend their animal nature by developing their higher nature."

The Guilt-Toward-Nature Complex

This complex is based on the false premises: "Humans are at the center of the universe and Nature is there to serve them," and, "Humans have to achieve domination and control over Nature." These premises separate humans from the consciousness of Nature, causing them to feel guilty, which is expressed in the phrase, "Humans are guilty for how they have mistreated Nature." The guilt then gives rise to the fear that "Nature retaliates for what humans have done to it."

The Guilt-Toward-God Complex

This complex consists of three components: The command-ment: "You must love, obey, and fear God," guilt and self-hatred for not being able to love God, and fear of God's punishment.

Guilt, as noted before, is a false concept that is not in harmony with the loving Cosmos. In investigating its origin, we found that it lay in the implications of the Biblical commandment Moses received from God, where love is mentioned only as a synonym for obedience: "For I the Lord thy God am a jealous God, visiting the iniquities of the fathers upon the children unto the third and fourth generation of them that hate me," and "showing mercy unto thousands of them that love me, and keep my commandments."[5] Here, love is combined with the threat of being punished severely for failure to heed God's commandments.

The Cosmos does not issue commandments because it is a system based on Principles of Harmony. When we follow our true nature, we feel the love of the Cosmos all around us as a supporting and caring energy. We do not feel love toward any-thing that is disharmonious, that is forced on us, that oversteps our boundaries, or goes against our feelings of wholeness. Be-cause the command to love God is so contrary to our nature, we secretly resent it. *Guilt* for being unable to love God is the resulting ego-emotion.

The Sage made us aware that guilt and self-hatred are the same ego-emotion; "guilt" is the true name of the ego-emotion Moses said we must feel towards God. Guilt is automatically attached to failing to fulfill any commandment.

This ego-complex shows that the ego concept of guilt and the idea of "original guilt" are one and the same thing: they both originate in a mistaken idea about the nature of love and the nature of the Cosmos.

In the context of Eastern traditions, shame or dishonor, rather than guilt, is implied in failing to conform to customs that specify the duties owed to parents and ancestors.

---

5 Exodus 20:5

The Hope Complex

This complex blocks the function of the psyche that acts as a facilitator for the Sage, by replacing feelings and sensations coming from the body with images of hope.

The Hope Complex is based on the spell, "You have to keep up your hopes." (The word "hope" has no Cosmic basis.) This complex produces an imaginary way out of guilt and also out of the fear of death.

Duty Complexes

These complexes inhibit the functions of the psyche that act as a facilitator for the Sage. Normally, the Sage assembles Helpers of our nature to aid the mind in its tasks. The duty complexes embroil the person in doing all the tasks the Helpers would do, so that the Sage's help becomes unavailable. The person with these complexes invests all his energies in trying to fulfill impossible tasks.

The Duty Complex (also The Helper, or False-Responsibility Complex)

This complex is based on mistaken ideas of what constitutes our responsibility: "It is my duty to sacrifice my own needs to help others"; "I am the one who can do it best (or "I am the expert"); "If I don't do it, something awful will happen"; "People can't take care of themselves"; "I am a person of responsibility (without measure)"; "You are responsible to your parents, siblings, children, friends, neighbors (without measure)."

The Duty Complex can also originate in commands delivered during childhood: "You must be a dutiful child," and "You must follow your duty to your parents, friends, family," and, "You must follow your duty to the community/nation by being a good citizen."

This complex is composed of an imp, demon, and dragon of duty and a dragon of justice that says we are to blame if we do not fulfill our duty. It creates the hidden anxiety that if we look inside ourselves, we might find that we have failed in our duty. The Sage verified that this anxiety is an important cause of illness.

The False-Responsibility Complex can also include taking responsibility for the harmful things people have done to the planet, other species, etc. The taking on of false responsibilities and then being unable to fulfill them leads to blaming the self for being inadequate, and/or blaming the Cosmos for "making us inadequate," or "flawed." This complex is energized by guilt, on which the egos, both in the person who has this complex and in those persons for whom he has taken responsibility, feed. It is particularly destructive to the love relationship.

Another version of the Duty Complex is the attitude of *noblesse oblige*, which is based on ideas of honor. This occurs in classes of society (the gentry) where honor is an important element, as in "old families of note," and in noble self-images such as that of the "gentleman" or "lady," or that of "the benefactor," "the tolerant, or patient person," or "the person of duty." Such people may do good deeds to build up indebtedness in others, and can be greatly offended when those others are not grateful enough. This complex can also be the reason for a person's refusal to receive gifts that would equalize the imbalance and the inequality they create through their benevolence.

A consequence of this complex is that it keeps people occupied with solving problems for others rather than solving their own; it also keeps those they help from asking the Cosmos for help.

The Selflessness-Complex
This complex is based on the spells, "You have to be selfless, otherwise you are egotistical," and, "You have to sacrifice your needs to the group."

Failure Complexes
These complexes block the function of the psyche that processes negative experiences by disturbing our sense of proportion.

The Failure Complex
This complex is based on the spells, "I have failed, therefore I have betrayed my family/clan and their expectations of me"; "I have disgraced them." This is accompanied by an image of oneself as a failure and as being stained with guilt and shame. Also part of this complex is an image of disgrace.

The Self-Defeat Complex

This is a complex of rationales that causes a person to sacrifice his abilities in order to be accepted by his group (family, colleagues, etc.): "I must not stand out; if I do they won't like me"; "A woman must not defeat a man in sports, or be smarter than her husband"; "a man must give the advantage to his superior"; "you have to play the social game correctly."

The Fate Complex

This complex distorts the *harmonizing function* of the psyche and thus confuses us as to what is in accord with our inner truth.

The Fate Complex is based on the mythical view that the stars determine human destiny. This false view allows the ego to blame the bad things it creates on the stars. Through believing bad things are predetermined, the person accepts unjust social conditions, and accommodates many other incorrect things by failing to say an inner No to them. Phrases connected with this complex are: "Your fate/destiny (your lot in life, high or low) is a pre-written script." "You are the kind of person you are because of where the stars were when you were born," and "there is nothing you can do about that."

In Cosmic terms, destiny means fulfilling one's uniqueness, whereas a person's fate is the result of his exceeding his natural limits, which are Cosmic in nature. Fate has the purpose of making him reflect on his disharmonious thinking.

Other phrases that can be part of this complex are: "Fate comes as a punishment from heaven, and must be accepted," or, "Fate is something that needs to be fought."

Another version of the Fate Complex is based on the spell, "I was born with a fatal flaw."

Another mistaken belief is the idea of karma, which posits that we carry forward from previous lives debts incurred by wrong acts. The projection that the person must pay back these debts creates a fate.

The False-Dependency Complex

This complex distorts the *organizing function* of the psyche by preventing us from seeing how our experiences have contributed to fulfilling our destiny. It also blocks the *passive and active transforming functions* of the psyche by causing us to depend on things that have no duration instead of depending on our inner truth.

This complex is one of the most important ego-complexes because it is based on our having dismissed as irrelevant what we know through our feelings (through being told that we cannot trust our feelings). Our inner truth, perceived through our feelings, tells us that we are ultimately dependent on the Cosmos for all things. By the one stroke of being told that we cannot trust our feelings, the majority of our bodily Helpers, which are feeling consciousnesses, are rendered unable to help us.

This complex begins with the false statement: "You cannot trust your feelings." It gives rise to the "dragon of essentials," and to spells that stipulate an accepted list of helping sources to which a person must turn when in need: "You can only rely on what you can see, and what is palpable"; "We depend on people and policies to fulfill our needs"; "Since the body has no sense of its own; it needs to be directed by, and depend on, the mind." To give weight to these false statements, we are presented with the mistaken belief, "We have no right to think for ourselves. We must let God think for us. We have to listen to what God says." This becomes an inner commandment that gets extended to our feelings, resulting in the spell: "I have no right to my own feelings."

Pragmatists who deny the existence of the Cosmic Consciousness and its helping energies, specify our dependence on other things: For our general needs: "It is essential to have money"; "It is essential to have a good lawyer, doctor, accountant," etc. "In business, it is essential to get clients/customers." For our security: "It is essential to have a fall-back position (savings, inheritance, insurance, particular people, family)."

One is inclined to say, "Of course, it is essential to have money, customers, etc." The problem is that we do not ask ourselves *what* it is that brings these people (or the money) into our lives. The "what" is the force of attraction through which everything in the Cosmic reality is achieved.

When we try to "make" money, for example, we think we are the ones who are making it. When, however, we realize that the money — just as all our other needs — comes from acknowledging our dependence on the Cosmos, the money can flow to us freely through various channels. The money can come *through* our job, *through* the company for which we work, but in themselves, the job or company are not the sources on which we can depend. Recognizing that we have blotted out our true dependency on the Cosmos makes us understand why the flow of money may be blocked. The attraction that was formerly there is missing because we have blocked the Helper whose job it is to provide us with sufficient money: the Cosmic Banker.

Another example can occur when we try to acquire clients; the idea of "trying" implies that we assume the force of attraction does not exist! By such beliefs we block the Helpers that easily bring us the clients we need when we ask them to help, as for example, the Marketing Helper for our business, and the Receptivity Helper on the prospective client's end. The Receptivity Helper cooperates with the prospective client's Personal Helper. Before such Helpers can be engaged, however, we need to deprogram the False-Dependency Complex.

When we are looking for the "right" doctor or lawyer, it is useful to ask the Sage to point us to the one through whom the Cosmic Doctor or Cosmic Lawyer can best work. That is the criterion for our choice.

The poison arrow, "The body doesn't have any sense of its own and needs to be directed by the mind," denies the existence of all our inner senses of perception, and our metaphorical senses. This poison arrow has a seriously harmful effect because it blots out our whole system of inner guidance, upon which the mind is dependent for a complete perception. Once divorced from the inner senses, the mind, in and of itself, has no guidance to offer. This leaves it open to the influence of the prescribed rationales which direct us to look to the collective ego and the body of knowledge it has collected, for guidance.

The Work Complex

Because the Work Complex is based on "doing it all ourselves," it prevents us from engaging the *passive transforming function* of the psyche. This function, when engaged, frees us from certain ego-emotions such as grief, hopelessness, self-blame, fears, doubt of the Cosmos, resistance, hatred, arrogance, reverence, ego-enthusiasm, depression, boredom, envy, and feelings of possessiveness. In the *I Ching* this function is pictured as a "big wagon" onto which we can load all these emotions. Doing so transforms them, thus freeing the psyche from the burdensome feelings they create.

The Work Complex is based on the spell, "You have to do it all yourself." Other spells connected with it declare work to be either the essence of virtue or the essence of duty: "It is your duty to work before you enjoy life," "Your lot/purpose in life is to work," and, "My work defines who I am." "Your work needs to be given first priority," "You need to sacrifice your body's needs to your work," "You must not rest until you have become somebody (through your work)," and, "Your work makes you special." This complex may also include the image and curse from the Bible: "In the sweat of thy face shalt thou eat bread, till thou return unto the ground; for out of it wast thou taken."[6] This gives rise to other spells, such as, "Work is hard," "A thing is not worthwhile if you haven't worked hard for it," "People who don't work are no-good," and "No pain, no gain."

Obviously, this complex has many elements of self-punishment, where the ego puts blame for the person's feelings of insufficiency onto his body. Such a complex can make it very hard for him to get out of the work mode, enjoy leisure time, take the time to learn new things, enjoy relationships, or get to know himself.

Social Complexes

In their healthy state, the *focusing function* and the *linking/harmonizing function* of the psyche concentrate our physical energy and harmonize it with Cosmic energy to realize creative

---

6 Genesis 3:19

undertakings. The following ego complexes imprison the focusing function and force it to fulfill the narrowly defined social roles prescribed by the collective ego. The linking/harmonizing function becomes blocked.

The Woman Complex

This complex shows the woman's place in the hierarchical social structure in these examples: "The place of a woman is in the house," "A woman obeys her husband," and, "A woman must be the one who yields." The precise definitions depend on the culture from which the woman comes.

The Man Complex

This complex shows the man's place in the hierarchical social structure in these examples: "The place of a man is outside the house," "He is the head of the family/clan," and "He must be the strong one, and the provider." If he is the father, he must be "the captain of the family ship." The precise definitions depend on the culture from which the man comes.

Emotional Complexes

These complexes block the *active transforming function* of the psyche that would normally complete our undertakings when they are in harmony with the Cosmos. As a consequence of this blockage, the success of our undertakings gradually erodes, because ego-emotions block the Helpers.

The Fear Complex

This complex contains the false statements, "Fears are a natural part of life," "It is good and proper, and even sensible to have fears," and, "Who are you to have no fears?" This complex confounds fear and caution: Fear is the consequence of the ego's blotting out the invisible Helpers in our lives, thereby depriving us of their help and protection. When they have been blotted out, the body knows that it has been made vulnerable, hence it fears. Caution, on the other hand, is one of our metaphorical senses that protect us by drawing our attention to a danger in time to avoid it.

The Fear-of-the-Future Complex

The following projections and poison arrows make up this complex: "The future is uncertain, therefore you have to make plans," "You have to be in control of your future," "You have to provide for old age," and, "You need to be certain about things, and nail them down."

The Complex of Returning

This complex causes a person to return to the mistaken ideas and beliefs of the collective ego because he doubts that the Cosmos would want him: "The Cosmos will not want me because I am not good enough." In this case, the person mistakenly believes the Cosmos expects and rewards only perfection.

He may also falsely equate returning to unity with the Cosmos with "falling out of the world." The ego in him asks, "How can I give up my place in the world?" It then introduces the fear of leaving the parallel reality behind by saying, "If I do not play the game, I will be excluded from the collective."

The person may also equate the collective ego with his vision of doing something useful and worthwhile.

Or, when he discovers that the Cosmos offers the "easy way" of attaining success, the ego in him objects: "It can't be any good if you haven't had to work for it," "You have to earn your keep."

Returning to the fold of the collective ego may also be initiated by thoughts of how much the person has already invested to attain success: "If I follow the Sage, it would mean that my years of school and work were a sham and worth nothing. I'll be standing here with nothing." "What else might I find out that really doesn't exist?"

How Ego-Complexes Form a Complex Support System

The creation of ego-complexes fortifies the ego's logic so as to make it difficult for the individual to see its deceptive nature. Seeing it with clarity is made even more difficult by the way groups of ego-complexes form yet other complex support systems. Nevertheless, the Sage has guided us to see how these complex structures can be made transparent.

The Capital With its Defensive Walls

Six of the above-mentioned ego-complexes form the individual ego's "capital."[7] The capital is a metaphor for the ego's residence in the psyche, from where it rules the personality. The rest of the complexes act as the wall that defends the capital.

The capital itself consists of the Self-Doubt Complex, the Guilt Complex, the God Complex, the Self-Punishment Complex, the Punishment Complex, and the False-Dependency Complex. The function each of the six serves is as follows:

The first complex making up the capital is the *Self-Doubt Complex*, which divides our wholeness and thereby pits us against our own nature by proclaiming, "human nature is divided into good and evil."

The second is the *Guilt Complex*, which proclaims, "humans are born guilty," in the sense of "being born with an inextinguishable stain on their nature." This complex makes us feel guilty whenever we want to express our true nature.

The third is the *God Complex*, or *Spirituality Complex*, which sets the mind on a quest to attain the knowledge of good and evil, thereby to attain a final place of knowledge that is equated with God and the idea of immortality. This complex gives the mind the task to be ruler over the personality, and also over Nature, and the Earth. Hidden behind the flattery of being given this role is the fact that the collective ego is using the mind to press as much energy out of the individual as possible. This is achieved by different means, all of which are described in the complexes that defend the capital.

The fourth is the *Self-Punishment Complex*, through which the mind exercises its rule over the personality. This complex causes the mind to totally internalize the collective ego's false values.

The fifth is the *Punishment Complex*. Because the self-punishments are so unbearable to the psyche, the guilt is thrown off

---

7 See Hexagram 42, *Increasing*, Line 4, "It furthers one to be used in the removal of the capital."

onto others by seeing them as culprits.

The sixth, the *False-Dependency Complex* causes us to put the dependency for all our needs on the social fabric. Once we are cut off from our inborn system of support, we look outward to the collective ego for the fulfillment of all our needs.

The combination of these six ego-complexes, once installed in the psyche, make up the ruling structure of the individual ego. Because in their totality, they completely obliterate our natural recognition of the Cosmos, we are left to wander through meaningless paths in the maze the collective ego calls "reality."

The Capital's Defensive Walls

Each group of ego-complexes that defend the capital represents a different defense strategy: they either keep us busy (as in the Work Complex and the Duty Complexes), make us fall into denial (as in the Emotional Complexes and the Hope Complex), flatter us (as in the Superiority Complexes), conjure up external threats (as in the Complexes of Evil, the Complexes of Conflict, and the Nature Complexes), or they make us look up to authority figures (the Inferiority Complexes).

The mindset thus created by the human-centered view of the universe described above causes fate after fate. The *I Ching* calls our attention to this fact in Hexagram 56, *The Wanderer,* Line 1: "If the wanderer busies himself with trivial things, he draws down misfortune upon himself." The 'trivial things' are the concerns of the collective ego with which we busy our minds. They are mentioned in the six ego-complexes that constitute the ego's capital, in particular the God Complex, the Guilt Complex, the Punishment Complex, and the Self-Punishment Complex.

Because of the frequency with which we create fates and because of the threat these fates pose to the ego's credibility, the Fate Complexes are composed of rationales that place the cause of Fate outside the responsibility of the ego. Fate is declared to be either due to a flaw in our nature, as in a "fatal flaw," or to a pre-written script, or to the way the stars were constellated at the time of our birth, or to being punished by a higher power. Thus, the Fate Complexes serve to prevent us from reflecting on the untruths on which we have based our lives.

The Right Time to Free Ourselves from Ego-Complexes

Although we tend to accumulate ego-complexes throughout our lives, the right time to free ourselves of any one cannot arbitrarily be chosen. We generally become aware that an ego-complex may be involved when a specific symptom manifests, either a disturbance in the psyche or in the body. The disturbance is itself an indication that we are ready to face and deal with the one or more ego-complexes that are causing it. Any ambitious effort to go on a hunt for ego-complexes before such symptoms show themselves would come from the ego. Our presentation of ego-complexes in this chapter is meant to provide the reader with sufficient clarity about the place a particular ego-complex has within the whole ego-structure. The fact that the complex has created a disturbance or physical symptom is the most obvious proof of its unhealthy nature.

A physical illness can be an indication that one or more ego-complexes have burned out. The burnout of an ego-complex can be compared to the blowing of an electric fuse, which happens when we overload the line. For example, when a person tries to fulfill to perfection the duties expected of him under the *Duty Complex*, he is bound to overload himself to a degree that the fuse blows, manifesting in his total physical exhaustion.

It can also happen that a person is ready to free himself from all the complexes that make up the ego's capital. This is referred to in Hexagram 11, *Harmony/Peace/Prosperity*, Line 6, in the words, "The wall falls back into the moat. Use no army now. Make your commands known within your own town." The situation is one in which the main aspects of the defensive walls of the ego's capital have been battered down by a fate. This is a most propitious moment to free ourselves from the rule of the *collective ego*. What we, Carol and Hanna, described in the first two chapters of this book was such a fate. At the time, though, we did not know about ego-complexes, and were not capable of freeing ourselves from the ego's capital. It was a process that continued over many more years.

The ego wants us to think that our lives are over because the highest values to which we have clung, have turned out to be empty of their promises. The words, "Use no army now" is advice to not allow the ego to create new defensive structures to fight the fate, because this would be fighting what is coming to our rescue. It is also important not to accept the mistaken beliefs that it is virtuous to endure a fate, or that a fate is a Cosmic punishment we must accept.

The words, "Make your commands known within your own town" counsel us to rally our will in the service of our inner truth. Our will has an enormous potential since it is the total energy of our psyche. Once freed from the command of the ego to suppress our animal nature, our will can be directed by the Sage to further deconstruct the ego.

Through deprogramming ego-complexes, our task of deprogramming aspects of the ego becomes easier because each complex contains a number of ego-elements. We also break up the collaboration that exists between some complexes.

The Danger of Creating a New Ego-Complex

Once a particular complex has burned out, the ego will attempt to install a new complex to keep its illusion of power in place. It can do this, for example, by suggesting that what we are experiencing is not a fate, but that God is testing our faith by putting us through trials. Through this rationale it installs in us the *Devil*, or *Job Complex*. (See the description above.)

"Perseverance Furthers"

The words, "perseverance furthers" resound throughout the *I Ching*. The Chinese character for this expression has two meanings, the one being "to persevere," the other "to be firm and correct." It is repeated to make us aware that although we may have been deprogramming an ego aspect, it would be an illusion to think that we no longer need to pay attention to what may still reside in our psyche. Our personal experience has been that the Sage works with us to bring these negative elements to the surface as we are ready and able to deal with them. As we

165

continue with this process, we feel ever freer and more joyful.

In the process of freeing ourselves, it is not helpful to look at the ego as a force bigger than ourselves. With this attitude we forget that a whole army of invisible Helpers stands by our side to protect and defend us when we are firm and correct in our attitude. This means we say an inner No to any ego thoughts and emotions in ourselves, and to any ego encroachments by others over our boundaries. We do not tolerate, by accommodation or excuse, ego displays; we say the inner No, then withdraw inwardly so as to give the ego no energy. We simply do not play its games, as when we fall into the delusion that "there is nothing we can do about it." The Sage makes us aware that saying the inner No and inwardly withdrawing, and turning the matter over to the Cosmos is by far the most effective means of dealing with the ego. The word perseverance also has the meaning of not letting up in our efforts to call on Helpers in all matters.

The reader, on having been introduced to the many false rationales and ego-complexes listed in this book, may feel overwhelmed by the seeming power of the ego-mindset, which has the intention to make us feel helpless.

We are helped out of this helplessness when we remember that we are dealing with habits of mind that hold on as long as they can, but which cannot stand up to a resolute inner No.

One great safeguard against the ego's incursions is gratitude. By this we do not mean a ritual of thanking, rather, it is a thankfulness that needs no display, only a remembrance and appreciation of the gifts we have been given.

A further safeguard is the practice of consulting the *I Ching* with some regularity. Such a practice can be viewed in the same light as regularly cleaning our house, to free ourselves of ego-emotions that crop up, of unprocessed stored traumatic memories that cause involuntary ego behaviors, and habits of thinking that lead to depressed thoughts, and the like. By following these practices we will find ourselves progressively free of ego, and consequently enjoying our lives to the fullest.

14. Help is Closer Than We May Think
The Helpers of Our Psyche

The ego would like us to think that the psyche is helplessly subjected to its takeover and domination. However, there are venues through which Cosmic help is given to free us from the ego's control. One of these venues is dreams that warn us of imminent dangers coming either from inside ourselves or from outside. Consulting the *I Ching* to find the inner truth of an actual problem is another. Fates, inasmuch as they bring us back to modesty, are also a venue. The modesty that these fates create opens us to the path of our Cosmic destiny.

The psyche appears to be helpless to the ego's takeover only as long as the mind remains under the delusion that *it* is the leader of our personality. This delusion is caused, as we have indicated in previous chapters, (1) by the collective ego's flattering the mind that it is superior to the rest of the body, and (2) by the ego's repression of the Helpers of Our Psyche.

The remedy begins with the fates mentioned above, which poke a hole in the hot air balloon of the mind's arrogance. This decrease can lead to wanting to know ourselves. In the course of this effort, the mind may realize its limitations enough to recognize that Helpers are available to support it. Once these Helpers are enlisted with the Sage's aid, it is possible to free the psyche of the ego's dominance.

However, as mentioned in the previous chapter, shedding the ego in one fell swoop is impossible. Deconstructing it entails a process of taking back the consent we have formerly granted the self-images and phrases of which it is composed. We may not be aware of how we have given our consent; this is because the consent was given in a manner that was unconscious to us. We are unaware, for example, that ideas we have only wondered about, and not actively rejected, are accepted into our psyche by default. At first they are put in a sort of holding place in the psyche, where they wait for a further reason that would either verify or dismiss them. However, they are then forgotten and become accepted in the psyche by the default belief that they are "probably okay." This okay is an unconscious Yes. In order to free ourselves from them, we take back this Yes, by saying a conscious No to them. This No engages Cosmic help to free the psyche of these ego components. It also frees the space around us of their negative consciousness.

The first order of business in this endeavor is the freeing of the Helpers of Our Psyche. For this we need to know these Helpers and their functions.

The Sage

We have already described in Chapter 8 how the Sage uses the psyche as its workplace to help the mind understand and correct human mistakes. It also coordinates the various functions of the psyche so that they work together harmoniously. In another of its functions the Sage facilitates the connection between our body consciousness and our mind. In these capacities the Sage is both a Helper of our Psyche and a Cosmic Helper.

As a Cosmic Helper, the Sage is the Helper that connects us with all the Cosmic Helpers we need at a given time.

Another function of the Sage is to communicate with our mind through meditations and dreams. For the Sage to be able to communicate through meditations, we need to ask it to provide us with the clarity we need for the moment. (See Appendix 4: Exercises: A Meditation to Attain Clarity.) In meditating, we approach the Sage to attain clarity. In dreams, the Sage approaches us. Dreams can give us messages of various kinds: premonitions of future events, opportunities along the path of our Cosmic destiny, warnings of imminent dangers, messages informing us of mistaken ideas and beliefs, and of harmful thoughts coming from others. (See Chapter 21, "Wake-up Calls.")

The Sage's capabilities are engaged when we acknowledge our relationship with it and seek its help. Hexagram 4, *Youthful Folly*, defines this relationship and the conditions we need to meet for the Sage to be able to help us. These conditions are not met when we approach either with an arrogant or a slavish attitude. An arrogant attitude is expressed as "knowing better," or, "I will see what the Sage has to say," said with an air of superiority. The attitude of slavish obedience is described below. The attitude that engages the Sage is one of respect and an inner neutrality when asking a question; we achieve the correct attitude when we put aside our distrust of what the Sage will answer.

The Sage, as the reader will discover, is first of all a friend, not a master who dictates to us our every move, or who will abandon us if we do not adhere to every word. We can ask any number of questions and get advice on how to do things, but we are to regard the answers as just that — help offered; this help is also meant to engage and support our commonsense. Once we get into the kind of relationship with the Sage where we make it the master, we begin to get answers that come from the ego in us, rather than from the Sage. Then the ego, in the guise of the Sage, is experienced as a taskmaster. The toss of the coins will then only further support this mistaken idea of obedience until we feel totally enslaved to what we think is the Sage. The ego is the cause of this experience, in its seeking to divert us from our true path that leads not to enslavement, but to inner freedom. This enslavement is described in Hexagram 29, *The Abysmal*, Line 6, as "Bound with cords and ropes, shut in between thorn-hedged prison walls: for three years one does not find the way. Misfortune."

If or when we begin to feel "bound" to the answers received, leaving behind our commonsense, it indicates that we have a fear, or a "chip"[1] containing a traumatic memory of some sort that we are carrying into our work with the Sage. Such a fear or traumatic memory often originates in a childhood incident in which a parent or teacher told us, "Do what you are told." This was accompanied by the threat of a severe punishment if we did not comply. The Sage also protects our mind from getting overwhelmed by fears or guilt stored in the subconscious.

The Helper of Inner Truth

This Helper is an aspect of the *transmitting function* of the psyche. It transmits to the mind feelings of inner truth that

---

1 See Chapter 19, "Stop Chips."

the Sage has translated into words. When we feel blocked from accessing our inner truth, we can call on this Helper to break through that blockage. We can also call on this Helper to help another person, to bring his inner truth to the surface of his consciousness. However, this Helper will not be engaged if we have even the slightest desire for retribution or to bring harm.

The Helper of Creativity

This Helper is activated when the mind asks for help when it is working on a creative project. This Helper then uses the *focusing function* of the psyche to focus all the energy of our mind and body on the project. (The focusing function is driven by the energy of our will.)

The *I Ching* defines creative activity as the process by which something inspired by our inner truth manifests into form. Such activities are initiated by dammed up Cosmic Helpers that are ready to break through with their energies. They are all lined up and waiting for the mind to become involved. Once the mind asks the Helper of Creativity for help, their energies are free to flow in cooperation with this Helper.

Calling on this Helper is essential for the executing of any creative project. This Helper also responds when it is addressed as "The Muse," or "The Helper of Inventions" or "The Helper of Paintings." The name we give Helpers is not as important as the sincerity with which we ask for help.

The Helper of Our Original Image

This Helper reconnects us with the original image of us that is stored in our psyche. In doing so, it reminds us of who we really are, and of the validation of our existence given to us by the Cosmos. This Helper flashes our original image into our mind when we are in the danger of losing ourselves. Asking this Helper to restore us to our original image helps damaged parts of our body to heal. Doing this revives the chi energy in those damaged parts, and frees them from the damage done to their chromosomes. However, before we can call on this Helper for help, it is necessary to find and deprogram the cause of the damage in its form as a phrase, image, or a chip.

In meditation, this Helper can lead us to a body part that needs a "slight repair." To relate an actual experience, a man who for many years suffered a back problem that periodically rendered him nearly unable to walk, was shown his backbone in a meditation. It appeared before him as if he was looking at it from behind. He noticed that one vertebrae in his lower back protruded out to the right. He then saw his hand go to that place and push the vertebrae back in place. Thereafter, and for the rest of his life (some 30 years), he had no more back problem. In the meditation experiences of other people, including Carol, shriveled, closed, and hardened hearts were seen to be restored to their full size and health. As a result of these experiences we have included in the Appendix a meditation exercise in which we ask the Helper of Our Original Image to help us "sit in this image," which is possible because it is a hologram. As may be expected, the effect is restorative. (See Appendix 4, Exercises.)

The Helper of Freeing

The Helper of Freeing is the psyche's *protective function*. It wards off disharmonious and harmful consciousness coming either from our own mind or from outside sources. This function is like an opaque mirror that causes ego thoughts to bounce off. It also frees other Helpers without the involvement of our conscious mind. It can also be asked to free us from prepossessing fears.

This Helper is the same as the one we have called "the Helper that Frees People from Guilt." Because guilt pervades the psyche and at the same time hides its presence there, this Helper, when asked to do so, seeks out its hiding places and negates its existence, thus deprograms it for us.

The Helper of Processing

This Helper helps us process negative experiences. When invoked to help us during or just after a negative experience, it gives us the key insights we need in order to process that experience; thus it enables us to avoid the damage that would otherwise be done to our psyche. During the processing it also draws on our sense of proportion by showing us what the ego calls "important" as trivial when seen from the Cosmic perspective; and vice versa: what the ego wants to discard as of "no consequence," is shown in its importance.[2] (Also see the description of the *processing function* of the psyche in Chapter 8.)

Our Personal Helper

This Helper helps us fulfill our Cosmic destiny. We can compare our destiny to a picture puzzle we are putting together. Our Personal Helper attracts us to the subjects we need to explore that are important to putting the puzzle together. It also draws the people and events to us that bring us key pieces of the puzzle. These may be partners in our endeavor, or simply passersby whom we meet only for a brief time and leave behind. This Helper organizes these disparate experiences in such a way that the overall design of the carpet of our destiny becomes visible and clear. Thus, our Personal Helper provides the thread of continuity to our life that gives everything that went before meaning. We see this continuity only in retrospect.

When our Cosmic destiny becomes visible, we feel a strong motivation to embrace it and go forward.

The Helper of Fate

This Helper has the function of bringing us back to the path of our Cosmic destiny when we have obstinately turned our backs on it. It does so by bringing back to us the negative energy created by our disharmonious thoughts and actions. The fate is to make us feel, in a physical sense, their disharmonious energy. Experiencing a fate gives us the opportunity to reflect on those thoughts and actions and to correct ourselves accordingly. When we have done this, the same Helper ends our fate by re-harmonizing us with our inner truth.

This Helper is present both in the psyche and in the physical world. In the physical world it is part of the laws of physics, and

---

2 See Hexagram 56, *The Wanderer*, Line 1, "If the wanderer busies himself with trivial things, he draws down misfortune upon himself."

in this context, it is also called the Law of Fate.[3]

The Helper of the Love Relationship

This Helper is connected with the *receiving function* of the psyche. It allows the love energy coming from the Cosmos to be received by the love partners. When they believe the love comes only from themselves, this Helper is excluded; as a consequence, the flow of the love energy becomes blocked. Little by little, each finds himself alone and alienated from the other.

When called upon to be active in a current situation, this Helper blocks any ego-elements active in the love partners' relationship. When asked in the context of deprogramming, this Helper erases any negative memories they may have of each other. When regularly asked to be present in their lives, it protects them from the intrusion of future ego-elements. When needed, this Helper also engages the Helper of Cosmic Protection on behalf of the love partners.

This Helper is present at the beginning of all love relationships that are Cosmic in origin. It attracts the two prospective partners, and helps them, through their experiences with each other, to correct their mistaken ideas and beliefs about the Cosmos and its relationship with humans; it also helps them to correct their relationship with their inner truth.

This Helper makes the love partners aware that one of the purposes of the love relationship is to free their true selves from the dominance of the ego. When they consciously join in doing this inner work, their love achieves duration.

This Helper maintains the inner channel that is created between the two love partners when they are first given the Cosmic gift of love. The channel facilitates their inner communication, releasing them from the need to say things outwardly when things go wrong; outer attempts to correct the other bypass this channel and only arouse ego-pride.

As may be seen from the above, ignoring this Helper inevitably leads to the failure of the love relationship.

---

3 See Hexagram 56, *The Wanderer*, Line 6, "The bird's nest burns up. The wanderer laughs at first, then must lament and weep."

An important related Helper is the Helper of Duration, which is a Cosmic Helper. During times when the ego in one partner has intervened in the relationship, it is important for the other partner to temporarily close his heart to prevent his love from being appropriated by the ego in the other. He can then ask the Helper of Duration to protect and hide his love until the other has returned to sincerity. When that happens, he needs to ask the Helper that Reopens the Heart to do that for him. (Note, this is different from allowing the ego to close one's heart, which leads to hardening of the heart and alienation.)

The Helper of Completion

This is the Helper of the *active transforming function* in the psyche that brings things to completion through transformation. It is the subject of the last two hexagrams in the *I Ching*. We need this Helper when we have done our best and put sincere effort into achieving something. At this point we are advised by the hexagram called "Before Completion," to cease all further effort, let go, and turn the matter over to the Helper of Completion (also called the Helper of Transformation). Only then can this Helper perform its function. When we have truly turned the matter over to this Helper, it connects what we have done with the Cosmic energies that imbue our work with life force. Thereafter, the energies that have been collected are transformed in the atomic realm, creating a success that is capable of enduring.

The hexagram called "After Completion" makes us aware that one thing alone can damage the duration of the success. It is the gradual appropriation of the success by the ego, when we allow it to claim, "I did it."[4]

The Finding Helper

This Helper uses the *communicating function* of the psyche to find a phrase or image that has imprisoned a particular Helper of Our Psyche. When we call on this Helper to bring to mind the

---

4 See Hexagram 63, *After Completion*, The Judgment, "At the beginning good fortune. At the end disorder."

pertinent phrases, it asks the imprisoned Helper which phrase or image has imprisoned it; the Finding Helper then informs the mind so that those phrases can be deprogrammed.[5]

The Cosmic Family[6]

The Cosmic Family is the name for the totality of consciousnesses that make up the Cosmos. By *Cosmos* we mean both its invisible aspect, and its visible aspect called *Nature*. Nature is comprised of the so-called inanimate matter, such as rocks, and animate matter, such as plants, animals, and humans, each of which has its own unique consciousness that contributes to the Cosmos as an alive organism. The invisible aspect of the Cosmic Family includes the Cosmic Helpers, those individualized aspects of consciousness that enable the Cosmos to function as a harmonious whole. The *I Ching* emphasizes the "Principle of Firm Seclusion Within the Family," pointing to the need to not allow elements that deny the existence of the harmonious order of the Cosmos to lead us astray and put us in opposition to the Cosmic Family.

Each human being is by nature part of the Cosmic Family. When we recognize this wonderful fact, we no longer need to feel unwanted if our parents felt that way about our existence. We also know where to turn for all our needs. What is a burden to our human family is never a burden to our Cosmic Family. As long as we ask for help with fulfilling our true needs, the Helpers joyfully respond. If, however, we come with ego-demands, or with the false hopes and desires of the ego, the Helpers retreat.

The Cosmic Family complements the Helpers of Our Psyche, thus supports us in all undertakings that lead to fulfilling our Cosmic destiny.

The Myriad Helpers

The Sage is the only Helper we consult when we have questions. The other Helpers are engaged through asking for their

---

5 See Hexagram 40, *Freeing*, The Judgment, "If there is still unfinished business, it furthers to bring it swiftly to an end."
6 Also see Hexagram 37, *The Family*.

help in specific matters. They are available to help only when we regard them with sensitivity and respect. They also need to be asked because the act of asking is an acknowledgement that we need help, which puts pride aside. They never tire of doing their work and indeed, they enjoy it. It is impossible to ask too much of them. They do not stand around waiting for our appreciation, but they enjoy it when we give it. They are available for every true need.

They disappear when we are haughty, proud, and demanding, or if we are indifferent. They do not respond to expectations. They will never compromise their dignity. They return when we are truly sorry for transgressing, but they may approach us with hesitation after we have done so, to be sure we are truly free of that negative energy. They do not take kindly to being worshipped, as that is embarrassing to them. They are rich in the energy of love, but will not throw one tidbit of that away on the ego. The reason is that being aspects of the Cosmos, they are unable to violate the Cosmic Principles of Harmony on which they are based. When we ignore them, as if they don't exist, then they cease to exist for us. If we cynically turn our backs on them, they put roadblocks in our way in an effort to wake us up to the fact that we need their help.

As their names show, we have been led to call them by the expertise they have, or by the expertise we need. Thus, the name of the Sage indicates that the Sage is our teacher that helps us understand all the things we need to know. Other Helpers have names, such as: The Helper of Mind Cleansing, that cleans out our mental trash; the Helper that Clears the Psyche frees the psyche of chips and such after we have processed and deprogrammed them; the Helper of Dissolution dissolves rigid structures in both our body and our mind; our Personal Helper of Deprogramming helps to increase the effectiveness of saying the inner No during deprogramming; and the Cosmic Helpers help with a wide variety of tasks, including deprogramming.

When we are not sure of the names of Helpers that are needed in a particular situation, we can ask the Sage to draw these Helpers to us. It is not up to us to determine which Helpers are needed when we approach a problem or task. We ask the Sage, "Is the Helper of Dissolution needed?" "Is the Helper of Mind Cleansing needed?" etc.

The Helpers are just what the word indicates; they help, but we need to meet them halfway and do our part. Doing our part is called "Joint Approach" in Hexagram 19, which has that name. It is not enough, for example, to ask for help to be freed of a pain (the symptom only). We do our part by searching for the cause, which may be in ourselves or in someone else whose consciousness is aimed at us (as in poison arrows). The deprogramming of these causes is facilitated by asking these Helpers to assist.

The following are a number of other Helpers we have recognized:

- Our Feeling Manager (it coordinates our psyche and body through harmonizing our heart beat with that of all other aspects of Nature, and through regulating our blood pressure, our lymph system, the production of hormones, etc.)
- Our Health Helpers
- The Cosmic Doctor, Cosmic Surgeon, Cosmic Dentist, etc.
- The Helpers of Healing
- The Cosmic Banker (to help supply our money needs)
- The Helper of Accounting (when doing our taxes)
- The Helper of Travel (when going on a trip)
- The Helper of Protection (it temporarily protects us from spells, etc., coming from others, until we have identified and deprogrammed them)
- The Cosmic Helper of Time (it manages our time)

Doubts that Block the Helpers

Doubts that imply the nonexistence of the Helpers are poison arrows that immobilize them. Examples are statements such as, "you can't rely on things you cannot see," or, "I only believe in what has been scientifically proven." Doubts in the efficiency of the Helpers also cause them to retreat. Examples are statements such as, "How do you know the Helpers will come in time?" "I can't see any result (of my deprogramming) yet." Other doubts are those that imply that we "do not deserve to be helped," or they contain the conclusion that we are "helpless." Such doubts come from the demonic element we have called "the doubter." (See Chapter 11, "The Darkening of the Light.")

Attitudes that Engage the Helpers

The *I Ching* shows us that the way of the Cosmos is the "easy way." Easy means *simple*. It is easy and simple because it is completely in accord with our innermost nature. The various Helpers of our nature, when not blocked through disharmonious ideas or beliefs, automatically attract the Cosmic Helpers as their complements. What makes things complicated is the ego.

Our inner firmness to not tolerate ego behavior, either in ourselves or in others to whom we are relating, brings the Helpers joy, and motivates them to help us. They honor our sincerity in ridding ourselves of aspects of the ego by bringing us help in many unexpected ways. Our gratitude for the help we receive automatically holds the Cosmic Helpers to us. These attitudes express themselves in certain efforts we make, such as

- giving up our pride by recognizing that in and of ourselves we cannot do what the Helpers can do
- turning over to the Cosmos our distrust of the Helpers
- rejecting the ego's interfering with judgments and doubt, with complaints and criticisms, and with ego-emotions such as impatience and ambition

When we fail to reject the ego's interference, we are forced to struggle with our task. This struggle creates frustration and anger, which are too often turned toward the Sage and the Helpers, rather than toward recognizing the ego as their source. We reject ego-emotions and the phrases put forth by the ego by saying No to them three times. (See Appendix 3, "Deprogramming.")

15. "If You Are Sincere, Whatever You Do Succeeds"
Our Thinking and Imaging Minds

The positive title we have chosen for this chapter on the thinking and imaging minds is taken from the Judgment text of Hexagram 29, *The Abyss/Danger*. The name of the hexagram refers to the danger incurred when the mind is divorced from sincerity, which comes from our body's true feelings. The Judgment text shows that the way out of the danger created by the mind's arrogance is to return to sincerity as the only way to success.

The Mind's Place in the Personality
When we speak of the mind, we are here speaking of the two frontal lobes and their thinking and imaging capabilities.

Of these two aspects, the imaging mind preceded the thinking mind in their evolution. Its existence was the necessary precondition for the development of language. The Cosmic purpose of language is to express the inner truth of things in images and words, and thus increase the possibilities of expressing Cosmic truths; language also makes it possible, as in the case of the *I Ching*, to pass on these truths from generation to generation.

Since each situation in the material world differs in time and place, and includes factors that cannot be seen, we make a mistake when we describe them in absolute terms. Furthermore, to correctly express a truth, our language needs to be in accord with the Cosmic Principles of Harmony, meaning, it cannot contain words that have no Cosmic basis. We know we are in harmony with these Cosmic principles when what we express in language is both just and moderate.

The Thinking Aspect of the Mind

The thinking mind is the latest development in the evolution of the animal kingdom, and thus is the least experienced faculty held among the animals. The *I Ching* refers to this fact by calling it a "young fool." This is not a pejorative statement; rather, it is a reminder that the mind needs to acknowledge its degree of inexperience.

The body, with its possession of inner truth/DNA, freely offers to the mind its wisdom of what keeps us in harmony with the Cosmos, and its collective knowledge of human existence. What the mind needs is the humility and openness to learn from the body's wisdom. This is not possible, however, so long as the mind remains caught in its delusion of not needing the body's wisdom, and so long as it has locked up that wisdom through slandering the body.

People generally assume that what they do with their minds corresponds with the purpose the mind is meant to serve. This assumption proves false when we begin to ask questions such as: why do people often feel overwhelmed, tired, depressed, hopeless, and helpless? There is no doubt that at that moment a litany of negative thoughts and a parade of negative images are crossing the mind. It would appear that these feelings are due to what is being observed outside; however, if we investigate further, we may find that these negative emotions are coming up from the psyche, from where they are coloring the present experience, as if the person is wearing dark glasses. In this case the mind is unconsciously "drinking from the well of remembered insults, injuries, injustices, guilt, hurt pride, and other negative memories,"[1] and is a victim of these memories. Like an automaton, the mind is reacting unconsciously to its conditioning.

To give an illustration, a woman shared with us an experience she had on finding again her favorite children's book that she used to read at Christmas time. On re-reading it, she began to cry, and remembered that every time she used to read the book it produced in her sad and hopeless feelings, even though the story ended happily. She noticed that others who read the story had an entirely different, even cheerful response. We read the story for ourselves and realized that it contained a superabundance of emotionally laden words that, although they were poetic,

---

1 From Hexagram 48, *The Well*, Line 6.

connected her with a situation in her childhood that had made her feel hopeless. In this case, her mind became a victim of a stored feeling of hopelessness that was reawakened by the dark, foreboding words that preceded the happy ending in the story. These words had created a spell in her mind.

To keep ourselves, or our children, from being brought under such spells, we need to understand the true functions of the mind, and how the mind, for many of us, has been brought under the control of the ego. We also need to understand that an early traumatic memory can be processed and the person freed of its negative consequences. (See Chapter 20.)

The True Function of the Thinking Mind

The mind's true function is to be present in the outer world, and at the same time, to keep tuned to what our body feels; our mind then gives expression to that feeling in *words*, be it in thought or speech.

The mind's analytical abilities, on receiving these messages, is analogous to a conference table where all the input received is subjected to analysis. The analysis then becomes the basis for actions that are based on commonsense.

An exception to this process occurs during emergencies, when the mind is bypassed by way of the *involuntary response function* in the psyche. This function takes over and directs the body's response. We understand the wisdom of this division of functions when we learn that researchers have found that the mind has the ability to process approximately 40 bits of information per second, while our feeling consciousness has the ability to process roughly 40 million bits of information per second.[2]

There is also a constant interchange between the mind and the psyche; the mind reflects and draws on the positive experiences stored in the psyche; the psyche reflects these memories to the mind in situations of need; it also reflects insight-flashes to the mind coming from the Sage.

---

2 Bruce Lipton, PhD in his audio program called "The Wisdom of the Cells (Sounds True 800.333.9185) speaks of the ability of the conscious mind to process 40 stimuli per second vs. the "subconscious mind" at 40 million stimuli per second.

The Thinking Mind's Natural State

The mind's natural state is to be *present*; this is also to be in a state of *inner neutrality* and *innocence*, free of pre-conceived ideas and anticipations. This inner freedom and neutrality gives the mind complete access to all the resources that are available to it from the psyche, to respond in the most effective way to every situation. In this way, intimations of what to do come spontaneously to us at the most propitious time.

While we often need to make a plan, such as choosing a theme for a lecture, if we too rigidly preconceive every sentence and paragraph, we lose our ability to "seize the moment" and reveal what it has to say. Too much mental preparation prevents us from being in touch with the inner truth of the moment, which is necessary for a correct judgment and response. Such preparedness makes it likely that the response is either an overreaction to the situation, or one that is unrelated. These preparations keep the mind busying itself with anticipations of various sorts, while additionally blocking the Helpers of our nature.

Keeping tuned to what the body feels prevents the mind from being taken over by the ego, which focuses exclusively on externals. This attunement allows the body's feelings to participate in our awareness of what is harmonious and what is not. Thus we go with what is harmonious and withdraw from what is not.

When the thinking mind is in its natural condition, it listens to the Sage, which conveys to it the wisdom of the body, via the psyche. Under the conditioning that creates the ego, this process is reversed: the mind no longer looks to the Sage; it gives commands to the body.

The Sage's Functions in the Thinking Mind

Certain functions in the thinking mind are reserved to the Sage. The mind needs to recognize its limitations, and acknowledge its dependence on the Sage in these matters. These functions also require the cooperation of other Helpers. Any interference by the mind causes a blockage.

One of these is the *adapting function*. This function allows us to adapt to changes in the environment that are necessary for our survival as a species. It is of great importance that the mind not appropriate this function, which happens when the ego says, "you have to accept adverse conditions." If we accept this idea and tolerate those conditions (by failing to say an inner No to them), the necessary transformations are prevented. For example, when we have become ill, and the doctors do not know how to remedy the condition, they may say, "There is nothing we can do. You have to adapt to this condition." It is never appropriate to consciously decide to adapt to something that is disharmonious. We may not yet know how to resolve the difficulty, but we can, and we need to say an inner No to its existence. This engages the Helper of Transformation. When the mind takes on the task of "adapting," it actually prevents the real adaptation, which involves transformations in the human DNA that only the Helpers of our nature can perform at the Sage's request.

Preparation for Freeing the Thinking Mind

If the mind is to be restored to its healthy functioning, it first needs to recognize that the image it has of itself as superior is the cause of self-imposed stress. If not corrected, it would ultimately self-destruct. The mind also needs to recognize that the pride it invests in the idea of its superiority is used by the collective ego to control it; the use of the word "superior" shows how the mind can be manipulated by words.

Thus, freeing the mind requires that we understand and pay attention to the intentional use of false words and the feelings they create. We notice how, just as the word "superior" creates an ego-emotion of inflation in us, the word "inferior" creates the ego-emotion of deflation, or depression. We also notice how these emotions initiate other ego-emotions: pride invites haughtiness; self-righteousness and shame invite self-hatred, and the hatred of others. We also notice how pride initiates the illusion of power that, in turn, leads us to attempt to force our way in the world. *Noticing the way words create energies* is vital to freeing ourselves from the collective ego's influence, for the ego primarily controls our behavior through words that create illusion and support it with bravado and other ego-emotions.

In order to return to innocence, the mind next needs to "put on a shelf" every presumption it has had of what it knows: its firm convictions of what is right and wrong, and its adherence to the values of the collective. In this way it will open up to the body's inner truth.

None of this can be carried out by merely reading about it. The Sage likes to teach us through experiences in the context of everyday situations. We need to practice opening our mind and listening to our inner truth the next time we encounter a difficulty. Gradually, through this practice, the mind can free itself from the flattery that its job is to manage the personality, and situations in general. As this flattery is released and Helpers of our nature are freed up to do what they know best to do, the mind also becomes freed from the burden of doing what it is truly not suited to do.

Freeing the mind also requires that we realize how the collective ego has used a language trick to get us to depend only on our eyes "to see the truth." This idea shuts the mind off from all our other senses of perception, in particular those known as our *inner* senses. We thereby become disabled from gaining a complete assessment of the truth.

The next thing that needs to be done is to *free the body* from the slanders that have been put on it. The body's wisdom is not available as long as it remains in a demonized condition.

These acts free up the mind to the body's commonsense — its natural advisor in all matters. The commonsense is then able to advise the mind as to what it needs to say "Yes" to, and what it needs to say "No" to. Yes is to be said to what feels harmonious, No to what feels disharmonious. What feels harmonious indicates the direction in which progress can be made. What feels disharmonious indicates the need to retreat and disengage.

Our inner No, when said from our whole being to something disharmonious, can be depended on to penetrate on the inner plane to others with a harmonizing effect. It is important to say it to all negative intentions, since such intentions invariably come from the ego. When we keep our mind in a state of attunement, our bodily senses make our mind aware of such intentions. Saying the inner No takes away their negative energy.

By keeping attuned to our body's awareness, our mind's natural defense against the encroachment of disharmonious ideas is restored. Keeping attuned also prevents our mind from falling under the spell of others who would like to dominate us. These others can only succeed if we have self-doubt, or if they can create self-doubt in us. The words the ego uses to create self-doubt are often hypnotic. They begin by claiming to offer us an "important truth" that will give us power over our lives (and power over others); the hidden catch is that by looking up to people for guidance who would like to dominate us, we put ourselves in their control. The *I Ching* addresses this in Hexagram 61, *Inner Truth*.[3]

When we are already an adherent of someone else, we need to recognize the words of the spell that has brought us under their domination. We also need to free ourselves from the original poison arrow that has made us fall under the illusion of their power; it is the belief that we need to find our truth through someone else. Behind this belief is the original poison arrow that proclaimed us insufficient in and of ourselves. To regain our inner independence we also need to free ourselves from the mistaken belief that we need a human master to show us the way.

The mind's most important resource for what it needs to know is the treasure chest of inner truth possessed by the body, as described in detail in Chapter 3.

The next step to freeing the mind from the dominance of the ego (whether it is the individual ego or the collective ego) is to recognize the danger of viewing the ego as evil, and as something we need to fight. To form an antagonism toward it is to engage in an unending negative energy exchange with it. It does not matter to the ego where it gets its energy; it only matters that it gets it. That is why seeing ourselves in opposition to the ego is foreign to the Cosmic Principles of Harmony. Similarly, the ego

---

3 Hexagram 61, *Inner Truth*, Line 2. This line describes "a person who is looking for disciples by saying, 'I want to share the good message with you.' If one follows that person, one would get involved in his fate."

wins our energy if we think we can defeat it by leaving society behind to become spiritual hermits. The correct way to separate from the ego's control is to not play any of its games, and to unfailingly say inner No's to what is disharmonious.[4] Doing so brings the Cosmic Army into action. Limiting ourselves to taking this inner action is what the *I Ching* calls "sweet limitation."[5] Holding back from "fighting evil" deprives the ego of our energy; simultaneously, it generates chi energy within us, nourishing and strengthening our self-esteem. Furthermore, the Sage makes us aware that when we truly let go after saying the inner No, the Cosmos becomes activated to correct matters.

The mind needs to take responsibility for the kind of thoughts it allows. Every time it is tempted to depart from our inner truth, it receives warnings from our inner truth to stop and reflect on the consequences. This is the moment when the mind needs to make a clear decision whether it wants to move toward inner freedom or toward continued enslavement and self-destruction. If the mind wants to free itself from the control of the ego, it needs to be resolved to say a firm No to the ego's temptations.

The Role of the Thinking Mind in Healing the Body

The mind's participation in the healing of the body is essential. Since the causes of illness often lie in faulty thoughts that the mind has accepted as true, the mind needs to cooperate with the Helpers both in finding the sick-making ideas, and in deprogramming them. Is it also an important part of healing that the conscious mind treat the injured parts (cells, organs, etc.) as "brothers" and sisters" or as "children" that are wounded or in shock. Under certain circumstances, the imaging mind can participate in healing physical conditions, as when it shines a healing light on injured cells, or imagines healing water, healing earth, or healing fire being applied to a sick body part. It can also help by visualizing the disturbed body part as healthy and whole, and by comforting the injured, sick, or weakened body cells.

---

4 See Hexagram 14, *Possession in Great Measure*, Line 1, "No relationship with what is harmful."
5 See Hexagram 60, *Limitation/Self Limitation*, Line 5, "Sweet limitation brings good fortune."

Summary

At first it may seem to the thinking mind that this work on itself will deprive it of certain benefits and privileges, especially as it has been put in the position of the Lord of the Manor. However, it needs to be reminded that in this position it is still in the service of the King, the collective ego.

If we look at the backside of being put in a high position, it becomes apparent that the mind becomes loaded with super-human tasks that only the Helpers can do. It is like being put in the position of swimming across the ocean while a boat that we cannot see, because we are so intent on making it to the other side, is riding alongside, offering us a ride. The mind, under the dominance of the collective ego, is deprived of all the helpful resources available to it from the Cosmos to make life a joyful and happy experience for the whole personality.

When the mind is willing to give up its pride, it gains the support of the Sage so that its crossover to the Cosmic way is made easy. The ego, the only thing with something to lose in this process, offers resistance, but so long as the mind remains modest, the Helpers prevent the ego from being successful. On making the effort to put aside that pride, the mind begins to experience an ever lighter and happier unity within the personality, and to feel in harmony with the Cosmos, as well.

The Imaging Aspect of the Mind

People connect the imaging mind mostly with fantasy and creativity. Creativity is not simply a matter of "imagining" something; Cosmic Helpers are always involved in the process. Works that are supposedly creative but only massage and titillate the ego are actually perversions.

When the mind is involved in creative work, we more or less begin with a blank mind, waiting for a thought or image to come to mind. The image that appears can be a memory of an event that has meaning for us, or an image of a way of improving a process, or the image of a device that would make our work easier. It can also be a musical phrase written on paper that sets in motion a musical composition.[6] Once the image appears in the mind, the process takes on a life of its own. Interfering with this process with an intention to "make it sell," "bring us fame," or "appeal to a certain public" halts the creative process.

Fantasy is useful in creating the structure of a play, and in creative writing, but only if the fantasy is guided by the Helper of Creativity. This Helper is engaged through the mind's openness to being helped. Then the fantasy images that come to mind spontaneously illuminate the parallels between one thing and another. In these situations the activity of the imaging mind *precedes* that of the thinking mind, and actually leads it along.

We often are unaware of the role the imaging mind plays in learning language; yet in learning to speak, someone points our attention to an object while saying its name, such as "tree." This sound becomes associated with the image of the tree pointed to. In the rather long process of learning to speak, we tend to forget that behind each word is such an image. The ability to create an image that replicates the tree in our mind is not unique to humans, for every animal has these images of things that populate its world. Only the ability to refer to trees and other objects abstractly is unique to humans.

The imaging mind is one of the first targets of the ego because during childhood it is easy to instill images in it that create fear and doubt. Introducing the word "hellfire" to a child is an example. While an actual example of hellfire is nowhere to be found in our lives, this imaginary fire is instilled with such fervor that it becomes far more threatening than actual fire, and more feared than the burn we experience on touching something too hot. Hellfire not only burns unnaturally hot, it burns forever, vindictively, and relentlessly and inflicting on us an excruciating pain if we do such and such. Fantasy images of this sort have a demonic quality once introduced into the mind that repeats and repeats subliminally in each situation where we might possibly violate the prescribed rules. These images of the fire, and

---

6 Mozart reported that he "heard" his compositions in a complete form before putting them on paper. Asking the Sage to clarify this, we learned that the Cosmic Helper of Creativity played this music into his psyche, and from there into his mind.

the "afterworld" where it supposedly is located, are fanned into huge dimensions by the child's imagination. The intention of those who put such ideas into the child's head is to lock him into automatic behavior patterns. These "locks" last lifelong or until such time that they have been deprogrammed. The fear of hellfire and other fantasized threats displaces our natural ability to judge events on the basis of our inner truth.

Another example of how words desensitize our natural feelings through inserting indelible images in the mind, is the experience of an innocent boy, who, on seeing an older boy blow up a frog with a firecracker, felt horrified. The older boy quickly branded the younger as a "sissy" and further justified his cruelty by saying "animals have no feelings." Since being seen as a sissy was shameful, the younger boy became locked into an inner conflict about this experience. The *image* of horror remained trapped in his psyche until he told his mother of the incident. Fortunately, she helped him process it by pointing to the incorrectness of the older boy's act, and to that boy's using the false word "sissy," to make the younger boy feel his act was okay, because it was "something boys do." She also reconfirmed that animals do indeed have feelings, to reinforce the boy's true feelings about that. The mother also suggested that the older boy might have experienced something similar when he was younger, and therefore became afraid of being called a sissy. Indeed, such unprocessed experiences are behind the acceptance of cruelty — an acceptance that creates an enduring conflict in the psyche. The conflict festers until such time as it is processed and the true feelings that accompanied that event are recognized and validated.

To give another example, it is widely recognized that there is a natural aversion to killing another person. This natural aversion is such that police and soldiers are required to practice shooting at the image of a human figure on the gunnery ranges to overcome it. This aversion, which is not officially stated, is the reason for the practice. Words of justification follow.

Words that justify killing are most obvious on the run-up to a war, where human beings are no longer spoken of as human beings, but re defined as "less than human." They are further defined by other abstract words such as "enemies," "evildoers," "terrorists," "a plague on humanity," or even as "vermin," with the aim being to distance people from their natural feelings. Other words hype the "national interest": "We are being invaded, our resources are threatened, if we do not respond with overwhelming force," and "they may escape to destroy our whole way of life."

Those of us who are exempted from the battlefield may never consider the tremendously destructive effect on the psyche of the individual soldier who makes the step from the imagined killing at a shooting range to an actual one. Once the actual killing has occurred, the inner conflict created within him lasts lifelong. For many soldiers, repeating and unforgettably horrifying images accompany this inner conflict. In all these cases the inner conflict is fuelled by the self-hatred created by their going against their true nature. The self-hatred is often extended to include those people closest to them, such as their wives and children, with whom they identify, and is the cause of spousal abuse.

Not only does the psyche of the person who commits acts of violence become disturbed, the observer who may only read about it in the newspaper may also become disturbed, although not to any similar degree. This is especially true in cases of collective violence (as in the bombing of cities) where the suffering of the civilians is dismissed through being referred to as "collateral damage," or, "the unfortunate consequence of a necessary action." The images that are created by these words allow the newspaper reader to read about the event and lose no sleep over it. This case shows clearly how language can be intentionally used for political purposes to dismiss the feelings we would naturally have about an event.

The Imaging Mind in its Relation to the Feelings

In its healthy function, the imaging mind forms images based on feelings coming from our inner truth. Our *inner sense of seeing* is part of this process in that it relates these images and feelings to other experiences we have had.

The imaging mind has at its disposal a mirror similar to a three-paneled mirror on a dressing table. The mirror receives the images coming from our *inner sense of seeing* that shows us the inner truth of a situation. The mirror then shows this image to the thinking mind, whose function it is to express it in words.

The separation of the imaging mind from our feelings happens through the elevation of the mind by the mistaken idea that "the mind is superior to the body." With the acceptance of the mind's superiority, the two outer panels of the mirror are folded in so that the mirror becomes completely closed. As a consequence, the imaging mind is no longer able to reflect to the thinking mind the images of inner truth that would otherwise come from its inner mirror. Thereafter, both the thinking and the imaging minds are left on their own on the stage of life. Being out of touch with the body and its feelings, the mind now sees itself as "the all." At this point an *ego mirror* is created that replaces the mirror meant to reflect our inner truth to the thinking mind. This new mirror only reflects the "glory" of the mind.

The Ego Mirror

With the creation of the ego mirror, the imaging mind is turned into an appendix of the thinking/word mind. In this position it is assigned to do a number of tasks, the first being to create an image of who we are. This image has the role to compensate for being made to see ourselves as "lacking by nature." To prove that our newly created false self exists, the ego mirror positions itself in the eyes of others. It is there that we are to look for the reflection of whether and how our new image self is being accepted; the feedback that comes through their eyes now determines whether this image is taken as real, and how good it is in comparison with others: Are we better, or worse? Are we higher, or lower? etc., in a unending search to make real a false image of what we are.

How the Inner Senses of Perception are Changed to Suit the Ego

In the healthy personality, what we see with our outer eyes is

191

informed by what we perceive with our inner eyes. The inner eyes process what the outer eyes see in the light of our inner truth. Our outer senses of hearing, feeling, taste, and touch are likewise informed by our corresponding inner senses. The judgment they render as a consensus is what is commonly called our intuition.

The Sage has informed us that of these senses, only the inner senses of smell and taste can be overtaken by the ego. However, as far as our inner sense of seeing is concerned, the ego can replace the images coming from our inner truth with distorted images. To dismiss those inner senses it cannot overtake, the ego suppresses our intuition by saying it is not to be trusted because it cannot be subjected to tests that prove its reliability.

For the mind to be able to develop a correct perception of the outer world, our *inner* senses need to be fully operative. This correct perception is vital to our survival as a species. The capabilities of these senses to help the mind arrive at correct judgments of reality, are the result of millions of years of human development and adaptation to principles that lead to success: these are the Cosmic Principles of Harmony. Humans have adapted to them through intuitively realizing that survival depends not on attaining superiority over others, but on judgments that correspond with Cosmic Principles of Harmony.

The Perversion of the Functions of the Mind by the Ego

With the ego's takeover of the mind, both the thinking and imaging/fantasy minds are altered in their functioning.

The order at the "conference table," where the thinking mind normally takes into consideration what the body knows through its inner truth, is replaced by a wholly different one: now, the mind has made the imaging mind its secretary, and the body the receiver and executor of its commands.

The thinking mind, under the spell that "the truth can only be seen through the eyes," still has a need to explain things that are invisible, such as the "afterlife." It gives this job to the imaging mind, which is no longer able to receive the correct images from the inner eyes. In its helplessness, it produces an image that is an exact replica of the outer world order that has been erected by the collective ego. It thus produces the myths of how the world began, descriptions of a heroic past, of the afterlife, of how things supposedly work, and all the justifications that uphold the illusion of power and the false glorification of human achievement that dazzle and flatter the mind away from our commonsense.

The imaging mind is also given the job of creating images that manipulate people to buy things they neither want nor need.

Another of its jobs is to imagine worst-case scenarios under the pretense that we need to protect ourselves from the unknown future. It may further create images that show us as helpless and divorced from the protection and help we would receive from the Helpers. Examples are images from dreams and meditations that show our being imprisoned in a room or cage without a door, or standing in front of a solid wall, or an insurmountable mountain. These images are demonic elements called "grabbers." (See Chapter 16: "The Devil's Country.") As their name suggests, they grab and block the Helpers that can help us with the difficult situations that occur in our lives. When combined with the mistaken idea that "we have to do it all ourselves," these grabbers seriously break down our will to go on with life.

The worst-case scenarios produced by the imaging mind get worse the longer the mind has been disconnected from our inner truth. This disconnect is caused by spells that either elevate the mind, or put down the feelings. (See the list of such spells below.) To illustrate the effect of these spells on the large brain, the *I Ching* uses the metaphor of a "dry poplar."[7] Under healthy circumstances a poplar draws a lot of water from the depth of the Earth. The same would be true for the way the large brain draws up the nourishment that is available from our inner truth, via our brain stem (the "roots"). Our feelings are instrumental in accessing that nourishment. A large brain that is cut off from this vital source slowly but surely dries out. The fears of

---

7 See Hexagram 28, *The Preponderance of the Great*, Line 2.

the mind that it will die are real. The remedy for the mind is to return to humility and to reconnect with the body and our feelings. When this return is not initiated through a person's inner work, a fate in the form of a life-threatening illness can bring him to his senses.

The Act of Freeing The Mind

When we see with clarity the falseness of the ideas and beliefs that have created conflict between our mind, psyche, and body, we can proceed to deprogram them, one by one. (See Appendix 3, "Deprogramming.") As they become deprogrammed, our mind is returned to its original innocence, and our body is freed from its demonized state. The ideas and beliefs in question are:

- Humans are special because they have the ability to think and to speak language
- The image of the mind as being special
- The truth can only be seen through the eyes
- The mind needs to search for the truth
- Commonsense is based on the wisdom of the ancients
- We need a human master to show us the way
- The mind knows what the body needs
- The mind needs to control the body
- The mind is our higher nature, the body our lower nature
- The body does not have any intelligence of its own
- Thinking is superior to feeling
- You cannot trust your feelings because they are only subjective
- Your feelings don't count
- The mind is the all
- Human animal nature is the source of evil
- Humans are guilty because they have an animal nature
- The body is lowly, and the cause of all our trouble

Our experiences, both with ourselves and with other people who have chosen to free themselves from the ego's dominance, have shown that the enormous burdens put on the mind by the ego can be lifted away. Swift to come, when we do this, are the many Helpers of our nature that have been freed. Swift, as well, come the Cosmic Helpers as their complements.

16. "The Devil's Country"[1]
Demonic Elements in the Psyche

Demonic elements in the psyche have long been observed in mental illness. We tend to think they only belong to the mentally ill, and therefore put as much distance as we can between "us" and "them." This is because we do not understand what they are. They are in every person's psyche due to the development of the ego, although, in the average person, they are not as obvious as in the mentally ill. What we observe in mental illness are demonic elements that have become visible through occupying the entire stage of consciousness, so that the person has no more room for his own thoughts and feelings.

What the ego does not want us to see is that the ego and the demonic elements that make it up, are not part of our nature. They are foreign elements. So long as we think they are part of our nature, the sense of shame they create causes us to deny their presence.

Once we realize that these elements are indeed foreign to our nature, we are able to distance ourselves from them, which is the first step toward freeing ourselves from them. First, however, we must get past the fear we have to look at them, and the fear that by looking at them, they can do something to us. For this, we need to know that all demonic elements owe their existence entirely to the false words, phrases, and images we have accepted as true, and thereby taken into our psyche. As we have mentioned in previous chapters, this acceptance is often neither a conscious nor a willing act; rather, it often happens by default through not knowing whether those words and phrases are true. This ambiguity ends in being a subtle acquiescence in their validity simply because someone has said they are true. Taking things into our psyche by acquiescence is also the way we accept fears, self-doubts, and crazy-making fantasies.

---

1 See Hexagram 63, Line 3, and Hexagram 64, Line 4. What Wilhelm translated as the "devil's country," Wu Jing-Nuan translated as "the demon regions."
Wu Jing-Nuan, *Yi Jing*, The Taoist Center, Washington, DC, 1991,pp. 213-216.

Perceptive writers such as L. Frank Baum, author of "The Wizard of Oz," have shown how these ideas trap the psyche in fear and doubt, but also, how the demons they create in the psyche may need only a little cold-water thrown on them to free us from their hold.

The Land of Oz was a good paraphrase for the land of the psyche where the inhabitants were held in awe by a wizard, who was revealed to have created the illusion of power through cheap tricks. The tornado that lifted Dorothy's house and killed the first witch, is a metaphor for the effect of shock in breaking the spell that made Dorothy feel helpless in the face of the threat to her dog. She woke up in a land populated by Helpers who had come to help her resolve her problem.

This story is not just a fairytale for children. It describes a number of things about the psyche. The first Helper one meets in the psyche, the Sage, appears in the guise of the "good witch." She makes Dorothy aware that the slippers worn by the fallen "bad witch" (the collective ego) were really Dorothy's. The shoes stood for the abilities possessed by her true self to draw the Helpers she needs to make progress in every aspect of her life. Through creating fear and doubt in Dorothy that she could hold onto her animal nature (represented by Toto), the bad witch had stolen the shoes from her.

In the course of Dorothy's journey home (a metaphor for her inner truth), she meets imprisoned Helpers of her nature that are represented by the scarecrow, the tin man, and the lion. Each needs to be freed from a spell that has been put on him — spells that had made each doubt his abilities. The remaining wicked witch that needs to be killed, before Dorothy can return home, represents the aspect of the collective ego that wants at all costs to take away the shoes. The shoes are what enable Dorothy to tread the path of her Cosmic destiny. The witch's focus on killing Toto indicates what the collective ego most fears: her animal senses that keep her in touch with her inner truth.

That these threats, presented in demonic form, are encountered by Dorothy, an innocent young girl, shows that they are not different from the threats presented to all children by the collective ego at an age when they are unable to process them. Remaining in the psyche, they become, in adulthood, the fear of being unemployed, of not having health insurance, money, food, old age care, etc.

The student of drama or literature will recognize that these different demonic figures, with their phrases, rationales, and justifications, are often represented as individual characters. Often, each states a particular rationale to the main character, who is suffering from an inner conflict between these voices and his true feelings. The fact that they have access to him indicates that he has not developed a strong-enough sense of authority over his inner boundaries to slam the door shut on them. They are therefore able to intensify his self-doubts. As members of the audience, we ask, "Why doesn't he see through these arguments? Why is he so weak? Why doesn't he take a stand?" When, in the end, the main character does so, we feel thankful and satisfied. The stage, or novel, at its best, is a mirror of these conflicts within ourselves, which is why we find ourselves so interested in them.

The self-doubts of the main characters tell us they are giving their energy to some sort of self-image. It may be the image of "the polite person" who doesn't speak up, "the person who maintains good form" at the expense of principle, or "the open-minded person" who ignores blatantly illogical statements.

The arguments and conflicts in Dicken's novels provide a good example of demonic elements being represented as people. Equally, the TV comedy series featuring Mrs. Bouquet in "Keeping Up Appearances," presents an exaggerated, but nevertheless real example of the inability of people (such as her husband and neighbors) to maintain their boundaries against the transgressions of someone who represents the collective ego. The characters show the absurd degree to which the neighbors, who represent the average person, have been conditioned to follow all the "virtues" laid out for them by that same collective ego, even while it is grossly abusing them.

As these examples demonstrate, all demonic elements have

their basis in the collective ego, which has the ultimate goal of diverting us from following the path of our inner truth, and to keep us frightened into adhering to its goals.

How We Came to Discover the First Demonic Elements: Imps, Demons, and Dragons

Carol had her first encounter with demonic elements in her psyche in two meditations that occurred a few weeks apart from each other during the 1970's. As the first meditation began, she experienced herself being pushed off a stool and falling onto the floor. Immediately, she looked around for the cause and saw a pixie-like small man half her size dressed in lederhosen, a green alpine cap with a feather, and shiny black shoes. His eyes were sharp and black and his nose hooked. He was looking at her with pursed lips as if to shame her. She immediately asked, "Why did you do that?" referring to his pushing her off the stool. He replied, "because you weren't supposed to be leaning on it." The meditation left her wondering what the meaning was. Had she been inappropriately leaning on something? If so, what was it? This meditation was far different from previous meditations in which the Sage's presence was invisible, but always felt as kind. Although authoritative, the counsel was always clear and felt harmonious. Giving this experience no further thought, Carol dismissed it as something that would reveal itself to her later.

Some weeks later the pixie figure appeared again. This time it was minuscule, about four inches tall. It was crossing a doorway at the other end of a room so quickly that she had no time to bring it into sharp focus. However, she did notice that its appearance and disappearance coincided with an obvious ego admonition that was voiced in the back of her head. Upon noticing this relationship between the movement of the pixie and the thought, the scene was replayed. This time a tall, friendly figure stood beside her, with a bow, and an arrow that was drawn and immediately released, killing the pixie before it disappeared from sight. Furthermore, she was aware that she had been allowed to sight down the arrow to see that it aimed straight onto the pixie, and that the aim was unerring. Now, the word "imp" came with the realization that this pixie-like figure, now dead, was a demonic element that had been in her psyche. It was the source of those back-of-the-mind thoughts that pronounced what she should and should not do, and that reminded her frequently of what she was doing wrong, all from the standpoint of what she had been conditioned to think. The bowman, she also realized, was clearly of Cosmic origin, and what we later were to identify as a Cosmic Helper.

It was some time before another meditation made her aware of another demonic element. This one appeared the morning after Carol had a conversation with a dinner partner at a party, who was getting his psychoanalytic degree. Jokingly, Carol asked whether he was a Freudian or a Jungian. He replied with surprising vehemence, "Jung! I have nothing to do with Jung. He was crazy!" Carol's son, who was also at the dinner party, on seeing that she was feeling put down, pointed out to her that her dinner partner was wearing two different colored socks! Now, having something to laugh at, Carol spent the rest of the evening feeling vindicated. The next morning's meditation began in a darkened place, perhaps a cave. She could hear a sound that reminded her of a coal-fired locomotive sitting idly on a track, puffing slowly. Then, suddenly, floodlights came on, revealing the sound to be coming from a sleeping dragon. Now the sound reminded her of the "Humph! Humph! Humph!" sound of vindictive indignation that she had heard in her mind the night before. Immediately, she realized that this was the "dragon of vindictiveness," and it was time to kill it, while it was still asleep. Finding a spear in her hand, she drove it into the dragon, killing it.

We later realized that dragons in the psyche include not only ego-emotions such as vindictiveness, but also controlling elements that were installed in the psyche during the formation of the ego, which repress our inner freedom through the fear or guilt they generate. Among such dragons are monumental images such as those of a vindictive, punishing God, and the image of hellfire.

After these early experiences in meditations, we learned that demonic elements also appear in dreams. They can appear in both human and animal forms. The next demonic element that appeared in meditation was a monkey-like figure that was repeating a fear over and over in Carol's mind. She realized that this harassing repetition, often active in her psyche at the time, came from a demon. This mindless repetition is characteristic of demons, and is often associated with fears and ego-emotions such as hate, envy, jealousy, guilt, hopelessness, and helplessness. The demons use these emotions to drive us, as in ambitious striving, or in avoidance, or fleeing. The only purpose of the demons is to steal our life energy through arousing emotions that sustain the ego.

We further learned that these demonic elements are the result of the common fears and self-doubts that are instilled in children. While the threats parents use in training their children may seem necessary to the parent, such as telling a child "what will God think when you behave like that," the child's imagination magnifies such a remark the way a movie projector magnifies a tiny picture frame to fit on a big screen. The psyche stores those images in the gigantic form in which we first experienced them. Once the ego gains control over the psyche through such threats, it plays them back lifelong. This activity of the ego happens outside our conscious awareness.

An example of such elements in the psyche was revealed in a dream reported by a woman during a counseling session.

"I was to drive a car from Berlin to Frankfurt. When I wanted to enter the car, there were already four or five men and women crowded into it; two of them were even crouching in the rear where baggage usually is stored. I was quite taken aback, and thought 'this is not a good situation at the start of a trip.' But, I was not firm in refusing to take them. I thought I had to put up with the situation.

"When I wanted to get into the driver's seat, one of the men was half squeezed into it. I said, 'you have to make room for me in the driver's seat.' He made a little room, but I still could hardly seat myself. The car was already running at low speed and we quickly came to a very narrow spot where a cart was occupying most of the street. The street also looked messy. I said, 'We can't go through there. Put the brake on!' But the man simply steered right through. I managed to put my foot half on the brake, but the car was still driving ahead, and forced its way between things. I woke up with the feeling that I needed to put my foot down and refuse to take anyone with me in the car."

When looking into the dream with the Sage's help, we found that the people in the car stood for four particular demonic elements in the woman's psyche: One was an imp that suggested, "We are part of you, you cannot get rid of us"; the second was a demon that aroused in the woman feelings of obligation toward the members of her family with whom she was, at the time, having problems; the third was a dragon that told her, in effect, "its your car, but I am the one driving it." (This dragon represented the collective ego.) The fourth, another demon, was the self-image the woman had of being a "noble-hearted person" who tolerates everything.

Other Demonic Elements

For several years, imps, demons, and dragons were the only kinds of demonic elements we knew. After we began to work together on our book, *I Ching, The Oracle of the Cosmic Way,* we were led to recognize others, including the changelings, which we have described in Chapter 12.

Over time, we encountered still others that were not imps, demons, or dragons. We simply called them "other demonic elements," or ODE's. One of them was the "doubter" mentioned in Chapter 11. Another was the "grabber of sleep." These are demonic elements that everyone can recognize. We found that discovering their names took away much of the control they had established over us. This fact reminded us of the fairytale of *Rumplestiltsken.* Freeing ourselves completely of them, however, requires a deprogramming procedure that involves Cosmic Helpers. Doing so takes away the possibility of their returning in a new guise.

Demonic elements in the psyche, as these examples show, serve the ego's purpose of keeping our true self locked in the subconscious, and of keeping us within the fold of the collective ego. They do so by reiterating the dangers of listening to what we know from our inner truth. They replay, on the back-of-the-mind screen, the threat of being abandoned by the family, and of being excluded from society. As the above dream shows, while we are made to believe that we depend on our social structures for our security and protection, in reality, these elements take a ride at our expense, and subject us to many unnecessary dangers.

Teams of Demonic Elements

There is a saying that "one evil rarely comes alone," and this is actually true for the way demonic elements form "working teams." For example, when we strive to fulfill any self-image of perfection, that self-image automatically creates demonic elements of guilt, because there is no way we can ever achieve an abstract standard of perfection. On pretending we have achieved such a self-image, we find it is accompanied by a demon and dragon of self-righteousness, a dragon of judgment, an imp of moral rules, and changelings that put forth rationales that support each of these elements. For example, the "Changeling of Measuring Us by a Standard of Perfection" plagues us with the question, "Am I good (meaning selfless, responsible, dutiful, loving, caring, etc.) *enough*?" Its twin, the "Changeling of Reversal" prosecutes us with statements of what we are *not* or *are no longer*, as in, "you are ruthless, uncaring," or "you are not as responsible as you used to be," etc.

How We Unwittingly Energize Demonic Elements

Demonic elements thrive on being seen as real. We energize them when we think of them as cute, clever, brilliant, tricky, or frightening, and when we believe they have the ability to overwhelm us. This danger is demonstrated by certain kinds of films and books that are geared toward giving reality to fantasized demonic elements. Indeed, so long as we see them as real, their size and importance is greatly magnified. Their ability to overwhelm was shown in the panic created by the famous radio broadcast in 1939 by Orson Wells, in which he described as if real, Earth's invasion by inhabitants of Mars.

Some demonic elements, hidden from our view, appropriate our talent for humor in order to laugh at and humiliate others. Other demonic elements appropriate the mind's ability to invent ever more terrible weapons to kill and maim. Still others appropriate its ability to reason, in order to justify lying, cheating, killing, and torturing. They likewise use our own minds to impress us that we are being possessed by elements so clever that they will always be able to outwit us. In like ways they make some people believe they owe the success of their creativity or talent to them, causing them to fear that they would lose their creativity if they gave them up.[2]

When, however, we speak or think of them in ways that reveal that they arise from words, phrases, and images that have no Cosmic basis, and when we also consider the damage such a false use of language does to us, they shrink in size and potency. Their big secret has been revealed.

A Sampling of Other Demonic Elements (ODE's)

ODE's are often composed of two or more demonic elements that collaborate to serve the ego in two ways: to arouse energy to sustain the ego, and to form coping mechanisms within the mind.

Spells and poison arrows, as we know, have the effect of fixing certain functions in the psyche, making them partially dysfunctional. To overcome these dysfunctions, ODE's are created by the mind to allow the person to somehow function while under these spells and poison arrows. Because the mind is not a feeling consciousness, it can only create coping mechanisms that make us function mechanically.[3]

As Carol's meditations indicated, demonic elements need to be "killed" in order for us to be freed from them. In the first meditation, a Cosmic Archer appeared that had unerring accuracy in his aim. In the second, Carol discovered she had a

---

2 We have mentioned this in Chapter 10, in reference to Stefan Zweig and his book, *Der Kampf mit dem Dämon: Hölderlin, Kleist, Nietzsche.*
3 This is referred to in Hexagram 10, *Conducting Oneself*, Line 3, "A one-eyed man is able to see. A lame man is able to tread. He treads on the tail of the tiger. The tiger bites the man. Misfortune."

spear in her hand, and the dragon's sleeping state offered the opportunity for her to kill it. In Appendix 3, "Deprogramming," we describe a number of Helpers that can be asked to kill those we have identified as responsible for problems. The killing of the demonic element is part of the process of deprogramming and freeing ourselves of it.

In the descriptions of the ODE's given below, the spells and poison arrows behind them are not directly visible, nor are they indicated by their names. Their names point mainly to their activities. We have pointed to some of their hidden roots that need to be deprogrammed along with the ODE's.

The Doubter

The first ODE is "the doubter" that creates the individual ego. It installs in us the initial doubt in our wholeness through the statement, "In and of yourself you are not special enough." Thereafter, the doubter's job is to keep that initial self-doubt in place. It has already been described in detail in Chapter 11.

The Grabber

The grabber can appear in different forms. The most common is "the worrier-grabber." Worry is the result of being separated from the Cosmos either through our disbelief in a loving Cosmos, or through having our wholeness divided by self-doubt. The consequence of this separation is that we are left to our own devices. The worrier-grabber takes up any conceivable subject we might be concerned about, and presents it in the light of what might threaten or ruin us. In response to other people's reassurances, it says, "but, what if…," becoming a devil's advocate against any view that offers the possibility of safety.

The "nightly grabber" is most noticeable at night when, after awakening for some reason, it then keeps us awake by bringing to mind situations that arouse fears and worries; it then proposes what we can do about the problem or threat and keeps us examining these 'solutions' until we realize they would be ineffective. Just as we let go of the question, the grabber introduces a new problem and keeps the mind looking for solutions to it. It continues in this way *ad infinitum*. The nightly grabber is the chief cause of insomnia. The subliminal worries, fears, and feelings of hopelessness that the grabber inspires are often the cause of hot flashes and nightly sweats.

The nightly grabber is based on the poison arrow, "Humans are responsible for everything that happens." This phrase, buried in our psyche, keeps us from remembering to ask for Cosmic help. The result is that we take on the task of Atlas, to carry the world on our shoulders.

Typical things the grabber brings to mind are situations we can do nothing about, but "are responsible for": human damage to the environment, wars abroad, natural disasters, crimes, social and educational deterioration, and all the negative news and predictions written about in the media. Also typical are knotty family problems that keep us awake, thinking what we might say or do; it then follows these with reasons why the solutions we imagine would not work.

Another grabber may play on fears, such as the fear we won't get the help we need, and fear of the unknown, as in, "You don't know what will happen." It can also haunt the mind with images that show no way out, as in being confronted with a brick wall, or it focuses obsessively on someone we see as doing something wrong. When this obsession becomes extreme, it can lead to the person's tracking and haunting another.

A grabber can also introduce open-ended obligations that make us feel responsible for everyone and everything. When the phrase is open-ended, the sense of obligation can be limitless, as in the phrase, "You are obligated to take care of the wellbeing of your family." The mind reads such phrases as a command to disregard any limits that would be set by appropriateness and commonsense. The weight of such responsibility keeps us awake at night, thinking of all the things we need to do, and also of all the things we have not done. What we have not done becomes a constant generator of guilt. Through guilt, the grabber keeps the ego firmly in control of the personality. Guilt can also be the cause of nightly sweats.

Other expressions of grabbers are: "There is no guarantee" (in regard to getting Cosmic help), or, "Maybe it isn't worth it" (referring to following the path of our inner truth).

Looking at both the doubter and the grabber, we see that the phrase of the doubter, saying we are "not enough," and the phrase of the grabber, saying we are "responsible for everything," put before us an impossible task that consumes our life energy. The only beneficiary of the effort this costs, is the ego.

The Torturer Team and the Torturer Team Complex

The torturer-team is a combination of a dragon and two other demonic elements. The dragon acts as the "supreme judge" that pronounces us as guilty and as needing to be punished. The other demonic elements are a "prosecutor" and a "torturer." The prosecutor continuously brings forth claims of our guilt, and the torturer carries out the punishment by torturing our body cells, as for example by hitting or pulling on them (through tics, muscle spasms, and bone aches), or by getting them inflamed (as in all illnesses that contain the suffix: "itis"). The torturer is always connected with a poison arrow coming from the inner judge that says, "When you make a mistake, you deserve punishment," "You have to pay for every mistake you make," or, "You have to pay forever for your mistakes."[4]

The Torturer Team can have been initiated by a parent or caretaker who believed in absolute right and wrong, and who gave the child the impression that he would fail in life and be abandoned if he did not live up to that absolute standard. His fear of failing to fulfill that standard draws others to notice his deficiencies and to tell him what he must do to make himself "right." They also focus on his failures, or slight him, or give other signs of disapproval. The pressure of this disapproval, in turn, makes him feel he cannot stand to be around those people. His emotions not only give those people control over him, they also give the egos in them his energy.

The torturer aspect of the team consists of an imp that nurtures the person's fears of being judged for making mistakes. It also reminds him of the threat of abandonment that he experienced during childhood. These fears attract to him the very people who play the ego game of now giving him approval and

---

4 In Franz Kafka's "The Trial," the torturer is referred to as "The Whipper."

now withholding it. A demon is also part of the torturer aspect, It creates the feeling of unbearable pressure by repeating the phrase, "I can't stand this anymore"; this pressure eventually spills out and over to the oppressing person. Once the person with the ODE is away from the oppressor, another demon in him plays the victim and the complainer by indulging in complaints about the oppressor to others.

A person who fits the above description may, in childhood, have developed the "abused child myth" to soothe the wounds created by his caretaker's constant criticisms.

As mentioned, the root of this ODE is the mistaken idea that there is such a thing as an absolute right and wrong. It is coupled with the idea that the wrong needs to be rooted out through punishment.

The Right/Wrong

This ODE is related to "The Torturer Team," and differs in that it is based on the phrase, "You have to be in the right...," i.e., the right party, the right movement, etc., or you need to have the right opinion, etc. The threat of abandonment, stored in the psyche since early childhood, is behind it.

The Upholder of Family Duties

This demonic element is created in a person by a feeling of indebtedness to members of his family that makes him give in to their pressures and demands. This ODE gives rise to a demon of shame that comes over the person whenever he fails to uphold these duties. It is accompanied by a swarm of feelings of guilt.

The root of this ODE is the mistaken belief, "You owe everything to your family."

The Cloud that Blinds

This demonic element is the creation of a changeling that shuts a person off from the true feelings that come from his heart, by covering them with a cloud. The cloud is made possible through the rationale, "it is dangerous to have feelings." (Particularly for men in our culture, this can be, "it's embarrassing or even shameful to have feelings.") Through blinding the person to his true feelings, the changeling is then able to change those feelings into ego-emotions, as for example, changing true feelings of anger into vindictiveness, or hatred; or changing true feelings of justice into self-righteousness; or changing neutral feelings into indifference. The ego-emotions created by this changeling become coping mechanisms, as illustrated by "The Demonic Army" (see the following).

The Demonic Army

The demonic army is a hoard of angry fighters within a person's psyche that seek ways to avenge an injustice once done to him. This army keeps him awake at night thinking of how he can pay back the person responsible for the injustice. By allowing this angry hoard to dominate his psyche for even one day, a memory chip is created that becomes the cause of passive-aggressive behavior against unrelated parties. It is *passive* in that he needs to keep up the image of being the victim. His hidden aggressiveness brings out an aggressive response in others, which then gives him ever more reason to feel that he is the victim of injustice. The presence of the "demonic army" maintains a vicious circle, the real victim of which is the person's true self.

This ODE is a mechanism created to cope with the person's faulty perception of that original injustice, which has never been processed.

The Haunter

The Haunter comes when we do the "unspeakable" (break taboos) in the eyes of the collective ego, as by walking away from a friendship/marriage/parent/sibling or any relationship where it is a taboo to walk away. The root of this ODE is the phrase we have internalized at one time or another, "What you did will come back to haunt you."

The Prideful Predictor

This demonic element is connected with the prideful self-image of one who knows the future, especially the bad things that are going to happen. It can be recognized by phrases such as: "As soon as one bad thing is gone, another comes," and, "Evil is always lurking somewhere." In relation to an illness that has just been healed it says, "It may come back." This ODE often formo a microchip and memory chip that cause different pains in the body that imitate the previous health condition, so that the person thinks it has come back. (See Chapter 18.)

As a coping mechanism, this ODE prepares the person for the "next bad thing" that is expected. His expectation creates the "next bad thing."

The Predictor of Bad Luck

This ODE predicts a negative outcome that is in accord with conventional views such as those taken from science, religion, morality, etc.[5] Predictions of this sort are likely to create the negative things that happen. An example is the prognosis in an illness, "You have about three months to live." Even though we may be determined, in our mind, to fight the prognosis, the will of our body cells to live is defeated unless the prognosis and this ODE are deprogrammed.

The root of the predictor of bad luck is the false belief that "people need to know the truth so that they can get prepared."

The Breakthrough and the Defeater

These demonic elements form a team in which one says, after there has been a breakthrough in a situation, "Finally, this long-standing problem is resolved." Immediately, "the defeater" objects, saying, "You have dealt with this before and nothing happened." An imp then says, "You should already be seeing results." A dragon that demands proof often accompanies this team.

This ODE has the belief, "you can only trust what you see."

The Self-Deprecator and its Partner

The "self-deprecator" says, "You will always be a failure no matter what you do," whereupon its partner adds, "No one will believe you are not a failure until you have proven otherwise." The comment of the self-deprecator is a spell that fixes the person as being a failure; the comment of its partner causes the person to cope by striving, although fruitlessly, to overcome the spell. The benefit of the energy spent goes to feed the ego. The comfort given to the person in this case is that "he is good at

---

5 Hexagram 43, *Resoluteness*, Line 6, makes us aware of the presence of this demonic element through the words: "No cry. In the end misfortune comes."

striving," even though his efforts are fruitless.

The Monumentalizer

This demonic element makes a mountain out of a molehill. It does this by focusing our attention on the size of the problem rather than on its cause, which is usually a mistaken idea, belief, or image — something the *I Ching* refers to as "a small matter." It thus discourages us from ever starting to look for the cause of the problem.

The root of this ODE is the word "problem." The person who has this ODE has associated the word "problem" with the image of a mountain and with the thought, "how can this mountain be moved?"

The Knocker

This demonic element is only active at night and causes sleeplessness. It is always combined with the ego-complex called "The You-Need-to-Be-on-Guard Complex." The only phrase of that complex is, "You need to be on guard against the ego." It gives the mind the task to be on guard, but of course the mind is not capable of carrying it out while asleep. It therefore creates the "knocker" to stay awake. This is a perfect example of the absurdities that result when the ego — via the mind — is given the task to protect us from the ego.

Note: This knocker is not to be confused with the knocking of a Helper that is trying to wake us up to the fact that we are sleepwalking through life, and if we continue, we will have "missed the whole trip."

The Interrogator

This ODE asks, "What are YOU doing about all the misery in the world?" It is connected with an imp of guilt. Because of the trap created by this kind of question, we look to the Cosmos/God with the same question: "What are you (Cosmos/God) doing about it?" The interrogator thereby reinforces "The False-Cosmos Complex." (See Chapter 13.) The coping mechanism, in this case, projects our guilt for not doing something about the misery in the world onto the Cosmos/God.

Guilt for Wanting to Be Healed

This ODE was seen in meditation as a big black tarantula. It is the result of the mistaken belief that we become guilty for wanting to be healed as long as other people are suffering. Behind this belief is another mistaken belief that wanting to be healed while others are suffering would mean that we are "special," which would make us feel guilty.

When, in looking for the cause of a hindrance to healing, we discover a "demon of doubt that we can be healed in time," we need to ask whether the ODE called "Guilt for Wanting to be Healed" is preventing the healing.

The Censor

This ODE makes negative personal remarks that aim to keep us from doing something we feel is important to do, to fulfill our destiny. An example is the remark, "You'll never be a writer," or "your feet are too big to be a model." The "censor" shows itself in the involuntary lifting of one eyebrow. It also acts as an inner censor when we feel drawn to do something that would lead to our personal fulfillment.

This ODE is sometimes combined with a "dragon of censorship" that calls to our mind a strong religious or social prohibition against doing what would lead to our personal fulfillment. It is also an example of a coping mechanism that pretends to protect us from defeat by telling us that we cannot attain the "standard" required to succeed in that particular field.

The Resigner and the Beater to Success

This ODE is composed of a team of demonic elements that can become active when the rational mind has run out of explanations for a situation. The team's goal is to force its point on another person by one means or another. Each tactic is led by a demonic element. Example: a person wants to get a particular idea across to another to satisfy the ego, but does not succeed. At this point, a changeling causes him to utter a sigh that accompanies his thought, "I have no explanation; there is nothing I can do." This activates the dragon of the idea that there is an explanation for everything; it says, "There *must* be an explanation," effectually commanding the mind to come up with a further rationale. This, in turn, activates the demon of repetition that keeps things going for the ego by starting all over. At this point, a changeling takes over that dresses the old rationales in new clothes, and starts to put these forth in a new attempt to get the point across. When nothing else works a changeling exclaims, "The situation is what it is!"

This same dynamic can also play and replay within a person's mind as a subliminal dialogue between these same demonic elements during sleep. It does not keep the person fully awake, but at the same time does not allow him to have a sound rest.

This ODE is based on the belief that a "sound argument must be made, otherwise wrong beliefs will prevail that are the cause of disorder in the world." This belief is rooted in the mistaken idea that if we do not make this argument, we will be personally responsible for the disorder. Further behind this idea is the human-centered view of the Cosmos, which puts human existence up as the most important thing.

The Wound Licker

This ODE is composed of a demon and dragon of self-pity. Behind self-pity is a feeling of hopelessness and helplessness that comes from a criticism of life itself. One needs to look for a memory and/or microchip that contains the memory of a traumatic event in which these two ego-emotions were created.

The Only Opportunity

This ODE is a team of several demonic elements that is active in a person who is needlessly taking up the time of another. A demon in him says, "You need to take advantage of this time, as it is the only opportunity you have to spend time with them." A changeling says, "seize the moment." Part of this team can be a self-image such as that of "the lonely person." Other elements may be a "demon of boredom," and a "dragon of the only opportunity."

Behind the idea of "the only opportunity" may be a poison arrow put on him by someone who has said, probably during youth, "You have to keep close contact with people, otherwise they forget you." The idea, in this case, has implied the threat of abandonment.

The Image of Things Being Complicated

This ODE keeps the image of things being complicated in the forefront of a person's mind, and thereby fixes him in a kind of mental stasis. The hidden root of this is the mistaken belief that "the mind is superior and therefore has the capacity to untangle difficult things." This belief invariably leads the mind in such a person to either create balls-of-conflict, which it cannot resolve, or to be attracted to them so that the mind can make an effort to solve them. The exercise keeps the mind busy because the person's pride is invested in proving the superiority of his mind. (See "A Ball-of-Conflict" in Chapter 12.)

The Act

This ODE causes a person to substitute his natural behavior with an act that he puts on. An example is a person's putting on an act to please someone. The hidden cause is the poison arrow contained in the belief, "you are insufficient in and of yourself." The negative self-image this creates in him makes him put on acts that present him as comical, sophisticated, intelligent, talented, or whatever he imagines will impress his designated audience. At the root, he clearly does not feel at home within himself. He feels at home only in the acts he likes to put on.

When such a person experiences a fate as a result of rejecting himself (the shock of which has the purpose of breaking this pattern), the ODE thwarts that purpose by allowing him to change his identity, like a chameleon. He also has a mistaken view of Fate. He believes it is his fate to put on these acts.

The ODE of Revolution

This ODE says to a person, "You need to make radical changes in your life." (When transferred to the outer world, he hears it saying, "Revolution is the only remedy.") This ODE keeps the person from addressing the root of his dissatisfaction by keeping him focused on making external changes in his situation. There are many possible causes for the person's dissatisfaction. The specific cause needs to be researched with the help of the *I Ching*, or the Sage.

The ODE of Incompetence

At the root of this ODE is the mistaken idea that the "ordinary individual is incompetent to free himself from a fate, and that he therefore needs a specialist (shaman, spiritual guide, or master)." This idea keeps a person separated from the Helpers he needs to end his fate.

The Standard of Perfection

This ODE is a dictate installed in the mind that in order to be someone the person needs to fulfill the standards of perfection set by the collective ego. He is constantly measuring himself against these standards so that he feels he exists. It makes him rigidly adhere to form.

It also causes him to say, "I hope I never get that ailment/economic problem, etc." This hoping draws that very ailment/economic problem, etc.

This ODE negates the uniqueness of the person.

17. What Is It That I Feel?
Our True Feelings vs. Ego-Emotions

We generally think that whatever we feel is an expression of our nature. The reader, by this time, will have realized this is not so, and that we need to distinguish between our true feelings and those that come from the ego. Moreover, our true feelings are often falsely accused as "getting us into trouble." This is due to a lack of distinction between true feelings and ego-emotions. It is ego-emotions such as hatred, vindictiveness, and self-righteousness that get us into trouble.

In our childhood conditioning, we experience that our true feelings "get in the way," as when we feel wronged by an adult, and then must either hide or repress our true feelings. The repression of our true feelings is, in fact, an essential tactic of the collective ego in taking away our sovereignty, by making us feel apologetic for our true feelings, and even to feel that they are wrong.

Our true feelings include feelings of love, caring, sadness, joy, anger, tenderness, peace, and harmony. Feelings that disturb our inner peace indicate the presence of the ego. Ego-emotions occur when the ego seizes our true feelings and turns them into devices that serve its purposes. Other ego-emotions such as helplessness, hopelessness, vindictiveness, envy, and jealousy originate directly in mistaken ideas coming from the collective ego.

The biggest difference between our true feelings and ego-emotions is that our true feelings are *Helpers of our nature* that are supported by Cosmic Helpers in case of need. By contrast, ego-emotions block both the Cosmic Helpers and the Helpers of our nature. The Helpers of our feelings get blocked, for example, when we allow the ego to claim, "I am a loving/caring person." Such a phrase makes our true feelings part of the prideful self-image it wants to show the world. Ego-emotions are meant to have an effect on others in order to engage the ego-emotions in them, such as a false acquiescence, pity, guilt, pride, or an attitude

216

of defensiveness, helplessness, or intimidation.

When we say we are moved by a true feeling to do something, we realize that all true feelings express an inner truth, be it in words or actions, or simply in a bodily expression. They are an innocent expression of our true nature. Ego-emotions, on the other hand, rather than expressing our true nature, allow the ego to steal our chi energy, and, if possible, engage the ego in others so as to multiply the gain for all egos involved. For example, the collective ego expects us to exhibit specific feelings on specific occasions. When we do not fulfill that expectation, we feel guilty for not showing what we "ought to feel."

Our True Feelings

Love

The source of all love is the Cosmos. Love is its primal energy. Being part of the Cosmos, human beings possess love in their nature. Cosmic love is the chi that supplies all living things with their life force. It may be seen as much in the alligators that rest their heads on each other's bodies as we see it in human beings. The Cosmic Helper of Love brings chi to the individual human.

Feelings of love come to the heart from the Cosmos when the heart is receptive. Receiving love from the Cosmos is made possible when we respect our dignity and worth to the point where we are not willing to compromise it. This is the meaning of loving oneself. When a person has this communion with the Cosmos, he always feels loved, even though he may be alone. Feelings of love flow to others when they, likewise, are receptive, and respect their dignity and worth as equal to others. Feelings of love are by nature tender and sensitive, and include fairness.

What prevents or kills feelings of love are ego-elements of all sorts. Because love tends to make room for people to make errors, it is a prime target of the ego in its search for energy. The collective ego has invented numerous ideas about love to enable it to gain this energy. Among them is the idea that love is to be given unconditionally. Another is the idea that love and sexuality are two unrelated things. When a person acts upon this idea, the ego humiliates the true self, and thereby gains control both of the psyche and the heart. Another mistaken idea is, "to be loved is our right." This implies that the Cosmos owes us love. Other ego-based ideas concern the love relationship: "Love has to be sanctified by authorities, otherwise society has the right to block it." Another is the moral view that, "You have only one true love in your life." In addition to these ideas that restrict love, slanders put on love allow the ego to draw energy from yet another angle. Examples are statements such as, "Love does not last," "Love is for fools," and "True love does not exist."

Love, being the primal energy of the Cosmos, maintains and furthers every aspect that is part of the harmonious order of the Cosmos. The reason the Cosmos does not give its love energy to the ego, is that the ego violates the Cosmic order and its Principles of Harmony by seeking to replace them with its values, all of which negate true love.

Sadness

Contrary to common belief, sadness is not a negative feeling. In fact, none of our true feelings is negative. Each one is an appropriate expression of the inner truth of a situation. The Helper of Sadness, for example, helps us when we have become shut off from our connection with the other Helpers that normally support us in many loving ways. This Helper helps us by creating a shelter for the feelings of our heart in the psyche until such time as our true self has been freed from the ego's dominance.[1]

We also feel sad when someone we love is taken out of our lives; when we allow this feeling, it draws the Helper of Comforting. This Helper reassures us of the other's wellbeing, and brings us relief. In due time, the Helper of Sadness attracts the Helper of Joy to enable us to continue our lives joyfully, knowing that the person who died is on his own path, while we, too, follow our own unique path. If it is the path of our inner truth, we are never lonely in treading it.

---

1 See Hexagram 56, *The Wanderer*, Line 4, "The wanderer rests in a shelter."

The ego, however, would turn our sadness into grief by calling it a "loss." The *I Ching* makes us aware that there is no such thing as "loss," as in death, since death is a passage into an invisible dimension, but not an end to life. What the deceased meant to those left behind is not changed. There is no doubt, however, that the person's presence is missed for some time. If the one left behind does not have a strong connection with the Cosmos, the Cosmic Family brings him reassurance, and little by little, the feeling of being loved.

To feel sad is also a natural response to seeing someone we care about drift away from his true self, or make a mistake that we feel will incur a fate. Sadness, in this case, is a form of caring about them. Our natural response is to ask the Sage-in-that-person's-presence to help the situation. The ego would lead us in the opposite direction by either suggesting that we need to rescue the other through words or deeds, or that we give up on him as hopeless, or tell him he is on a path toward failure. In all these cases, the ego causes us to put judgmental projections, spells, and poison arrows on the person that fix him in his erring ways. The ego can also make us feel disdain, disaffection, or hardness toward such a person.

The tears that normally accompany the feeling of sadness are an expression of the Helper of Sadness. These tears have the same qualities as the "liquid light" we use in a healing meditation that facilitates the process of transformation.[2] They are tears that transform sadness into joy.

However, it is not normal when we cry without end. Then, the ego has seized our feelings of sadness and distorted them with ego-anger. Ego-anger is a reaction to the word "loss." When we see the departure of someone who was dear to us as a loss, we develop anger at being abandoned. This can be anger at the person who departed, or at the Cosmos for "taking him away." We often notice how these tears spring forth spontaneously when we touch upon a memory of stored-up anger at a perceived injustice we have suffered. In this case, the tears help

---

2 See Appendix 3, "Deprogramming," i.e., *Deprogramming crystallized ego-emotions.*

us to access the memory chip and/or microchip containing the components of that event.

The *I Ching* refers to tears that are connected with ego-anger as "bloody tears." Bloody tears can also flow when we have given up on ever reaching a goal that is important to our true self, such as the goal of freeing our true self, of being united with another, or of ever finding the job that would fulfill us.

In "crying at the happy ending," tears are released that have been suppressed by feelings of hopelessness. Watching a movie that reflects an experience in our own lives that left us with a feeling of hopelessness, and then seeing the story take an unexpected turn toward a happy ending, brings us relief and the awareness that unexpected turns toward a happy outcome are possible.

"Bitter tears" can be the result of self-blame for bringing shame upon ourselves for not observing ego-values. They come from the true self that has falsely taken on the blame. These contrast with the tears of remorse that flow when we realize that we have gone against our true nature.

Bitter tears are also connected with regret for something we have done or failed to do, such as failing to listen to feelings of hesitation of leaving our child with someone, only to find that the child was harmed in the process. These are tears that come upon realizing we have created a fate. It is important, in this circumstance, not to allow the ego to seize the emotion and use it to create an everlasting self-blame. When we realize that we have created a fate, we need to look for what has caused us to act the way we did, deprogram it, and ask for Cosmic help to erase that blame and its effects.

Bitter tears can also be caused by feelings of being betrayed. This can include someone we have trusted, an official or agency responsible for our insurance, security, or money, or feeling betrayed by the Cosmos. Bitter tears can also flow when a person experiences a fate that he thinks is undeserved.

When either bloody tears or bitter tears flow, the *I Ching* counsels us to retreat and examine what role the ego may be playing in these emotions.

Depression is a condition in which the ego has combined ego-emotions and true feelings of sadness with the conclusion that the situation is hopeless. Leading to this conclusion are mistaken beliefs that say, "that's the way life is," "that's the way people are/the way I am," or "I'm born under a hostile constellation," or "depression is due to brain chemistry that cannot be altered."

Caring

We often do not realize how much caring feelings are natural to humans. This is true even in people whose feelings have become fairly hardened. It is shown in their natural inhibition to run over an animal that suddenly comes into the road. It is shown likewise in the adult who suddenly sees a stranger's young child wander into the road. Caring is a feeling caused by the Helper of Caring that each person possesses within his nature. In emergencies this Helper causes us to call for Cosmic help. It enables us to do what we are capable of doing under the circumstances.

Natural feelings of caring become perverted when someone takes on the image of "being a caring person," or when he believes he ought to be compassionate. Striving to fulfill the self-image of "the compassionate person" keeps him from saying the inner No to wrong conditions and their causes. It also exposes him to feeling guilt when he cannot do anything directly to help "the starving children in the world," or the maltreatment of animals, trees, the earth, etc. Compassion is based on the assumption that there are no Helpers available and contains the self-flattery that it is noble to be compassionate. Acting from any self-image comes from the ego and creates a fate.

Caring, or empathy, which is to understand and share another's true feelings, is not to be confused with sympathy. Having sympathy with someone who suffers or is in a difficult situation has the problem of locking us into the helplessness, hopelessness, or pain the other feels. It does not bring help to the situation. Sympathy is different from caring, which calls for help. Another name for the Helper of Caring is "the Helper of Biting Through"

221

because it brings the help needed to "bite through" the idea or belief that is causing the suffering. "Biting through" means saying a firm inner No to that idea or belief.

The Helper of Caring makes us recognize where help is needed, and in what form. For example, when we see someone locked in fixed behaviors that continually put him in a bad light, this Helper helps us search for the underlying causes, so that we can deprogram them on his behalf.

This Helper also helps us to deprogram incendiary words used by nations that are in conflict to describe each other, such as "evil," "culprits," and as "too rigid to change" in regard to certain behaviors.

This Helper also helps us deprogram spells and poison arrows put on Nature, and the animals around us.

These examples show that true caring does not mean to sacrifice our needs for others, to jeopardize our safety in demonstrations for a cause, or to intervene outwardly to correct situations, for these are not in themselves caring acts. They are rather political stands that energize the opponents by pointing fingers at them. The self-righteousness of those holding up a cause obscures the fact that viewing anyone or anything as an opponent is not in harmony with the Cosmic order. By contrast, true caring responds to the needs of the moment on the inner plane, to free the situation from the spells that have created the problem.

Caring, in such a situation, does not mean deprogramming only one side of a conflict. It is to deprogram the spells and poison arrows at the root of the conflict on all sides with impartiality. To fail to do so creates the danger of leaving intact the source of renewed conflict. This is the danger referred to in Hexagram 21, *Biting Through*, Line 5.[3]

Gratitude

The feeling of gratitude we have comes from yet another Helper of our nature, the Helper of Gratitude. Carol remembers

---

3 Line 5, "Biting on dried lean meat one receives yellow gold. Perseveringly aware of danger. No blame."

an event that became what she later called her "benchmark of gratitude." In 1952, she and her family had spent the summer on a farm they hoped to buy after selling the crops they planted. The main crop was to be 100,000 onion plants which they grew in a hotbed sixty feet long. The day they began planting them, with a crew of helpers, was the beginning date of a drought that lasted more than thirty days. Every day of the planting was hot and dry, and when there had been two weeks without rain, and the first onion plants were dying, they stopped, and began investigating whether they could continue without installing a large watering system. The fact that they lacked the capital and help was decisive and the project failed. By the end of the summer, only a few other crops succeeded and they saw the end of their attempt to be farmers. Then one day when Carol walked the quarter mile to get the mail, she looked back over the farm from the small hill where the mailbox was. She heard the beautiful sound of the birds and felt the peace and quiet of the lovely surroundings. She suddenly noticed that she had come to this place because of its beauty, but had become so consumed with all the plans and work that she had not heard the birds, nor had she taken the time to feel the place, or just stand in the quiet sunshine or listen to the rippling river nearby. Everything else had intruded. Suddenly, the depressed feeling of failure lifted; she felt the beauty of Nature pouring in, and gratitude for the gift of being alive. She later noticed that from that day forward events took a different turn — upward, leaving behind despair and regret.

Gratitude, she noticed, was something she often forgot, but at key moments of despair, this Helper returned. Eventually, she began to notice that whenever she felt the slightest negative mood, remembering the wonderful moments in her life quickly dispersed it. This remembrance was not like that preached during her childhood in the church, or like the "grace" said at the family table before eating. It was not thanks for something imagined, or hoped for, but was an alive and heart-warming feeling of remembrance.

Carol realized that in earlier times, the dark moods that ac-

223

companied her negative experiences would totally eclipse her natural cheerfulness. The ego had pulled a veil of forgetfulness over all her experiences of gratitude. It did so by replacing these memories with thoughts of "how bad things are." Then those bad memories led to fears of new negative experiences, which would actually happen. Fortifying herself "for the worst" produced even more negative experiences for which her preparations against them were always inadequate.

One day, while observing Nature, a curious image came to Carol of how gratitude occurs in Nature. It was the image of a cow relishing the lush grass she was eating. It occurred to her that the cow's enjoyment was actually the most pure expression of gratitude. From the Cosmic perspective, she learned that the simple recalling of Cosmic gifts connects us with Cosmic beneficence.

Cosmic beneficence is available to us at all times. Connecting with it requires only that we see it is there. What stops us from seeing it is the ego's human-centered view of the Cosmos and of life, and the arrogance and lack of modesty those views create. The ego has added to this blindness by describing the Cosmos as a tyrannical and uncaring overlord, and by describing the human mind as "the light of creation." To such superlatives are added degrading descriptions of human nature as "greedy and lustful." All such descriptions, when believed, isolate us from the Cosmos and its beneficence.

The Helper of Gratitude is unblocked by shock — as in the kind of shock by which the world around us is destroyed while we are left standing. This is demonstrated again and again, as when a fire destroys every house on a block but one. Such demonstrations remind us that the Cosmos was there, protecting that one person or family. The ego would say the Cosmos is unfair, but in such cases there is an inner truth that we do not yet know.

Joy

Another Helper of our nature, the Helper of Joy, brings joy to us. True joy is a feeling we experience on discovering a Cosmic truth, because it lifts us out of an oppressive idea that has been stored in the back of our minds. We also feel joy when we have discovered the true name of a thing — the name that expresses its essence. Joy is often connected with language since we feel it when we find the words that fit the inner truth of a situation. Joy also comes when our true self is in communication with another's true self, and when we have a feeling communication with an animal or any other aspect of Nature.

Joy is perverted when the ego uses it to convince others how joyful we are, and when we cultivate the self-image of being joyful. Behind this is the idea that this image will make us "popular," and "win friends and influence people." A self-image of this sort always comes across as "too much."

Joy is given a perverted meaning when we accept the mistaken idea that true joy can only be found in the afterlife. This idea excludes the possibility of our experiencing true joy while living in a body. It further taints our experiences with embarrassment when we do experience joy. Carol remembers visiting her cousins who lived on the farm of their great-grandparents; the great-grandparents were buried in a family cemetery on a hill overlooking the farm. The cousins, six in number, liked to dance to Glenn Miller's music, but would always comment while pointing to the hill, "Great Grandmother would turn over in her grave if she saw us dancing in her house."

Joy is also perverted when it is connected with mentally conceived ideas such as "serving others," "being in the service of God" (or of a cause of any kind), "spreading good news," and with falling into a state of ecstasy or delusion achieved by a progressive excitement that hypnotizes the person. True joy is simple, not spectacular, or the result of being hyped up.

True joy is also experienced in the intimate love relationship where there is no need to contrive feelings, and where each is sensitive to the other. It is both a bodily experience of joy and a joy of the heart. However, when love is either absent, or is polluted with ego, or divided into divine versus earthy love, the joy of bodily love becomes perverted.

People speak of the joys of victory, as when they win a lawsuit or war. Such emotions are clearly ego-emotions that come from the mind, not the heart. True joy can never be at the expense of another, as in seeing them vanquished, or as in *schaden-freude*—seeing someone getting their comeuppance.

The same applies to the supposed joy a person has at success-fully fulfilling a self-image, such as that of the "successful writer," the "great actor," or "the powerful politician." The ego-joy experienced over such things is short-lived because the fulfillment of every self-image is accompanied by a fate. All such successes are stolen from the Cosmos and are to be repaid in one way or another. These repayments do not fit what the ego would pronounce as just. The danger of taking joy in false things is referred to in Line 6 of Hexagram 29, *The Abyss/Danger:* "Bound with cords and ropes, shut in between thorn-hedged prison walls: for three years one does not find the way. Misfortune."

Anger

True anger is an energy that flows to us from the Cosmos under the following circumstances: when we have been treated unjustly or with careless indifference, when people have encroached over our boundaries, or have intentionally harmed us, or when we witness harm done to other people, to animals, or to Nature. The anger energy comes from the Cosmos because these acts are first and foremost committed against the Cosmos. Therefore, true feelings of anger are meant to make us recognize that something incorrect has been done.

Feelings of anger have the purpose of initiating the correct response: saying either an inner No to the aggressor, or an outer No, depending on the situation. After having said the necessary No, we then turn our anger over to the Cosmos, which transforms it into an energy that comes out later in exactly the way needed to correct the aggressor. The transformed anger energy is also used by the Cosmos to heal the injury. For the person wronged, forgiving or not forgiving is not his job, because the aggressor's act is first and foremost an offense against the Cosmos. When we turn matters over to the Cosmos, Cosmic justice *will* be served. When the aggressor has true remorse, it corrects his relationship with the Cosmos. For a detailed discussion of Cosmic justice, see Chapter 7.)

Acts of aggression always create a fate that returns to the aggressor if not interfered with. When the ego in the one harmed seeks retribution, he interferes with the return of that fate, and further enmeshes himself in that same fate. He thus remains negatively connected with the aggressor, giving the ego in him his energy. It is important for the person harmed to ask the Sage to free him of any grief or other difficulty the wrong act has caused him. This cleansing of himself of these ego-emotions attracts the Cosmic Helper of Fate, which then comes to his defense, assuring a just and correct conclusion to the matter.

When anger is taken over by the ego, it is blindly thrust back at the aggressor, as in openly blaming, or returning the aggression. Doing so dissipates the anger energy so that it is no longer available for use by the Cosmos. Neither is the anger to be repressed, because that only turns its energy against the one harmed. Repressed anger becomes congealed in a microchip, which is lodged in a part of the body, or a memory chip lodged in the psyche. It eventually becomes the cause of a health condition. (Repressed anger is also sometimes combined with an inner command that one "ought" to forgive.)

Anger is also not meant to be vented through bitching about a grievance to a third party. It dissipates the anger energy and prevents the person from saying No, and turning the matter over to the Cosmos for correction.

Tenderness

Feelings of tenderness are a natural response to innocence, as when we feel tender toward the innocent child or a baby animal. We have such feelings toward an adult only when the adult is relating from his true self.

It is impossible to have tender feelings while the ego is present. For example, tenderness is prevented by ego-emotions such as possessiveness and dominance. When the ego is absent, as in being knocked unconscious in an accident, we feel tender toward the person as we stand by his hospital bed.

Genuine tenderness cannot be perverted by the ego simply because we are incapable of feeling tender toward someone who demands tenderness from us. Any attempt on our part to comply with that demand causes our feelings of tenderness to withdraw. Then, only compliance can take its place. Compliance comes from a desire to get along at any cost, behind which is a fear of offending, or fear of an aggressive reaction.

We can also have tender feelings toward ourselves.

Feelings of Harmony and Peace, or Feelings of Disharmony

The *I Ching* makes us aware in its first two hexagrams of what it means to be in harmony: Hexagram 1, *The Cosmic Consciousness*, speaks of the Cosmic way by which things manifest into existence: before this manifestation occurs, an image of it is formed in the Cosmic Consciousness. This original image is only harmonious and good. This is true for all life on Earth. Hexagram 2, *Nature*, refers to everything that has already manifested into form. The original image of everything that exists is stored within the individual thing. For example, our original image is stored in our psyche. It tells our body cells how to grow and is a reminder of who we are.

Regardless of how far away we depart from our original image, it remains true. We feel harmony when we are at one with it. It is like a hologram into which we can seat ourselves and feel at home. We also feel this harmony when we take our true place in the Cosmos as equal to all its aspects: both those that have manifested and those in the invisible realm.

When we are not in harmony, the Helper of our Feelings of Harmony can temporarily realign us with our original image, if asked to do so. This brings us back to peace within ourselves.

In relation to health, the Helper of our Original Image can be asked in meditation to correct the distorted images of us that show us as sick, deformed, or lacking. For example, the pains experienced by amputees are an expression of the image of the amputated part as "lost." In this case, the person needs to return to his original image of being whole and to reclaim the image of the amputated part.

Being in a state of harmony is also to be in the optimal state of creativity. We are here speaking of creativity as free of ego. *Feelings of disharmony* always indicate the presence of ego. We feel them when we ourselves are under the ego's influence, and also when the ego in others is present. Our sense of caution warns us when we are in the energy field of an ego. Compared to feeling in harmony, we have "jagged feelings." Any feeling of being disrupted from our inner harmony indicates that we need to find out whether that feeling originates within ourselves, or in others, or in both. On discovering the causes of the disharmony, we can then deprogram them with Cosmic help. This removes all the negative energy and restores harmony.

Feelings of disharmony that are caused by being injured, abused, or treated unjustly require saying an inner No to the wrong treatment and turning the matter over to the Cosmos, as has been described above under *anger*.

Ego-Emotions

All ego-emotions are felt as disharmony. Above, we have mentioned only those ego-emotions that *are created by the ego's appropriation of our natural feelings*. In the following we will speak about all those ego-emotions that *have their roots in the one mistaken idea that we are born lacking, i.e., we are not sufficient within ourselves*. The following list will show how significant this one idea is in creating disharmonious feelings. The arrows show how one ego-emotion creates others.
- Inferiority > superiority
- guilt > shame
- shame > abandonment
- Self-doubt > nervousness
- Self-hatred > hatred
- Envy > discontent and feelings of annoyance
- Ego-desire > possessiveness
- Ego-anger > vindictiveness
- Pride > hurt pride, self-righteousness, vindictiveness, indignation and resentment

- Self-pity
- Pity > pride in being good
- Lack of self-worth > reverence for others
- Awe > ego-enthusiasm
- Helplessness > hopelessness
- Boredom > depression
- Feeling obstructed > feeling despair
- insecurity > possessiveness

By accepting this single mistaken idea that we are born insufficient in ourselves, we form an image of us that contradicts the original image that is imprinted in the Cosmos and in our psyche. Moreover, we form an image of life that is in conflict with the Cosmic image of life as abundance. Thereafter, the false image of ourselves causes us to lose our natural self-confidence, our feeling of self-worth, our dignity, and our connection with many Helpers of our nature, and with the Cosmic Helpers. One can readily see why, through being possessed by this mistaken idea of being born insufficient, feelings of being helpless and obstructed can take over. These, in turn, lead to ego-anger, ego-desire, nervousness, and to all the other ego-emotions listed above. We can also see how feelings of awe and ego-enthusiasm become necessary to lift us out of our feelings of self-doubt and insecurity. Thus, feelings of self-doubt and insecurity cause us to strive to become superior, and when superiority is acknowledged in the public eye, it leads further to self-righteousness and pride.

Ego-Emotions That Are Extensions of Other Ego-Emotions
Aggressive feelings

These feelings can come from envy of what others have. They can be acted upon either individually or collectively. Individually, they characterize the thief and robber, whether the theft is of a material or immaterial possession, such as wealth, position, title, privilege, knowledge, insight, or discovery. An example is envious feelings that generate wars, with the aim being to possess the trade, wealth, or natural resources held by another nation.

Aggressive feelings toward one's partner, children, or other family members can be caused by seeing oneself as disadvantaged, overlooked, or suffering from a repeated injustice. They can serve to justify the person, or to bring retribution for insults and slights, or to correct perceived injustices by force.

Aggressions against the self are a form of self-punishment from having accepted the belief that one is guilty, blameworthy, inferior, unlovable, or ugly. It can also be the consequence of being abandoned by the parents or others. Self-aggression can also come from the belief that the evil in oneself can only be conquered by stringent self-discipline.

Aggressive feelings can also be based on the belief that progress is made only by pressing oneself and one's interests forward, or those of one's company. A sales person acts on this belief when he attempts to overwhelm a prospective buyer's commonsense. Lobbyists who pay to buy political favors follow this path, as do business monopolies that act aggressively by expanding and shrinking supplies to extract the highest prices for their essential services, and to squeeze the workers' wages down.

Feelings of aggression against Nature come from the human-centered view that Nature is there to serve humans. Rationales supporting these feelings are claims that "some parts of Nature are bad, or useless because they do not contribute to human needs, and therefore can be extinguished." Even those parts that are considered useful to humans are treated aggressively, as if Nature and humans are unrelated. The rationale behind this behavior is that Nature will not give us its gifts freely.

All aggression and use of force is based on inner feelings of conflict that have their roots in the belief in lack, which ultimately is due to denying the existence of Cosmic abundance and help.

Feelings of conflict

All outer conflict begins as an inner conflict. Feelings of inner conflict are caused by ideas and beliefs that are contrary to our true nature. Those ideas and beliefs are based on one or more of five false words that have no Cosmic validity: special, evil, guilt/culprit, power, and rights/duties.

Blaming

Blaming other things or people happens because the ego prevents us from seeing that the cause of problems lies in the ego-mindset.

An attitude of suspicion and defensiveness against Nature

This attitude is due to what appears to be the "fickleness" of Nature, and the prevalent ego-view that Nature is hostile to humans. This has led in earlier times to seeing the water and fields as governed by spirits or deities that need to be placated through sacrifices. These views cause Nature to respond with fates that can manifest as severe weather conditions and so-called natural disasters. It is in our makeup to live in a positive symbiosis with Nature, and not in fear of it.

Feeling victorious

This feeling occurs, for example, when we allow the ego to appropriate the cultural achievements that were possible only with the help of the Helpers. There are those who then say, "Humans have achieved yet another victory over Nature!" Indulgence in this feeling invariably creates a fate. The loss of humility brings about a gradual decrease of the gain.

Feeling victorious in war is another example. The ancient Chinese recognized the fate it brings, when they created the saying, "When there is a victory, it is a time for tears."

Feelings of anxiety about being judged a culprit

Feelings of anxiety about being judged a culprit engage a person's mind in observing what is wrong in others. The *I Ching* calls this activity "busying the mind with trivial things, thereby drawing down misfortune upon oneself."[4]

Guilt

The ego-emotion of guilt is created by the collective-ego's invention of that word. It falsely introduces the idea that an inextinguishable stain is put on our nature if we do not live by its values. The concept of anything inextinguishable being put on our nature violates the Cosmic order. From the standpoint of the Cosmos, we incur Cosmic blame when we go against our

4 Hexagram 56, *The Wanderer*, Line 1.

true nature. This blame gets erased as soon as we recognize our mistake, feel remorse over what we have done, and correct our thinking. This kind of learning from our mistakes allows us to make progress. Because guilt is so toxic and contrary to our true nature, it causes us, when we have been branded as guilty, to unconsciously cast guilt onto others.

The word guilt holds more control over people than any other word because it contains the threat that if a person is found guilty, he will be permanently branded by and potentially excluded from society.

The control of the collective ego over the individual goes even a step further with the introduction of the idea that "humans are born with original guilt/sin." The individual who is born into a culture that supports this idea finds himself under this spell simply by default. Like all spells, it locks the person into a pattern of behavior that is unnatural to him. The collective ego can then exploit the individual's feelings of guilt without measure at the expense of his life energy, because he feels guilty for whatever he does (or even doesn't do – thus the expression "you're damned if you do and damned if you don't.") The idea of being born with original guilt causes confusion inasmuch as it makes people look at the Cosmos as having created a defective order by putting guilt on everyone.

The collective ego offers a number of ways that will supposedly free us from guilt such as working for a good cause, redeeming ourselves in the eyes of God through devotion and prayer, or sacrificing our animal nature by suppressing our sexual needs in the effort to be "spiritual." All these strategies only serve two purposes: to supply the collective ego with even more of our life energy, and to keep us as individuals under its control.

The *I Ching*, by making us aware that the word guilt has no basis in the Cosmos, shows us the way out. We need to say No to the validity of this word and the image of the inextinguishable stain connected with it, and deprogram these with Cosmic help. We also need to deprogram guilt whenever we find that it is connected with a self-image, or a mistaken belief, or a chip that contains the memory of a traumatic event.

Self-blame

This ego-emotion keeps us attached to mistakes we have made. It has one simple phrase, "You are to blame." By this accusation, which has no time limit on it, we feel forever condemned as "wrong" and "bad." It therefore prevents us from looking for the true cause of the mistake in question, and deprogramming it. Self-blame is also a cause of illnesses and psychological problems.

Attachment

Attachment, when it is an ego-emotion, comes from the fear that something we are falsely depending on will be taken away. It comes from being separated from the true source of our security — the Cosmos — and the flow of blessings and gifts the Cosmos gives freely. Attachment creates the fate that we lose what we are attached to.

Attachment to mistaken ideas and beliefs that give us a false sense of security comes from being separated from our inner truth. In recognition of this fact, the *I Ching* does not ask us to give these up until we have seen with clarity that they are untrue.

The belief that we will obtain protection by performing a ritual or by placing a fetish in a certain place, is another example of a false attachment.

Another form of attachment is the attachment to the idea of non-attachment for its own sake, which is common to many spiritual beliefs. This idea prevents us from attaching ourselves to the one thing we need to be attached to: our inner truth.

Depression

The ego-emotions described above all have the effect of draining our chi-energy, and therefore gradually lead to feeling empty and depressed. The *I Ching* describes this condition as "sitting under a bare tree, staring into a gloomy valley."[5] This image shows a person whose efforts may have turned out to be fruitless, and who is accusing himself of being guilty for having failed, and who has now concluded there is "no way out." A

---

5 See Hexagram 47, *Oppressing/Exhausting*, Line 1.

grabber of self-criticism has collapsed his will to live.

What the person does not realize is (1) that his failure is a fate caused by having acted against his true nature, and (2) that the fate can be ended the moment he recognizes and frees himself from the mistaken ideas that have caused it. The ego in him has reached its monumental control by keeping him attached to self-criticism and guilt. It has achieved this through such phrases as, " I cannot get past this problem."

A person allows the grabber free rein because he is unaware that it is not his true self speaking, but an interloper that needs to be silenced with a firm will, by saying the inner No to each of its phrases. This is also true in addictions.

18. Harmful Microprocessors
Stored Memories of Shocking
and/or Traumatic Events

Shocking and/or traumatic events that are not processed at the time they happen become stored in the psyche, where they are hidden from view. They can be thought of as "chips." They are like microprocessors that trigger mechanical responses; the difference is that they only trigger *unhealthy responses.*

Chips

Chips contain the memory of an original event in complete detail in microform; they also contain the conclusions that were drawn at the time, and the fears, guilt, self-blame, and other emotions that accompanied the traumatic images. The automatic reactions they trigger override commonsense, and all mechanical attempts to suppress or change them (mechanical attempts being "mind over matter," "force of will," a "change of mind," and medications). Chips remain obdurately in place until such time as the event that created them, together with all its components (words, images, emotions, conclusions) have been successfully identified, processed, and deprogrammed.

By *identified*, we mean that the original components of the chip are identified and verified with the help of the Sage.

By *processed*, we mean the original events are shown and understood in Cosmic terms so that the fears, guilt, and other ego-emotions connected with them do not overwhelm the mind. The clarity thus achieved goes about three-quarters of the way to dissolving the chips. The final dissolution occurs through a transformation that is brought about by the Helpers when we deprogram the contents of the chips. This process frees the psyche and/or body of the chips permanently.

We have identified six kinds of chips: (1) *Memory chips* are memories of traumatic events stored in the *psyche*. (2) *Micro-chips* are memories of traumatic events stored in the *body*. (3)

236

Ego chips are memories of shocking events stored in the *mind*.
(4) *Birth chips* are traumatic memories stored in the *brain* and
body. (5) *Conception chips* are shocking memories stored in the
brain. (6) *Stop chips* are traumatic memories also stored in the
brain. (They are discussed in detail in Chapter 19.)
Why are all these chips relevant in this book on the psyche?
They are mentioned here because the automatic responses they
create override psychic functions.

The above-mentioned chips can be the causes of uncontrolled
behaviors such as stuttering, restless movements (twitching
of the legs, wringing or restless movement of the hands),
uncontrolled blushing, sweating, acts of violence, freezing in
fear, compulsory avoidance, and compulsions in general. A
chip can also be the cause of a depression that recurs around a
certain date in the year. That date may be when a close friend
or partner died. This unnatural memorial is due to guilt that
was taken on at the time: for not being there for that person,
or for thinking that one may have contributed to their death.
Chips are often the cause of uncontrolled emotional outbreaks,
sleeplessness, and mental disturbances. They can be the reason
behind repeated failures in specific areas, such as relationships,
professions, finance, or health.

Chips in the psyche and elsewhere are a sort of "envelope"
formed by the body, psyche, brain, or mind to contain the traumatic or shocking memory, in an attempt to protect the rest of
the body, psyche, or brain from its negative effects.

Memory Chips

Memory chips are lodged in the *psyche*. Using the metaphor
of the carpet that is in the process of being woven in the psyche,
memory chips are like objects, stains, or blotches in a section
of the carpet that block the weaving, or disturb an area of its
design. They control our behavior and filter our experiences in
such a way that they confirm, time and again, the false conclusions, fears, doubts, or guilt contained in the chips.

Memory chips are activated by situations reminiscent of the
traumatic event stored in the specific chip. The chip causes us to

respond in the same way as when the traumatic event occurred
It is activated before we can consider a different response. The
chip thus manifests in unwanted behaviors and disorders such
as blocks to learning, blocks to accepting help, and the automatic rejection of gifts, opportunities, and friendly acts. To the
bystander this emotional quality seems totally puzzling and
unrelated to the present circumstance.

The majority of these chips are created before we reach the
age of thirty; some are created even *in utero*.

Memory chips are often combined with a microchip created by the same event, which is stored in the body. While its
re-creation is not as traumatic as the original event, an allergic
reaction is created that triggers the emotions connected with
the original event. The fear that one will never get rid of the
memory, or the expectation that the event may happen again
causes the situations and things stored in the chip to be re-cre-
ated. Memory chips can limit our possibilities to experience
things beyond what the phrases, fears, and expectations they
contain, project.

The general conclusions contained in memory chips preclude
future positive experiences that are in the category of that memory. Examples are conclusions and misunderstandings drawn
at the breakup of a relationship, such as: "All men are egotists."
"This can happen to me again." "I will never again allow myself
to trust someone that much, or get so deeply involved."

When memory chips contain ego-emotions such as guilt or
repressed anger, they can be the cause of illness.

Examples of memory chips:

(1) *A memory chip as the cause of an allergic reaction:* The
memory chip was formed in a woman at age twenty-three when
her husband repeatedly criticized and rejected the way she expressed herself. The chip included phrases such as "You need to
think before you speak," "You've got to get rid of your backwoods
background," an imp of annoyance, and a dragon of self-righteousness. Long after the husband was gone the chip caused her
to flare into anger when anyone seemed ready to object to her
way of speaking. This led to conflicts and mutual blaming when

people close to her expressed a view that was different from hers. Examining the issue with the Sage, she found that the hidden reason for the conflicts was that the minute someone disagreed with her, the imp of annoyance and the dragon of self-righteousness in the chip would create in her the projection that "they behave exactly like my long gone husband."

(2) *A memory chip that caused difficulties in learning from the Sage.*

Barbara was a participant in a seminar on learning from the Sage. She soon became aware of a fear she had of the Sage. When asked to identify that fear more closely, she found that it was the fear that the Sage would abandon her if she were not "good." Her investigation into the origin of this fear led her to a memory chip created in the fifth grade. The traumatic incident involved her being verbally ganged up on by classmates in a back room, with the acquiescence of the teacher. The chip also contained the following conclusions: "It's dangerous to show my feelings," "I can't show myself," "I must hide," and, "I'm a victim." Because learning from the Sage requires revealing to the Sage the embarrassing incidents in one's life, the conclusions stored in the chip made her afraid of the Sage.

After freeing herself from this memory chip Barbara actually enjoyed learning from the Sage, because it is all about freeing the self from fears and other oppressing ego-elements.

(Many traumatic memories that create obstructions in our learning from the Sage originate in schooling experiences.)

Microchips

Microchips are lodged in the *body*. The memory of the shocking or traumatic event is encapsulated so as to contain all aspects related to the event.

The majority of microchips are created before we reach the age of thirty. This is because we tend to process such events better after that age. Like memory chips, microchips can also be created *in utero*.

Microchips are triggered by the fearful expectations of the body cells that were previously affected: the fear that the original event might happen again; the fear that one may never get rid of the memory; or the fear caused by a negative medical prognosis. Microchips can limit our ability to have positive experiences beyond what the prognoses predict.

A microchip, if left undetected for a long time, can manifest as lumps, basal cells, cysts, arterial plaque, and illness. They can also be stored in the tissues of the sexual organs. Furthermore, they can manifest as tics, twitches, unexpected blushing, sweating, stuttering, and unexplained pains that occur repeatedly in certain parts of the body. An example is a person's fingers moving involuntarily while in conversation, or feet and legs moving uncontrollably. Microchips can also be responsible for food, skin, and other allergies, and also for fears of a close relationship.

Examples of microchips:

(1) *Nightly sweats.* We were approached by a woman whom we shall call Jane, to help her find the cause of her nightly sweats. These had been occurring every night for some time. She would go to sleep easily, but wake up later drenched in sweat. Being new to the *I Ching*, she still tended to look at such problems as having a mechanical cause, such as having to do with what she ate, or the failure of some body function. Despite this, she was determined to keep her mind open to what the *I Ching* had to say.

Consulting the *I Ching*, we received Hexagram 57, *The Penetrating*, Line 5, and only this particular sentence: "This line also refers to the necessity of putting an absolute end to the imps, dragons, and demons that compose the ego and which rampage through the psyche in demonic form."

With the use of the *rtcm* we found that the demonic elements were sent to her by an aunt with whom she was then communicating by email, after many years of no communication. In Jane's youth, the aunt had come to live with her family in order to go to a better high school than was available where she lived. Although the two had a good relationship, as Jane grew into womanhood, she became aware that the aunt saw this period of living with her family in a dark light. The aunt had been heard to say, "Jane had advantages I was denied," "Her family could have sent me to college, too, but didn't," and, "I had to do chores they got out of doing." The *I Ching* made us aware that these conclusions of the aunt were spells and poison arrows she had put on Jane. They had simmered over the years into the principle myth of the aunt's life: that she was a disadvantaged person; in turn, these phrases had transmuted in her psyche into these imps, demons, and dragons: "God favored her and not me"; "She is part of the reason for my having to go into a big city alone at eighteen, to get a job," "Jane, the privileged"; "She was treated royally while I was treated like an alien"; "I can never forgive them." These words, and the guilt they had instilled in Jane, had formed a microchip in Jane's body, more specifically, in her sweat glands. During the period of non-communication, they remained dormant and were reactivated when Jane and the aunt began to correspond. At this point, the microchip manifested in the nightly sweats. As soon as Jane deprogrammed this microchip and its components, and pulled back from sympathetically seeing her aunt as disadvantaged since her youth, the nightly sweats completely ceased.

Jane was also shown by the Sage that the aunt's bad memories had formed a memory chip in the aunt's psyche that Jane could deprogram. It did not contain all the same components, but only the following: "Jane had advantages I was denied," "God favored her and not me"; "She is part of the reason for my having to go into a big city alone at eighteen, to get a job," "I can never forgive them."

(2) *A microchip ensuring the failure of a love relationship:* Jackie described her problem in a consultation as follows: She had gotten together with a former boyfriend. After they became intimate again, she found that he was having an affair with another woman. That ended their relationship once again. Two months later, feeling that the relationship had ended badly, she called him, asking to talk. He agreed and she felt that was also what he wanted to do. They became intimate again.

As she put it, "I wanted to reconnect and feel good with him, the way it was in the beginning of our relationship. Perhaps that's what he wanted too, yet we seemed to have perpetual inconsideration and misunderstanding to the point of leaving each other again, with quite a bit of ill feeling. I feel sad about this and guilty, and at the same time defenseless, and I would like to fix it. I think about it all the time to the point of being inhibited in what I do. I feel trapped by my own thinking to the point of not being able to connect with what is good in me and what I want to do with my time and my life. I can't move forward. Perhaps the biggest problem is connecting with my true self."

Consulting the Sage, we found a microchip in both people that was formed in the beginning of their relationship. Although their experience at the time had been a happy one, a fear had entered both that "it may not last." A second ego-element was formed by this fear: an *attachment* to the good memory of the experience. The fear that their happiness may not last caused the boyfriend to adopt yet another ego idea: "you need a backup in case this one does not work." When they got together again without having their mutual microchips processed, the doubt and fear these chips contained re-entered their relationship, preventing them from feeling the original good feelings they had for each other. On this account, each felt only further deceived, with the result that the feelings of deceit, guilt, and blame they put on each other were added to their original microchips. Jackie was able to deprogram the microchips for both of them, which gave their relationship a new chance.

Searching for the deeper root of what had happened, we un-covered the mistaken belief held by the boyfriend, "Happiness is illusory at best." Such a belief is behind many reservations of attitude (or suspicions) that people bring to their relationships; they insure the failure of the relationship through creating a progressive alienation.

(3) *A microchip and memory chip preventing a person from receiving chi-energy from Nature*

Daniel suffered from an extreme lack of stamina and emo-tional energy. This indicated a disturbance in his ability to receive chi-energy from Nature. The cause was found in a microchip and memory chip that were formed *in utero*. Both chips contained an image his mother had taken on by seeing herself as the one who provides the embryo with everything it needs. By adopting this image, his mother had put herself in the place of Nature, thereby cutting off Daniel's own relationship with Nature.

Generally speaking, we can easily imagine that a person with this disturbance might seek a partner who replaces his mother as the one who provides him with the energy he would normally get from Nature. Daniel had no partner and so had lost his energy.

Ego Chips

An ego chip is a chip stored in the *mind*. It is connected with the idea of *family* and clan-thinking. Ego chips can be created *in utero* and up to about the age of eight. An ego chip can be the cause of an illness. When this is the case, the illness is an attempt of the body to free the person from the ego chip. This purpose is thwarted if the illness becomes complicated by other ego interferences that cause it to become chronic.

Examples of ego chips:

(1) *Getting the family's approval.* Jennifer was observed as "always buying the wrong gifts." The following thought pattern was contained in an ego chip: "I need to get their approval. I need to do something they think of as important. It has to look big. It has to be impressive. For the artists it has to be odd."

(2) *A mother's boasting:* A woman in counseling said that she felt that her mother had projected all her bad qualities upon her; this left her with confused feelings about herself. The Sage pointed to an ego chip that was formed *in utero*. The chip contained the image of the woman's mother during pregnancy, pointing at her belly and boasting, "Look how God has blessed me!"

The Sage clarified that through boasting, the mother had diminished her daughter (a gift from the Cosmos), by seeing herself as special. Thus, she took away the child's sense of self-worth, and the child's sovereignty over herself. This replaced the natural bond between mother and child with a negative bond that caused the daughter to doubt herself. The mother, in effect, had taken possession of her. One consequence of this was that on a subconscious level the daughter identified with her mother's emotions, making the daughter feel that her mother had projected on her all the things she disliked about herself. Deprogramming the ego chip freed the woman from her emotional confusion and restored her sovereignty.

(3) *A father's boasting:* An ego chip was created in Conrad by his father's boasting of having fathered a child. Because a child is a Cosmic gift, and the father's boasting was an appropriation of that gift, it had the following consequences on the child: it created self-doubt in Conrad about his sovereignty, his wholeness was split, and it created doubt in him about his Cosmic origin. It also created a demon and dragon of resentment toward his father. The resentment caused him to feel guilty toward his father, which, in turn, contributed to his sleeplessness; he compensated for the resentment by trying to please his father.

Conrad's comment to the discovery of the ego chip was: "The insight that I had doubts about my Cosmic origin answered many questions for me. I was very touched to learn about this. When I deprogrammed the ego chip in meditation, I saw a suitcase that was now being opened for the first time. I was able to "unpack," I have arrived. The suitcase was like Noah's arc: everything that will bring new life to my true self was coming out of it. Some days ago, in a meditation, I even saw a white dove with an olive twig in its beak fly by!"

(4) *The family sticks together:* The contents of this ego chip were as follows: "We are a family." "A family needs to stick together." "You are a representative of your family." "You are responsible for what happens to your family." This chip had caused a fate for a woman in the form of repeated health problems. They began with her feeling drained of energy; this brought fears of getting ill, the consequence of which was to repeatedly get ill. Moreover, through seeing herself as responsible for the family (which included herself), she deprived the family of Cosmic Protection.

(5) *Monumentalized relatives:* This type of ego chip includes any monumentalized relatives with whom the person identifies in order to feel proud. "My grandfather/great grandfather/original settler in America, was so and so, and did such and such thing that made him well known and much honored." The

pride associated with such ego chips leads to the fate that the person is laughed at behind his back, or suffers another kind of humiliation.

The need to monumentalize relatives comes from the mind's attempt to create an escape from feelings of inferiority. Similar identifications can be with the clan, or tribe. The source of this inferiority comes from parents who have made their children feel small and insignificant, in comparison to their mythologized relatives, or clan.

The tendency to mythologize relatives can also go in the other direction, when a person who has "come up from the wrong side of the tracks" pridefully points to his achievements and success. If he has a high scholarly degree, for example, it becomes a weapon to put down others whom he views as having been born on the "right side of the tracks." The chip can thus be seen to contain old resentments toward those who were privileged, and towards himself for his "inferior birth." It also contains the self-image of the "one who made it."

(6) *One family member extending the boundaries of his personality to include all members of his family, or the extended clan*: the person thanks others for gifts they give to another member of his family, as if the gift was given to him; or, the person feels embarrassed for the bad behavior of another member of his family and apologizes to others for it.

In another version of extended boundaries, a woman made a pact with herself that if she had children, she would never allow to happen to them what happened to her when she was a child. The woman vigorously defended and covered up all her children's ego-behaviors in order to present to others the image of a perfect family.

(7) *Health problems that are supposedly inherited:* This ego chip was discovered to contain the phrase, "Certain things are passed on in the family." It led to physical symptoms being shared by other members of that person's family.

(8) *False humility:* This ego chip was discovered to contain the statement. "No one deserves luxurious things." The chip also contained guilt for wanting and having such things, but also for

having things that could barely be thought of as luxurious.

Birth Chips

A birth chip is a chip stored in the *brain and body* created during birth. Like an ego chip, it is always connected with something that has to do with *family*.

Example: Feeling oneself to be a stranger in life

The following chip was discovered while we were consulting the *I Ching* to find the cause of Beverly's feeling that she was "a stranger in life." The chip was due to her mother's thinking, during her birth, that the baby might be born dead. Added was her further thought that should the baby die, it would be for the best.

Behind these thoughts was the fact that she already had two children and dreaded having a big family. Her dread came from her own mother who had been abandoned, along with her eight children, by her father during the Great Depression. Being the second oldest in the family, Beverly's mother felt deprived of her schooling and her future. During the investigation, Beverly had a pain in her left chest that made us ask if we needed to look for something related to her heart. This was confirmed. It turned out that her mother's thought had given Beverly the feeling of her heart breaking, as she was about to be born. Her mother's thoughts also caused Beverly to have a fear of living, and for her to conclude, "I am a stranger in life." Fortunately the investigation also showed that her uncle, the first to treat her with love, came along at age four, healing much of this damage. Deprogramming the birth chip removed her fear of living and the feeling of being a stranger in life.

The Sage made us aware that the circumstances of a person's birth can also influence whether a person *feels safely grounded* on the Earth. This has to do with the role the Helper of the Earth plays during a person's birth. Under normal circumstances, this Helper welcomes the child on the Earth and gives him the feeling that this is a safe place and that he is loved by the Earth and by Nature. Under abnormal conditions, such as the one described above, this Helper is unable to do so. As a consequence the person feels ungrounded and "not at home" on the Earth. The Sage made it clear that birth chips are to be considered as the *most basic* "ringleaders of disorder" in regard to a person's feeling secure in life. False assumptions about the Cosmos, Nature, and about human nature add to this insecurity. Birth chips shape not only the person's feeling toward the Earth, but also the relationship between his mind and body. When his connection with the Earth is unimpeded, the slanders put on human nature by the collective ego have little ability to harm; however, when his connection with the Earth is disturbed, these slanders are able to have disastrous effects on the person's physical health.

Fortunately, the Cosmos always comes to help a person who, as in the birth experience, is stuck in a difficult situation. The help that Beverly received from her uncle's affection is an example.

When a person is afflicted by a birth chip, he needs to make connection with the Helper of the Earth, because this is the Helper that helps him move on with his life. When activated, it works together with the Helper of Transformation.

Conception Chips

These traumatic memories are stored in the *brain*. While other kinds of chips may cause a person to "blow up," a conception chip causes the person to throw a wall up around himself. These chips can cause malfunctions in the glands of the brain, and other brain malfunctions. They can affect the child's growth and maturation. They can also cause hyperactivity. A general characteristic of conception chips is that they derail the person from fulfilling his uniqueness, through fixing his primary reactions to the people around him. Instead of openly embracing the positive possibilities that come from them, he hides behind a wall of fear, self-doubt, shame, or guilt, or a combination of these ego-emotions.[1] The person may compensate for these negative emotions by taking on a self-righteous and superior

---

1 This wall is referred to in Hexagram 13, *Associating with People,* Line 4, "He climbs up on his wall; he cannot attack." The interpretation of the oracle saying makes us aware that the wall can become a place from where the person argues self-righteously rather than looking behind the wall for the cause of his problem. Therefore, he cannot "attack" it in the appropriate way to resolve it.

attitude, as in, "I know what is right and what is wrong." The sad consequence is that he does not seek the help of the Sage, and therefore cannot gain a correct approach to his problems.

Examples of conception chips:

(1) Bernard, a man in his 40's, characterized himself as someone who "thought a lot about what other people might think about him." In a consultation we uncovered the following components of a conception chip. It contained his mother's fears and guilt, which were expressed in the phrase: "I hope it (the pregnancy) won't show." Also stored in the chip were Bernard's guilt for being the cause of his mother's shame, and his decision: "I won't betray my mother." "I want to bring her honor."

(2) For Anna, the desire to be perfect was the constant source of self-blame. When exploring the cause of this desire, we found a conception chip that contained the emotional conditions of her parents and her older sister (who at the time was age four). Her father's feeling was of having lost the family home; her mother's feeling was of being abandoned; her sister's feeling was of emotional coldness coming from the people around them, because the family, being from a foreign country, was "unwanted." Anna took on all these negative feelings, and, in addition, developed a "grabber of fantasies" about what being unwanted means. The consequences of this chip for Anna were a fear of rejection, self-doubt about her intrinsic worth, and, to compensate for these, the desire to be perfect.

Crystallized Emotions

Unprocessed traumas can also leave behind crystallized emotions such as repressed anger, guilt, self-blame, self-hatred, and fears. As such, they are responsible for allergic reactions, which can be either physical or psychological; they are also responsible for pains located in the area of the body that was involved in the traumatic event. Crystallized ego-emotions can also be stored in the psyche, and can accompany a memory chip.

Examples:

(1) A boy had made a drawing of an atomic bomb exploding. The quality of the drawing was superb, but his parents were con-

cerned because of the subject he had chosen. Looking into the matter, we found that it was pointing to crystallized anger ready to explode. The cause of the anger was a poison arrow of envy a classmate had put on him to the effect, "I wish I could draw like him. But he is a failure in other subjects." The boy's parents deprogrammed the poison arrow and the crystallized anger on his behalf. Beforehand, the boy was withdrawn and uncommunicative; afterward, he was more friendly and outgoing.

(2) A woman who had gone to her annual physical check-up had a frightening dream that prompted her to come for a consultation. We found that the dream was making her aware of a memory chip that contained spells and poison arrows from the doctor who had said, "Things look serious. The result of the blood test can indicate several things: it can either be a bacterial infection, or something more serious." The memory chip was accompanied by a crystallized "fear of something serious." The dream was making her aware of the danger posed by these stored words and the fear they created. In fact, we learned that they can bring about the illness that is feared. Illnesses that are called "fatal" can be the result of an undetected crystallized fear.

(3) Nightmares can be caused by a memory chip that is accompanied by crystallized emotions such as guilt, fears, or anger. The repetition of shocks experienced in recurring nightmares have the purpose to free the dreamer of both the memory chip and the crystallized emotion.

Crystallized Memories

Crystallized memories are not the same as chips, because they are not contained in an "envelope." What characterizes them is that they always contain crystallized guilt for having failed. Crystallized memories can be recognized by the fact that they give rise to allergic reactions that are either physical or psychological. They can be stored in various parts of the body or psyche.

An example was a man's inability to do the inner work necessary to free his true self, although he clearly desired to do so. Our exploration showed that the cause of his impediment was a crystallized memory of a failed attempt, several years before, to do the inner work needed to free his true self. The crystallized memory included guilt for having failed, and the conclusion drawn from the experience, "I cannot do inner work." This conclusion protected the crystallized memory, keeping it untouched until he deprogrammed the phrase, "I cannot do inner work." Then he was able to deprogram the whole memory.

19. Stop Chips

As indicated by its name, this kind of chip stops a person from making further progress on the path of his Cosmic destiny. The chip is created very early in life by a remark, event, or treatment by a caretaker that prevents the child, and later, the adult, from growing in one area or another. The event can be:

- an attempt of a caretaker to forcefully subjugate a child
- an intense effort on the part of the caretaker to get into the child's psyche, as by insisting, "You have to tell me everything," or by insisting that the child have the "right" reaction to whatever is happening, thus neither leaving him any personal space, nor room for reflection
- A denial on the part of the adult that the child's inner truth is valid
- religious commandments
- the threat that "God sees everything," implying, "God sees the evil in you."

The above descriptions make clear that stop chips cause the child to lose his sense of privacy and sovereignty. By sovereignty we mean the possession of our personal space, our respect for our inner truth, and the security of our boundaries, all of which is maintained by our fundamental ability to say No.

Each of the stop chips we investigated and describe below had a negative influence on a child's growth in a specific area. The stop chips have the effect of putting a "stop sign" to an area of consciousness, and to the child's true feelings that says, "Don't go there!" The stop sign "walls off" that area and the feelings connected with it so that the collective ego has full access to, and control over it. As the examples show, there can also be physical effects. One is reminded of the great walls built by empires over centuries, the great walls of China and Rome, the Berlin Wall, and all the building of walls that is still going on today.

The fears stored in the stop chip can result in a hunched-over posture, difficulties in breathing, or self-deprecating or self-punishing behavior. In all cases, stop chips create an impediment to saying the inner No, be it to a parent or to another person of authority, or to ideas or beliefs that are "not to be questioned."

The fears stored in the stop chips can break through to the conscious mind when triggered by situations that remind the child, and later the adult, of the initial trauma. These fears can manifest as a sudden stuttering, blushing, a sudden increase in blood pressure, or a reaction of panic.

Fortunately, we have experienced how people affected by stop chips can be freed from them and their harmful effects by deprogramming them with Cosmic help. The Sage has made us aware that help constantly comes to the child throughout his growth, and indeed, throughout his life, despite these stop chips. While the Sage is not always able to protect the mind, which has been walled off by the chip, the Sage nevertheless acts on behalf of our inner truth, protecting and defending it when we are sincere. This is because sincerity removes obstacles between us and the Sage. When we are sincere, the Sage is busy taking down the wall, and helping the person to connect with his commonsense. For example, through revealing dreams, the Sage may show him that the thing he feared most, and which had stopped his development, is "not so bad, after all." In such small ways the Sage blows our fears apart and communicates our inner truth to our conscious mind outside the awareness of the ego.

To be sure, the mind's contact with our inner truth makes the ego insecure. In response to the newly gained awareness of the mind, the ego attempts to defend its hold on the personality by coming up with "yes-but" rationales to discredit the inner truth. When we are trying to free ourselves from stop chips, we need to be aware of the ego's resistance.

Example 1: The inability to make decisions about my life

In the first chapter, I, Hanna, described the shock I experienced when a friend asked me what I enjoyed doing. My friend thought that his question would help me find out what I would like to do with my future life, but instead, I saw only a deep dark abyss. Everything I had built my life on had collapsed. It was only recently, thirty-eight years later, that the Sage made me aware of

Example 1. The Inability to Make Decisions

two stop chips that were the deeper cause of my conundrum. Here is what I found:

I was five years old when my mother said to me, with a sideglance to my father, "Mothers have a much better ability to tune into the feelings of a child than fathers do." As a result, a stop chip was formed in me, causing me to no longer be in charge of my feelings. Believing my mother's words, I concluded that she knew my feelings better than I did, and thereafter I turned to her when I wanted to know what I felt. Shortly after this incident, an aunt whom I loved dearly and who lived in the same house, learned about something I had done that did not show me in a good light. (I do not recall what it was I did.) Wanting to protect me, she said, "Be sure not to tell your mother about it." This left me with feelings of guilt as the only feelings *I* owned. The Sage showed me that what my aunt said had combined with my feelings of guilt to create the second stop chip. With the Sage's help, I found that the conflict between the two stop chips had caused me to feel that I no longer knew who I was. To be sure, some other cause may have been behind my accepting my mother's view without question, but this knowledge was not needed to free me of these particular stop chips. I add this here to show that the Sage knows how to free us from a problem without requiring an exhaustive study of the problem.

The inability to sense who I was due to being cut off from my feelings, became the cause of a lingering depression. I still remember that from about the age of five on, I often did not know what to do with myself when I had the chance to play. I would then go to my mother and ask her, "Mutti, what should I play?" and then follow her suggestion. Another decisive moment came when I was about to finish school at age sixteen, and had to decide what to do afterward. I had no idea. Once again, the answer came from my mother. I was glad about her guidance and followed it like a dutiful daughter. The moment of truth came when at age thirty-five, everything collapsed, including the role of the dutiful daughter, as described in Chapter 1. At this moment, the *I Ching* came into my life to lead me back to my own feelings. It has been an ongoing process ever since. Many of the discoveries I made on my way are described in this book. They were made possible through the help of the Sage in that it revealed to me my inner truth in many other ways that went around the wall that separated my mind from my true feelings. Among these other ways were my dreams to which I paid much attention ever since the collapse. The messages I received from the *I Ching* were another way of connecting me directly with my inner truth. "Helpful coincidences" in the form of meaningful encounters with people, and learning opportunities were other means. Finally, help also came in the form of insight-flashes. All this is to say that the Sage was capable of teaching my mind the inner truth of things even though the stop chips were still in place. In addition to the above stop chips I have since found a number of other stop chips. At this writing, I am experiencing my feelings much more, and can say that I have been completely lifted out of the depression.

Example 2: A difficulty with breathing and a posture deformation

Jane, a woman in her fifties who had been working with the *I Ching* and our method of deprogramming, had long suffered from general difficulties in breathing, and wished to free herself of this problem. By difficulties, we mean her breathing was mostly superficial. At times, she would notice a deep sigh that indicated that something was holding her back from breathing normally. She found it was due to a stop chip, that, much to her surprise, was also the cause of an additional problem, her hunched-over posture.

The Sage led her back to an incident that occurred when Jane was five years old. At the time, she happened to be in the care of her father, and did not want to undress in front of him because, shortly before, she had been sexually molested by her uncle, who lived in the same house. Her father, unaware of what had happened, said to her, "It's okay to take your clothes off, Daddy won't harm you." The stop chip contained the conclusion she drew from her father's statement, that it would be better not to grow up because "as long as I'm little, Daddy will protect me." The chip also contained a fantasy that should she grow up, the danger to her would grow worse because Daddy would not be there to protect her. The fear of growing up was the cause of her hunched-over posture, and the fear of life itself as holding dangers to her personal sovereignty, were partly responsible for Jane's lifelong breathing difficulty. Another cause was a microchip that was formed at the same time. It contained Jane's conclusion, "If I don't breathe too deeply, I will stop growing." Repeated commands by Jane's parents to "sit up straight!" as she matured, only aggravated her condition, causing her to reply, "that's the way I am." After deprogramming the stop chip, the microchip, and the spell she had put on herself by saying "that's the way I am," her body was able to correct the deformation within a few weeks, without Jane's having to give it further thought. A few days after the deprogramming, Jane felt relieved of most of her breathing difficulty. Within a few months it disappeared altogether.

As this example makes clear, posture deformations in children are correctable by learning the inner truth behind them with the help of the Sage.

Example 3: Anticipated Obeisance

Greta, a woman who had been working with our methods for a number of years, told us of her finding a stop chip. She had noticed in herself a lifelong struggle with the fact that she persistently put others' needs ahead of her own, and wished to understand the cause.

The Sage guided her to a time when she was eight years old, and to her remembering a trauma that was still vividly in her memory. Her mother, an extremely hardworking woman, "took her migraine" every Sunday morning as permission to stay in bed. It had become the custom for Greta to bring her mother's breakfast into her bedroom. That Sunday morning, Greta had gotten distracted by her father and went to see her mother later than usual. Although she apologized, her mother was furious: "It is unforgivable to forget yourself like that!" Even fifty years later, Greta still vividly remembered how she had left the room and thrown herself on a sofa and cried inconsolably. Her crying contained all the components of the stop chip that was developed from this incident; her mother's words and Greta's conclusion, "there is an abyss of evil in me that can ruin me. It can come out without my being aware of it." Trust in the goodness of her nature was replaced with distrust and suspicion, and the suspicion that other people, too, might find things in her that were unforgivable.

All of this created an avoidance mechanism that answered her inner need to make sure that never again would she forget her duty to put others' needs above her own, which would be unforgivable. This mechanism was built on the rationale, "If I do what people expect of me, I can't make a mistake."

Another consequence of this experience was Greta's developing an ego-complex called The *Complex of Anticipated Obeisance*. Not only did this cause her to perform what people expected, she tried to provide what she *thought* people might expect. This complex is based on the projection and poison arrow: "You must sense what the other needs, and provide it." The Sage made Greta aware that this complex had become part of the above-mentioned stop chip, and that the stop chip had stopped Greta from validating her own needs.

Deprogramming this stop chip freed her from the compulsion to rush to help others without asking herself whether it was appropriate to do so; it also freed her from the guilt that she would have experienced had she not gone to help them, regardless of the circumstances.

The Inability to Say an Inner No

The ability to say an *inner* No is our natural means of protection from encroachments by the ego in ourselves and in others.

We emphasize the importance of the word "inner," because saying something inwardly is outside the hearing of the ego, and therefore does not engage it. Saying an inner No is an inner acknowledgement that something is disharmonious and that we are not willing to go along with it. *It is our primary way of keeping our inner border intact, and our primary protection from encroachment.* Saying the inner No also protects us from the ego's developing a stronghold within our personality. Failing to say the inner No to something disharmonious actually gives it validity, not only in our psyche, but it also validates disharmony in the external world. It is by such a simple omission that we as individuals empower the collective ego in the external world. Saying the inner No is everyone's Cosmic responsibility.

It is obvious that the collective ego wants yes-sayers who conform to its values. Less obvious is the fact that it also wants people who accommodate disharmony. People who outright deny the validity of the collective ego's values are not welcome. Our parents and their parents and grandparents have all been brought up with punishments for saying No, and rewards for saying Yes. Since parents do not want their children to get into conflict with society, most of them pass these values onto their children. When a child is forbidden to say No to his parents, teachers, and other figures of authority, he loses his ability to say No; he even loses his ability to say an *inner* No to them, and to the untrue ideas and beliefs he is taught not to question. All traumatic events that mark the moment when we lose the ability to say No, are stored in a *stop chip*. That event may be connected with an outright threat ("if you say No one more time, ... such and such will happen!"), or an authoritarian statement ("children must do what their parents say"), or the promise of recognition ("a good child does not say No"), or through subtle forms such as those shown in the above examples.

A stop chip can also be created when a child asks, "Why?" before accepting a statement as true (when he has not felt its validity), and the parent responds: "because I said so!"

It needs to be noted here that the person who has been deprogramming individual components of a stop chip, without knowing about stop chips, may in the process have actually deprogrammed the stop chip. Our focus on them here is to make the reader aware of how stop chips function to stop our growth, and how, on knowing about them, we may suspect that they are the cause of a difficulty we are seeking to understand.

How to Free Ourselves from an Impediment to Saying the Inner No

A person can have a partial or total impediment to saying the inner No. The first thing to find out by using the *rtcm* is whether the impediment is partial or total.[1] Partial can mean that the impediment only exists in relation to particular situations or people. What we then need to look for is a stop chip that contains the memory of the traumatic event that created the impediment. To identify the stop chip, we do not have to relive the traumatic experience; instead, we now look at it with our adult mind.

With the help of the *rtcm*, we find out (a) when it was created, (b) who was the caretaker or authority figure, (c) which words were used, and (d) possible conclusions we drew from the experience.

When we have assembled the contents of the stop chip, we ask the Sage and the Helpers (we do not need, in this case, to know their names) to free us from it. We check the following day whether we need to repeat our request, and do so until the answer is No, no, or No, no, no.

A Final Look at the Stop Chip

The examples of stop chips in this chapter show how they interfere with the individual's mental and emotional development. We can also see how the idea of evil being part of our nature is passed down from one generation to the next.

This idea is the biggest hindrance to our growing up. The growing up of the true self is only possible through getting to know our true nature. When we have seen through the falseness of the words that make up the ego-mindset and freed ourselves from them, we know from deep within that we can trust our feeling animal nature, and that we can trust life and the Cosmos. While we are in this freeing process, we are already fulfilling our Cosmic destiny.

We are not able to live in peace as long as we harbor the idea that there is evil in our nature. This idea creates a permanent

---

1 See the description of this method in Appendix 1.

restlessness for the following reasons: (1) one part of our nature is pitted against another part; (2) our mind thinks it needs to be on guard against that evil in us; (3) we are driven by the fear of becoming guilty for listening or giving way to the evil in us; (4) we suffer anxiety, because it was never made clear to us precisely, when we were young, what the evil is that we need to be on guard against. All these factors cause us to think that "we must do something" to avoid the presumed evil in our nature. This pressure *to do* something often puts us in a position of taking actions that are not appropriate to the situation.

As mentioned above, the Cosmos never leaves us helpless. The Sage comes to help constantly throughout our lives. When we make the sincere effort to free ourselves from the ego, and start on the path to find our inner truth, the Helper of Sincerity accompanies us on the journey to protect us from any dangers until our true self is safely established as the leader of our personality.

As long as a person has not decided to free his true self, the danger of being overwhelmed by fears coming from his subconscious is great, particularly when the things that have given him a sense of security collapse around him. The danger can be caused by a stop chip that contains a false sense of protection given by a parent that is later transferred to the institutions of society. These institutions can be an employer, an insurance company, a bank, or the government. This false sense of protection contained in the stop chips becomes activated by the death of a parent, the break-up of a close relationship or marriage, the loss of a job, or an economic crisis. The caretaker's statement, stored in the stop chip, that was meant to protect the child from anything in him that would create insecurity, now creates the very opening that allows his fears to come out. Now, the person is buffeted between two fears: one caused by the collapse of what had given him an outer sense of security, the other coming from the original fears about his true nature that are still stored in his subconscious. In this critical situation, the Sage comes to help with Cosmic nourishment that is given to strengthen the person's heart. The *I Ching* refers to this help in the words: "A jug of wine, a bowl of rice with it; earthen vessels simply handed in through the window. There is certainly no blame in this."[2] This was the circumstance for both of us when the *I Ching* was brought into our lives, as described in Chapter 1. When, however, we close our heart to the Cosmos by blaming it for our misfortune, we are unable to receive the nourishment offered.

---

2 See Hexagram 29, *The Abyss/Danger*, Line 4.

20. Conditioning vs. Processing

Conditioning

Conditioning is the process used by the collective ego to make the individual, from early childhood on, conform to the values and customs of the given culture and its hierarchical structure. The process is carried out by creating a picture of the way he is to see the world, and his place in it. Then the picture is placed in a frame that is thereafter fixed, so that he is prevented from seeing anything beyond the borders of that frame. The frame consists of instructions on how he is to measure and evaluate all his experiences. By the time he reaches adulthood, he is so dependent on making judgments on the basis of *what he sees*, that he is almost unable to think outside that frame. His perception has been reduced to that one sense so that he is prevented from obtaining a true sense of reality. He thus develops an unreflecting attitude about his experiences, believing what he has been conditioned to think about them.

The frame consists of a set of references that categorize his experiences: what he is to regard as happy, pleasant, acceptable and successful, or unhappy, tragic, terrible, frightening, and unsuccessful. His fixed frame of reference defines what is considered appropriate to his social class: his opportunities, liberties, and constraints; they also define what is appropriate for him in terms of his gender and race.

All these frames of reference determine how he responds to others' experiences. The effect is to deprive his mind of its innocence in evaluating situations, and to divorce him from his inner truth.

To understand the effects of conditioning on the psyche, it is necessary to recognize how conditioning takes place. Primarily, it is imposed on the child by rewards for conforming, and punishments for not conforming. Both means can be employed subtly, as by the warning of a raised eyebrow, or by withdrawal of rewards. They can also be grossly administered to the extent that some of the punishments constitute physical and emotional abuse. In all these cases, the result is psychological damage.

In sum, the damage done is to our nature, which becomes divided against itself because our mind becomes pitted against our true feelings. This division leads to a life of conflict in all our relationships.

The Role of Chips in the Conditioning Process

As shown in the two previous chapters, chips replace our natural responses to everyday events with pre-formed responses that are all based on negative conditioning experiences. In this sense, they create in us mechanical responses that take away our ability to know our inner truth, and thus also our humanity. We become divorced from our true feelings, and controlled by mechanical impulses.

Processing

Processing has the purpose of undoing the chips that have been created through traumatic events. It is done through engaging the processing function of the psyche and the help of the Sage.

With the Sage's help we are able to uncover the harmful components that are contained in the chips, without reliving the traumatic experience itself. These components consist of things that were said, thought, and done (without dwelling on their graphic aspects), the images and ego-emotions that accompanied them, and the conclusions the victim drew from the experiences. (The Sage has made us aware that when we are helping another person process such an event, it is vital to avoid encouraging the other to fall back into the original emotions and physical sensations, since this would prevent the separation necessary for the mind to process the traumatic experience.)

In processing traumas, the Sage connects our mind with our inner truth and shows us how the trauma has affected us. It engages our metaphorical sense of proportion so that the insights gained prevent an excessive emotional response to the event.

The processing function puts the components of the event in the Cosmic perspective. The clarity we gain from this already carries us three-quarters of the way toward becoming free of the chips; however, for the chips to be removed permanently, we need to deprogram them with Cosmic help.

Discernment

Once the psyche has been freed of the components of a chip, the mind is able to exercise its ability to *discern*.

Discernment is a mental activity that automatically takes us out of those conditioned attitudes that frame our experiences and prevent us from realizing that each experience is unique. Discernment puts experiences into words that express our true feelings towards them. Unlike judgment, which stuffs every aspect of an experience into a box that contains conditioned reactions, discernment sees the wider picture, which includes its inner truth. To give an example, a child who is helped to understand that a playmate who has hit him is reacting to a violence that was done to him formerly, is able to come to a moderate and just understanding of the situation.[1] Through discernment, cause and effect are seen in their true relationship. Judgment, on the other hand, looks only at the outer appearances: the "bad" child has attacked "because his nature is faulty."

The Role of the Parents in Processing

Processing shocking events for children is one of the parents' most important functions. We give the following traumatic experience as an example, which was not processed by the mother at the time when it happened:

The event involved a sexual abuse that had occurred to her seven-year-old daughter. It took place in a small town where everyone knew everyone else. The girl was filled with anger, felt humiliated, and put down. She also felt guilt for what happened, and shame because the abusers taunted her with it as a secret they held afterwards. She also felt betrayed by her girl cousin she

1 See Hexagram 30, *Attaining Clarity*, Line 2 for the difference between what the *I Ching* describes as the "white light of judgment" and the "yellow light of understanding."

was visiting, who suggested that her older brother wanted to see her "at the barn." It felt strange to her at the time that her cousin did not go with her, and that the mother, normally there, was absent. What followed was an entrapment by the older brother, aged sixteen, and several of his friends from the community.

How could the girl's mother have correctly processed this event? The first thing was to affirm the girl's true feelings and sense of injustice and betrayal. This, the mother did. Secondly, she needed to make it clear to the girl that under no condition was there cause for her to feel either guilt or shame. The mother did not recognize the importance of helping to release her from these ego-emotions. Third, she needed to state clearly that nothing the boys did to her could diminish her true worth. Fourth, she needed to state that what they did was a clear offense, not only against her, but against the Cosmos. Fifth, that its occurrence did not mean it would happen again. Finally, she needed to reassure the girl that the Cosmos always brings justice to the situation by hidden means. For this to happen, however, the girl needed to turn the matter entirely over to the Cosmos and let go of it. In this regard, the mother also needed to make it clear that it was not up to her as the mother, to take outer action on the girl's behalf, because no human being can satisfactorily bring the true justice needed. Only the Cosmos knows how to do that.

The mother, in this case, did not bring the matter out into the open, because she wanted to avoid having the girl be the center of a scandal, whereby she would ever after be viewed as sexually tainted in that small town. She did not even tell her husband about the event because it might have set off a permanent feud between him and the boy's parents who were his first cousins.

What was never processed were the girl's feelings of guilt, shame, her dignity being violated, anger, and betrayal. All of these were stored in her psyche as a memory chip and in the body as a microchip. Also never processed was the question that had haunted her all her life, "Why did the boys do it?" What we found with the help of the Sage was that the cause was envy on the part of the cousin's family. They, as a prominent family, had lost a lot of money during the depression, whereas her family had not. The son had taken it upon himself to express that envy on the part of the family. This fact also explained why her girl cousin accepted being an accomplice to her older brother.

Processing was also needed for the mother, herself, for her feelings of helplessness, anger, fear of shame, and guilt for not coming to an active defense of her daughter. The event left a memory chip in her psyche as well.

From the Cosmic perspective, processing was also needed for the boys. They carried the memory and microchips containing their betrayal of themselves. We learned from the Sage that this betrayal led to an inner death wish and a need for punishment. This played out in the boy cousin's being killed shortly afterward, in World War II. The others, mysteriously, were also taken out of the girl's life. Had the girl's mother fully processed the event, which would have included processing for the boys, they would have felt remorse, which would have corrected the matter, from the Cosmic perspective. Such a processing, we learned, would have freed those involved from committing further acts of self-betrayal.[2]

As the above shows, the thorough processing of an event has a correcting function for all parties involved. Everyone, in this manner, learns from the event, without any scars remaining. As similar cases of processing have taught us, unprocessed self-betrayal preceded by having been the victim of an act of violence, is one of the roots of criminal behavior and acts of violence by the former victim.

The first step in processing is to gain the Cosmic perspective of the situation. This perspective includes the underlying motive for the deed. In the above example, it was the envy of the cousin's family. The girl who was abused falsely took on guilt and shame; she also falsely concluded that her true worth had been damaged. This instilled the fear in her that something similar might happen again, and the conclusion that she was unsafe.

---

2 The Sage later confirmed that the boy cousin had himself suffered sexual abuse at an earlier time, and that this unprocessed abuse led to his choosing sexual abuse as a means of expressing his family's envy.

She also falsely concluded that the matter was only between the boys and herself. The Cosmos, and Cosmic Justice, were left out of the picture. All the following elements needed to be extracted from the event and deprogrammed:

- the cousin's envy, expressed in the statements identified by the Sage, "I'll show her her place," and "I'll take her down to size."
- the girl's feelings of guilt and shame
- the image of being laughed at while being violated and humiliated
- the fear, "it might happen again."
- the conclusion, "I am unsafe in this town."
- the feeling of being helpless, leading to the unspoken conclusion that "nobody comes to help"
- the anger she still possessed about the situation at age seventy-five

In addition to deprogramming these contents of the micro and memory chips, the processing included the woman's actively acknowledging her earlier inner feeling that the Cosmos had taken the boys out of her view.

Processing does not deny that something traumatic occurred. Rather, it corrects the view we have held of what happened, and above all, it transforms the emotional charge into positive energy that is now available for healing the wounds caused. As this example shows, processing is the first step in removing chips of all kinds from wherever they are stored. The second step is deprogramming them. (See Appendix 3.)

Before We Can Start with Processing:

When we suspect that a chip may be the cause of a disturbing symptom, we first find out whether this is true. If so, we need to find what kind of chip is involved.

The person who is suffering from the chip needs to realize that although feelings of guilt may be stored in the chip, and even be the cause for the development of the chip, *in no way* will the investigation be a matter of looking for something he may be found *guilty* of having done. Guilt and shame are words that cannot describe the inner truth of a situation. It is possible that the chip contains Cosmic blame, as in the case of the boy who violated his girl cousin. However, Cosmic blame becomes extinguished when there is true remorse for the deed, and when the thoughts that have caused the person to act in a harmful way are deprogrammed. In the above case, the boy would have had to deprogram his envy of his girl cousin, and the mistaken belief that "girls need to be shown their place." It needs to be noted that when Cosmic blame is incurred, the ego converts it into guilt, which also needs to be deprogrammed as part of the chip.

When guilt is contained in a chip, it can make it difficult for the person to remember the incident that created the chip. This is because guilt is defined by the ego as an inextinguishable stain on one's nature, and therefore is so unbearable that we blot it from our memory. The ego takes advantage of this fact to hide behind the guilt. When it is difficult to remember a traumatic incident because of guilt, we can ask the Sage to suspend the guilt until the chip has been identified and is ready for deprogramming. This makes it possible to access the hidden memory.

When investigating a chip, we are never asked to relive any painful experience. If it is necessary to distance ourselves from the emotional content of the chip, we ask the Sage to show us that particular event as if we were watching a film. As we see the images and the action, we become aware that we are an adult observer who is emotionally removed from the scene. If, at any point, the person with the chip falls back into reliving the traumatic event, we need to invoke the Sage to call the person by his name. Then the Sage calls him back to himself.

Identifying a Chip

To identify a chip, we need to find out the following by asking the Sage, with the help of the *rtcm*:
- what kind of chip(s) needs to be identified: is it a memory chip, microchip, ego chip, stop chip, birth chip, or a conception chip
- at what age was the chip created (include the time *in utero*)

267

- the context in which it was created, as for example, within the family, at school, with friends
- the other persons who were involved
- the actual event

Then the things contained in the chip need to be identified as closely as possible. The following list shows what things to look for:

- words, or phrases that were said
- images connected with the event
- emotions, such as helplessness, repressed anger, shame, ridicule, or embarrassment, vindictiveness, self-righteousness, hurt pride, envy, jealousy, and hate
- guilt, blame, self-blame
- possible conclusions drawn from the experience, as in, "there is no help," "I will never be able to get over this," "I can't trust anyone," "I need to be punished," or "I can never be forgiven for what I did"
- a self-image that was taken on as a result of the experience, such as, "I am a bad person," "I have been damaged for life"
- fears as in, "it might happen again"

Finally, we ask whether one or more changelings are connected with the chip.

21. Wake-Up Calls
Dreams — The Psyche at Night

The nightly activity of the psyche we are most aware of is dreaming. We have mentioned that the psyche is the Sage's workplace. Dreams are the means through which the Sage can communicate our inner truth to the mind when our normal access to our inner truth is blocked. The elegance of this communication is that it happens while the ego is "asleep." The language used by the Sage in dreams is one of metaphors, meaning it uses certain objects as representations of multidimensional meanings. An example is a *trap door*. The image of a trap door evokes a *feeling* everyone can relate to. It can also evoke a *memory*, or it can be a trigger for a *fear*, or *suspicion*. It is up to the dreamer to find out which of these possibilities actually apply. For this reason, dreams are always personal and subjective as to their meaning and do not allow for a one-time definition.

Other dreams concern the inner communication between parts of our body. They occur with the help of a psychic function called the *remitter function*. The name of this function reveals the purpose of this communication: it is to *remit a request* of one body part to another to help in some way. When such dreams come to the attention of our mind, they are also to be understood as a request to gain the support of the mind in the difficulty at hand.

A third kind of dream can come from the ego when the ego is kept awake, because it is afraid of losing control over our personality.

Dreams that Come from the Sage

Despite the fact that every dream needs to be understood subjectively because of its personal connotations, we can give examples of various types of purposes the dream is meant to serve. The Sage has helped us to draw up the following schematic. The purpose of a dream can be to make us aware.

• that we have either just created a fate, have an ongoing fate, or that a fate has just ended

- of a fear that has been created in us by a projection, spell, or poison arrow we have either put on ourselves or have received from someone else
- of a projection, spell, or poison arrow we have put on someone else (our angry reaction in the dream indicates that the person has sent us a projection, spell, or poison arrow in return)
- of demonic elements in our psyche, such as imps, demons, dragons, changelings, or an ODE (In the dreams, we are either bystanders observing them, or we are given help to deal with them.)
- of an ego-complex

Dreams coming from the Sage can also serve:

- to show us the solutions to a fear
- to warn us in time to ward off an illness or accident
- to give us creative inspirations
- to give us a vision of something that wants to be expressed through us as part of our destiny
- to teach us something, as about our own nature, about Nature, the Cosmos, or about the Helpers
- to give us an insight into a process going on in our psyche
- to reflect to us an ordering process that is going on in the mind under the direction of the Sage, as, for example, about a work-in-progress. (It is good to write it down, even if we cannot yet make sense of it; writing it down will help to make its purpose obvious, later.)
- to remind us of something we need to do
- to reveal something about the inner truth of a person close to us (often to make us aware that we are meant to deprogram something for that person, or ask for help on his behalf)

Dreams that Come from the Ego

As mentioned above, these dreams occur when the ego is afraid of losing its control over the personality. To regain its territory, the ego uses various tactics such as fears, confusion, or image tricks.

The following is an example of a dream the Sage identified as having come from the ego. It dates back to the time when we, Hanna and Carol, were about to complete our new version of the *I Ching*:

"In the dream, I (Hanna) and Carol were in a foreign country. We had walked through many shops, had looked at a lot of things that were for sale, but had bought practically nothing. We had employed the sales staff to show us things, but with one exception had left the shops without making a purchase. We were about to leave the country when a woman who it seems had followed us on the whole shopping trip, confronted us squarely by saying, 'You didn't buy anything,' in a tone that suggested that we had done something wrong. I said apologetically, that I did buy a two-piece dress for someone else 'with accessories,' and that I also bought drawing materials. The woman made us unpack these things. When I saw the 'dress,' which turned out to be just a flimsy skirt, I saw that I had totally overpaid for it. The woman, seeing my shock, pointed to the skirt seam and began to unfold it; as she did so, the dress top appeared. It was very primitively designed and I thoroughly regretted having bought it. The 'drawing materials,' when laid out on the table, turned out to be four very ordinary coloring pencils. The woman spoke German although it was not her native tongue. I answered her sometimes in German, sometimes in English, not knowing what to say or in which language to say it."

The Sage guided me to develop a hexagram to understand the dream. I received Hexagram 18, *Recognizing and Correcting the Causes of Decay*, Lines 1 and 2. In Line 1 the following text was pointed to:

> The line points to a person's habit of accepting statements that persons in authority, such as his parents, have said are true. Here, he is behaving in the image of the "good son," who brings no blame to his parents. He is also avoiding feelings of guilt—the danger mentioned— which he is conditioned to feel on questioning his parents. This line is telling him that he needs to say the inner No to the guilt, and that he can quickly check through the *rtcm.* whether a given statement is true.
>
> The son also represents the person who follows traditional beliefs because he likes or fears the father (tradition), thus excuses

what is incorrect. This favoritism creates the danger that he will not say the necessary inner No needed to correct the situation. If he remembers his responsibility to be firm about what is incorrect, everyone will benefit in the end.

The line can also refer to the person who is looking at the Sage as a monumentalized being, therefore, is putting a false distance between himself and the Sage. As Lao Tzu said, the Sage "does his work but makes nothing of it." (Verse 2.)

This line also indicates that a person needs to question the taboos set up by the collective ego to secure its power, and that act as its defense system. These taboos exist in the form of various musts and must-nots that are connected with the image of a mythical patriarchal or matriarchal authority.

Danger also refers to the ego, which upon realizing the person has learned the inner truth of a matter, seeks to draw attention away from itself by setting up something outside, such as an outer authority or tradition.

Hanna learned from this text that she needed to identify a seed phrase she had taken on as true and that caused her to be intimidated by the woman's confronting her. It was the phrase: "Might makes right." The second paragraph indicated that she had falsely transferred this idea onto her relationship with the Sage, thus making the Sage into an authority figure that wielded power over her. The dream came at a time when Hanna and Carol had just realized that 'power' was a concept created by the ego. The ego attempted to use this dream to draw her attention away from this realization.

The following text from Line 2 was also indicated by the Sage as relevant:

Setting right what has been spoiled by the mother. One must not be too persevering. The mother stands for the fear-dominated beliefs about the 'unknown' that the mother instills in the child, together with those beliefs that are forced upon children by threats.

The Sage informed Hanna that she needed to look for a threat, which she identified as, "You cannot leave the collective ego's world behind (the foreign country in the dream) without having bought into something that you will take with you." However, the dream had revealed the truth: that there was nothing of worth to buy into and that the few things Hanna had actually bought were either shams or something the collective ego would call "of no worth" (the coloring pencils).

Dreams that Are Requests for Help from One Part of the Body to Another Part and to the Mind

The night is the time for our organs and certain bodily systems, such as our circulatory and glandular systems, to become particularly active. When an organ or bodily system is either overloaded or otherwise unable to fulfill its normal function, it puts out a request to other parts of the body and to the mind to help. This request for help is sent out through the *remitter function* of the psyche. The Sage helped Hanna to gain a preliminary understanding of such a dream.

"In this dream, I, Hanna, was supposed to go with one group of people to meet another group. First, however, I needed to go to the toilet, which was in a big room where the others were waiting for me. I needed a lot of time, but still could not finish my "job." I felt pressed on the one hand, but I also felt that it was important to take my time. When I was finally finished, I began to assemble several unidentified things I needed to take with me, but was soon so overloaded that the things kept slipping out of my hands and arms. They seemed to be pieces of clothing, and other things that were not easy to hold together."

On waking, Hanna consulted the Sage and learned that it was a dream in which one part of her body requested another part to wait. More specifically her elimination function requested parts of her digestive function to wait until it had "done its job." The reason why the elimination function needed more time was revealed in the "things" that were difficult to hold together: these things were foods that do not nourish, because they are devoid of feelings. Her adrenal gland and kidneys, which are part of the elimination function, were unable to process these "things," so that another way had to be found to eliminate them. The dream did not show a resolution to this difficulty.

We later found that vegetables that do not nourish are those grown with chemical fertilizers rather than natural ones. The same is true for the flesh of animals used for food that are fed hormones and antibiotics. The reason for this is that "chemicals" are components extracted from natural materials that have a feeling consciousness. Once a component has been separated from its source material, it loses its feeling consciousness. Thereafter, the inner truth of the body/DNA has no way of recognizing that component. While we can ask the Helpers of our body to deal with such foods, the dream was also giving the message to avoid taking in foods that do not nourish, because the body gains its nourishment from the feeling consciousness of the food.

Examples of Dreams that Come from the Sage for Specific Purposes

(1) A dream revealing the purpose of a fate

Three days after having been in a major car accident, Ronald shared his reflections with us:

"Tonight I am feeling very grateful to the Sage, Helpers, and Cosmos for their sparing me from what could have been my death in the accident. Although it was shocking, I can feel with my entire being that the accident really could have been worse.

"Last night, I dreamed that my house was lifted off its foundation, moved to another location, and put on a new foundation. It certainly is an example for me of the economy of the Cosmos and how one is increased by events such as an accident, or what could be seen by others as a tragedy.

"I learned from the *I Ching* that the whole event was an opportunity for the Cosmos to shake me loose from old patterns."

(2) A dream revealing the end of a fate created by a birth chip

Shortly before turning fifty years old, Hanna dreamed the following: She was on a train that stopped at a station in the middle of the night. Since everyone was getting off, she also decided to leave the train. Following an intuition, she went alongside the cars all the way back to the last one, where a man with a lantern wanted to show her something. As she stepped inside the car, she saw, with shock, that it was filled with starving newborn babies, all of which were helplessly lying on the floor stretching out their little arms. It was a horrifying sight!

At the time, Hanna was undergoing psychoanalysis. She related this dream at her next session. Her analyst suggested that it might want to reveal something about the circumstances of her birth, and encouraged her to tell her what she knew about it. Hanna recalled what her mother had told her: As a child of German parents, Hanna was born in a hospital in Czechoslovakia soon after World War II ended. Germany had lost the war, and many Czechs still strongly resented being suppressed by German troops during the occupation of their country. The attitude of the hospital staff toward the mother and child reflected this resentment, since neither support nor adequate food was given either to her mother or to herself by the nurses. Her mother told her that one nurse had even said, "Let the little thing perish."

As Hanna was relating her sad story with her eyes closed, she felt more and more sorry for herself. Suddenly, she heard the clear voice of her analyst: "It is true that you almost died, but here you are! After all, you survived! What you just told me is the myth about your birth." Hanna was shocked on hearing her analyst describe her experience as a "myth." Was she doubting that Hanna had told the truth?

It was then that she learned that a myth is based on a half-truth; it monumentalizes one half of a story and leaves out the other half. Hanna realized that she had been building her whole life on the sad, but monumentalized circumstances of her birth. For a brief moment, she felt as if a rug had been pulled out from under her, but an instant later, she felt a huge relief: she was free to start a new life!

In her dream, the large number of newborns reaching out for food illustrated the degree to which she had monumentalized the situation. The dream also showed her that she had reached the end of the fate the myth had created. The Sage further clarified to her that as long as she had invested in the myth, it created recurring fates from which she was now free.

It was almost twenty years later that we learned about birth chips. The Sage then made Hanna aware that she still needed to deprogram several birth chips.

(3) Dreams that point to the presence of guilt

Because of the "sticky" quality of guilt, dreams concerning guilt often reflect this stickiness: the dreamer has to wade through mud, or is stuck in mud; the dreamer needs to use a bathroom, but then finds the toilet already overflowing with excrement. This indicates that the dreamer wants to free himself from guilt, but is caught in such a pile of guilt from the past that he does not know a way out. While dreams about mud point to guilt stored in the psyche, dreams about excrement point to guilt stored in a microchip in the body.

A demon of guilt can also show up as a large spider surrounded by hundreds of baby spiders. This dream image shows the poisonous aspect of guilt for both psyche and body. In this case, the spider is a demonized aspect of our mind, more specifically its memorizing function when it is under the spell of the notion of "guilty memories."

An underwater plant with tentacles that threatens to suck the dreamer into its embrace stands for the devouring aspect of guilty feelings.

(4) Nightmares coming from the Sage

As a rule, repetitive nightmares are caused by a chip that contains a traumatic or shocking memory. The chip can be accompanied by a crystallized fear or other ego-emotion. (See Chapters 18 and 19.) The nightmares reflect efforts of the psyche to break these chips. Every time we wake up with a shock, a piece of the chip is broken off.

A particular kind of repetitive nightmare can be caused by a memory of an event in which the dreamer has given up on another person as a "hopeless case." In the dream, the roles have been reversed, with the dreamer being the one given up on: he is being persecuted and threatened with death. The dream is showing him what it feels like to be "mentally executed" and written off as hopeless; it seeks to make the dreamer aware of the harmfulness of his thought (a poison arrow), and to give him an opportunity to deprogram it. The deprogramming, should he do it, will release the dreamer from the fate he has created, and remove the arrow from the person on whom he has put it.

(5) A dream about a ball-of-conflict

Many years ago, Hanna had a dream that was about her love relationship at the time. In it she was shown an apartment with two rooms. The door to one room was open, while the other door was closed.

Reflecting on the dream after waking, Hanna felt that there was something behind the closed door she needed to discover. In a meditation she actively imagined that she was back in the dream, standing in front of the closed door. She inwardly asked for a sign to be shown on the door that would tell her what she could expect to find in that room. Immediately, the words "No Exit" appeared on the door that seemed to warn her from going inside that room. Only opening the door a crack, she saw that the whole room was filled with trash up to the ceiling! 'Relationship trash' flashed through her mind, as she remembered the blaming each other that had taken place. Hanna realized that it was useless to go inside that room and evaluate each piece of trash before throwing it out. There was only one-way to get rid of it all: to ask for help to have it cleaned out.

At that time Hanna did not know about deprogramming, or about the Helpers, but she knew a method for clearing spaces. She envisioned a violet light filling the whole room, then after a while, she envisioned a white light in the center of the room that expanded gradually until it filled the room. At that point, the room became quiet and peaceful, like a room used for meditation. In the middle was a lotus blossom with a well at its center. Hanna realized the room had become the place of the Sage. She found herself sitting at some distance, looking toward the center. Her partner was also sitting, looking toward the center. With the Sage they formed a triangular relationship! At that moment, it became clear: She and her partner had not been looking to the Sage as the center of their relationship, but only at each other. They thought their relationship was only a matter between the two of them! That view had created all their difficulties.

We later learned that the "room with no exit" was something the *I Ching* calls "a ball-of-conflict." A ball-of-conflict gets started when we see ourselves or another person as a "culprit." The only purpose of that word is to get a conflict going and make sure it continues endlessly through blaming. Hanna's meditation showed her how it could be ended.

(6) A dream about replacing one ego-complex with another

Another dream of Hanna's came at a time in her life when she felt she needed professional help to find her way out of a depression. In the dream, she was in a large house that had been given up. An auction of its inventory was taking place. After observing this fact, she decided to leave, but then noticed a pair of boots that had been conveniently placed by the door. The boots appealed to her. She put them on, and then left the house. Outside, she followed an uphill-leading path, at the end of which she could already see a much bigger house than the one she had just left.

This dream was still vivid in Hanna's memory when, many years later, she learned to interpret dreams with the help of the Sage. To her surprise, she learned that the first house represented a Superiority Complex she had developed. Since it had not led to any success, she decided to leave it behind. The auction going on represented the activity of Cosmic Helpers that were evaluating the psychic inventory she possessed that they could transform into helpful skills. However, the help they offered was blocked by a changeling, which had placed the boots by the door. Her putting the boots on and walking toward the bigger house on the hilltop indicated that she had just adopted a new ego-complex: the Psychoanalysis Complex. The dream showed that the failure of one ego-complex does not necessarily lead to freedom from the ego's dominance; it can achieve that only if we actually deprogram that complex, and make sure that any changeling connected with it is also taken care of. By creating a new rationale/changeling ("Psychoanalysis will help me"), the ego "updated" its program. The *I Ching* calls this going from one conventional means of help to another, without getting to the root cause of the disturbance.[1] This example is not meant

---

1 See Hexagram 57, *The Penetrating*, Line 3. "Repeated penetration. Humiliation."

to dismiss the help psychoanalysis can offer. It is only to say that a lot more help would be possible if the ego-elements were deprogrammed.

(7) A dream calling one to help another person

In this dream, Hanna was invited to a house-warming party being held in a newly renovated house. The people were very friendly and showed her the new wooden panels that covered the walls that were painted with an elaborate design. Although there was plenty of food and many guests, she was not able to join in the party. Instead, she wandered around with different pieces of paper trash in her hands looking for a wastebasket. She went outside the main rooms and along big hallways that led to more halls and large rooms where other people were celebrating their family get-togethers. The people were mostly elegantly dressed. In other parts of this living complex, workers were busy restoring floors and other woodwork. They were producing lots of dust. The whole complex reminded her of those huge galleries in Italy that have glass domes spanning vast spaces. This made her conclude that she must be somewhere between Italy and Switzerland. She then climbed down steep, risky stairs, but got safely to the bottom. Weary, because she could not find a wastebasket, she stuffed the papers into an empty, deserted bathtub that was cluttering one of the hallways. Just before waking up, these words came to mind, "I have stalled feelings and don't know where to put them."

Investigating the dream with the help of the Sage, Hanna learned that the "I" in the dream was actually a young woman with whom she was connected through family bonds. The Sage was using the dream to make Hanna aware of a dangerous activity going on in that woman's psyche. Through the following communication with the Sage, she learned how she could help this young woman.

The words, "I have stalled feelings and don't know where to put them," reminded Hanna of the Self-Doubt Complex. The vastness of the "living complex" suggested that she had been shown an assembly of ego-complexes that the woman was seeking to update. Both intuitions were confirmed by the Sage. The renovations indicated that two new ego-complexes were about to be added. One was The Restoration Complex, that had the phrase, "I need to clean up my act." The other was The Revolution Complex, which says, "What I used to believe is not true; the opposite must be true."

The Sage pointed out that the young woman had been blaming herself: "With my education, I should be able to earn more money." "I should be able to afford a real vacation." These phrases suggested that she had believed in some untruth that did not fulfill its promise. It was the phrase: "Poverty is spiritual." She had now adopted a new (false) motto: "I must think positive." "I must think wealth." "I must think big."

The dream showed Hanna how the ego in a person can use false rationales to "update" a whole mélange of existing ego-complexes after they have lost their appeal. The updating, however, did not resolve the real question: where to put the stalled feelings that had been reduced to paper waste.

Some Help to Understand Your Dreams

The Sage helps us with understanding the message of a dream. For this purpose we use the *rtcm*. (See Appendix 1, "Using the Retrospective-Three-Coin Method.")

We first feel into the dream: does it give us the feeling that it contains a message? If we are not sure, we use the *rtcm* to put this question to the Sage. If the answer is Yes, we may want to clarify the source of the dream: Did it come from the Sage, from a body part, or from the ego?

The following suggestions can be used as a guideline to gain a further understanding of a dream:

Write down everything you remember from your dream and/or draw a picture. (Some people place a recorder by their bedside so they can listen to the dream later.) Pay particular attention to the feelings you woke up with. Are they true feelings, such as joy, gratitude, or anger, or are they ego-emotions, such as frustration, fear, guilt, etc. If they are ego-emotions, they most likely indicate the presence of a spell or some kind of chip.

You may find it helpful to determine the purpose of your dream by checking the list given at the beginning of this chapter under "The kinds of dreams that come from the Sage." This gives your further inquiry a direction. If, for example, you learn that the dream wants to make you aware of a spell, you can proceed as follows to identify it:

Ask if you have put this spell on yourself. If not, find out who has put it on you. Then ask the Finding Helper of your psyche to bring the spell into your conscious mind. To free yourself from the spell's harmful influence, follow the deprogramming instructions given in Appendix 3.

If the dream wants to make you aware of a traumatic memory stored in your psyche or body, follow the suggestions for investigating a chip. (See Chapter 19.)

On occasion, a dream can prepare us for other dreams that will eventually show a more complete picture. Dreams can also mirror to us how we are making progress in a particular area of our lives. This is especially true when we experience the end of a spell or chip that has been causing us nightmares. (See the example above: "A dream revealing the end of a fate created by a birth chip.")

It is important to note that the character we experience as "I" in the dream is not necessarily ourselves. In such cases, the Sage may want us to experience how another person is being affected by spells put on him by others, or by ego-complexes in his own psyche. The "I" in the dream may be a part of our own body that the dream wants us to understand, as described in Hanna's dream about her elimination function.

We need to remember that dreams use a metaphorical language and that metaphors are multidimensional in their meanings: they can have a concrete meaning, but can also stand for something invisible. For example, money can point to an actual money issue, or to an issue having to do with the true *value* of something, in the figurative sense.

Common Dream Metaphors

Time and Place. Since the contents of our psyche are not

subject to time and place, our dreams are not to be understood within these parameters. In a dream, w can be first in one place, and immediately after in a wholly different place. What the dream may want to show us is the relationship between *cause and effect*. This is illustrated in the dream about the elimination function described above: the "things" that were causing the elimination function to take more time, were shown *after* this function had finished its "job." The fact that the psyche is not subject to time, but contains the knowledge about cause-and-effect, allows for premonitions as well as flashbacks.

People in dreams can stand for aspects of actual people or for mistaken ideas they hold. Example: A drug dealer may stand for the idea that "we have to make deals to get what we need/want in life." This idea imprisons the Sage with the consequence that the Sage cannot gather the Cosmic Helpers that would support us in all respects. A person in a wheelchair can stand for a function of our body or psyche that has been made dysfunctional by a poison arrow. People in dreams can also stand for Helpers of our nature, or for Cosmic Helpers. In other dreams, people can stand for imps, demons, or dragons. For example, seeing our father can indicate the presence of a 'dragon of authority.' (Also see the car dream related in Chapter 16, "How We Came to Discover the First Demonic Elements . . . .")

Animals often appear in dreams. This fact reminds us that we are part of the animal kingdom and have an animal nature. In fact, our animal nature is composed of the consciousnesses of many animals, some of which we are familiar with, and some not.[2] Each of these animal consciousnesses has one or more particular functions in our body, psyche, or mind. It is important to pay attention to the feeling we get from the animal. When it is pleasant, the particular animal function wants to make itself known to us, as if saying, "hey, I want to show you what I can

---

2 The evolution of animals has progressed from the single cell to organizations of cells. We see this in biology where there are examples of "an organized stomach" such as coelenterates, and the organized intestine shown in worms. The human organism is an assemblage of such organisms, each of which has its own intelligence and feeling nature. These organisms have learned to live in a harmonious symbiosis with each other. Thus we humans share our biology, in one way or another, with all living forms.

do for you," and "I want you to know that I care for you." If an animal in a dream feels scary, or looks deformed, it is a sign that its function in our true nature has been demonized. Examples: (1) The spider was mentioned above in the context of the poisonous aspect of guilt. (2) An animal in a cage can indicate that its function has been imprisoned by a spell. For example, a tiger in a cage may be telling us that we need to free all our bodily senses. (3) If we see fish that are turning into humans, or into something else, it may indicate that we have put a spell on our *inner* senses of perception by denying their importance. (4) A dead mammal in a dream may indicate that a particular bodily or psychic function has been killed through cutting off the specific feeling associated with that bodily function. For example, if we dream of a dead mare, it may mean that our firmness in standing up to the ego has been undermined. A dead water foul may indicate that a particular aspect of our creativity has been killed off by a slander. Fortunately, all these functions can be revived. That is why we are being shown through the dream that help is desperately needed. We can give this help by finding out which spell or poison arrow has caused the sad state of affairs, and then deprogramming it with Cosmic help.

Large buildings or other structures may indicate ego-complexes that make up the ego's capital and the defensive structures around it. Being inside the building complex may indicate that we are enmeshed in an activity that is based on a particular ego-complex, such as the Self-Punishment Complex. When we find ourselves looking at a complex from the outside, it can indicate that we are in awe of the mistaken idea on which it is based. We may also be shown that an ego-complex has burned out. (Also see above: "Dreams that are calls to help another person.")

A forgotten apartment or room may want to make the dreamer aware of a microchip or memory chip.

A train usually points to a fate. A train runs on an existing track between two places. Because of this it is the perfect metaphor for the way a fate returns to its originator like a boomerang. (Also see the example given above, "A dream revealing the end of a fate created by a birth chip.")

A *bus* can have either a Cosmic meaning or an ego meaning. In its Cosmic meaning it can represent the unity of our body and psyche, with the bus driver being the Sage. To be offered a ride on this bus may mean that we are ready to return to unity with the Cosmos. It is characteristic of this kind of bus that no fare is being charged. In its ego meaning, the bus may stand for our longing to be whole, which indicates a separation between our body and psyche that was initiated by the original self-doubt that allowed for the development of the ego in our psyche.

A *car* can stand for the totality of our bodily Helpers, or for functions of our psyche. When functioning healthily, they operate as a feeling consciousness. This condition allows us to make smooth progress. When the car in our dream is functioning badly, we need to investigate the cause. For example, if the car has no lights, our inner senses of perception and our metaphorical senses are under spells.

A *bicycle* represents a slower means of making progress than normal. It tends to indicate that we are relying on rules rather than on our true feelings for whatever we do. (This can refer to our conduct in general, or the way we go about a particular project.) When the bicycle in the dream is in good condition, we are making some progress, but not as much as would be possible with a car (which can stand for allowing ourselves to be carried forward by our true feelings). When the bicycle needs repair, it can indicate a physical or mental condition of ill health that has immobilized us to some degree.

Landscapes in dreams can either stand for our own psychic landscape, or that of another person. The landscape is part of our "inner country" and wants to show us a particular aspect of it: one that wants to be seen for its natural beauty, or for the things that have been destroyed or falsely erected in it. (Also see "The Landscape of the Psyche" in Chapter 8.)

22. The Fork in the Road
Crossing Over from the Ego-Mindset into the Cosmic Reality

The Decisive Moment

There comes a point in our inner journey when it is time to make a conscious decision: Do I still want to live my life in the parallel reality created by the collective ego, or do I want to live in the Cosmic reality? The moment for this decision comes of itself; it is not made by our mind alone. Up to this point, we have had many experiences of having received the Sage's help: in healing an ailment, in finding a new job, or in ending a conflict in our love relationship. We were able to see how saying an inner No to ego-behavior in ourselves and in people who are close to us has had a harmonizing effect. All these experiences have allowed us to build trust in the Sage and in the support that is available to us from the Cosmos as a whole.

We refer to this moment as coming to a fork in the road. The fork differs from the image of being at a crossroad. The image of the crossroad suggests that if we choose one path, it will put us in opposition to the road not taken. The image of the cross-road is created by a changeling that would keep us within the mindset of the ego. This mindset falsely suggests that following the road of our inner truth means that we will automatically be in opposition to the collective ego. The path of our inner truth is not in opposition to anything, because the idea of opposition contradicts the Cosmic Principles of Harmony. By contrast, the fork represents the place where we depart from convention to take the unique path that we, in the company of Helpers, create for ourselves.

The ego may argue that our following this path will undermine the social order. This is its last attempt to make us feel afraid of becoming guilty. However, it is the other way around: it is the collective ego that has continually undermined the natural social order. Other arguments by the ego are, "by taking this fork in the road, you're betraying your ancestors, leaving behind your family and friends, and you will be left without support."

Once we make the decision to say Yes to living in the Cosmic reality, additional Helpers are created in our psyche, together with their Cosmic complements. A Helper that keeps doubts at bay comes to enable the Sage to bring us greater clarity. Another Helper comes to support our Personal Helper in helping us fulfill our Cosmic Destiny; as a result, we make faster progress on our path. We also enjoy more Cosmic protection.

Making this clear decision helps our true self grow up and take responsibility for our thinking and actions. That does not mean that the Cosmos will now require the impossible of us, or expect us to be perfect. By consciously saying Yes to our desire to live in the Cosmic reality we are saying Yes to our wholeness, and Yes to taking our true place in the Cosmos. This is to reclaim our sovereignty.

Bringing Unfinished Business to an End

In Hexagram 40, *Freeing,* the *I Ching* counsels us in the words: "If there is still unfinished business, it furthers to bring it swiftly to an end." The unfinished business referred to is *guilt.* We cannot make the crossover as long as we are tied to the collective ego by the false idea of guilt. In order to free ourselves from it, we need to have absolute clarity why it contradicts the Cosmic Principles of Harmony.

Of all the ideas the collective ego has created, the idea that there is such a thing as guilt that creates an inextinguishable stain on our nature, is the most destructive.

According to the logic of the collective ego, the *fear of becoming guilty* is what "protects" the individual from listening to the "evil" in himself. Another supposed benefit is that it keeps him striving to develop his "higher nature."

These proposed benefits of the belief in guilt serve to enslave us to the collective ego's service, whereby we devote our life energy to its purposes, and sacrifice our inner truth.

The bond by which the Cosmic Consciousness holds all its aspects together is a feeling bond. It is created by the attraction that exists between its complementary aspects. The Cosmos, for its part, employs no power, holds no threat over a person's head, and administers no punishments. To reunite with the Cosmos, people need to make no extraordinary efforts, do no extraordinary deeds, or make any pacts, promises, or confessions of having sinned, or rituals of cleansing. The Cosmos receives us where we are in our sincerity, and comes to meet us halfway. We need only the sincere desire to turn our backs on the collective ego that has pulled us away from our true home.

(To deprogram the false idea of guilt, and any guilt we have accepted, see Appendix 3, "Deprogramming.")

"This Above All, To Thine Own Self be True"

This counsel given by Polonius to his son in Shakespeare's *Hamlet* expresses that to which we owe our true loyalty. By being loyal to our true self we hold together with our inner truth, which connects us with Cosmic truth. Though this bond is invisible, it is felt as Cosmic blessings, support, and protection.

The Cosmic Principles of Increase and Abundance

In its Cosmic meaning, "increase" refers to the way everyone is increased who takes his true place in the Cosmos as an equal to everything else.[1] This personal increase contributes to the increase of the whole.

By contrast, the collective ego defines "increase" as the acquisition of wealth, power, fame, and knowledge. This form of increase serves only a few and decreases the whole. What is gained through such activity invariably comes with a fate attached that will eventually take the gain away. The collective ego sees nothing but "lack of resources" in the world, and therefore advocates the amassing of resources in the hands of a few. The ego-mindset revolves around fighting for the scarce resources — a fight in which everyone is out for himself.

Likewise, "abundance"[2] characterizes the relationship between the Cosmic Consciousness and everyone (and everything) who

1 See Hexagram 42, *Increasing.*
2 See Hexagram 55, *Abundance.*

takes his true place in the Cosmos; the Cosmos gives an abundance of nourishment, protection, support, and furtherance;
the Cosmos also has an abundance of patience with humans in
their learning process.

Gradually Leaving Behind the Ego-Mindset

When we learn to follow our inner truth with the Sage's help,
we tend at first to transfer onto the Sage the image of a higher
authority (such as God) that we have assumed to be part of the
"natural order of things." The Sage tolerates this habit for a while
because it knows how we have been conditioned to distrust our
commonsense; and it takes into account that we are only able
to gradually free ourselves from our doubt in the harmonious
nature of the Cosmos.

What the Sage does not support is our desire to have *it* make
all our decisions for us. This desire comes from a fear that we
will make a mistake and be found guilty; therefore, we adopt a
servile attitude toward the Sage as if it were a punishing God.
Making mistakes is part of our learning process, and guilt for
making them does not exist in the eyes of the Cosmos.

At first, it may seem impossible to leave the ego-mindset behind while continuing to live our lives in a world that is dominated by this very mindset. The ego would say, "if you want to
go on that path, you have to either withdraw into the solitude of
the mountains, or become a rebel who fights the system." Both
these "solutions" only hold us in that mindset because they are
based on the idea that following our inner truth puts us *in opposition* to the collective ego. Withdrawal from the collective ego
means that we no longer give it our energy; it does not mean
putting ourselves in opposition to it, which would be to give it
our energy, and hold us in conflict with it.

The *I Ching*'s counsel is expressed in the words, "It furthers one
to have somewhere to go." The place to go is inside ourselves. We
reside in our inner center, keep counsel with our commonsense
and with the Sage, and meet our friends, the Helpers, which the
Sage gathers around us. Keeping our inner counsel before we
undertake things in the outer world means that we ask to be

shown the Cosmic way before acting outwardly. Being shown the inner truth of a difficult situation we would like to resolve means that we allow ourselves to be shown the causes of the difficulty that lie in projections, spells, poison arrows, demonic elements, self-images, or ego-complexes. On learning these influences, we proceed to deprogram them with Cosmic help and then ask the Cosmic Helpers to do what is necessary to resolve the difficulty. We also refrain from talking about what we have found to be the inner truth of the matter. (We can talk about such things only with people who are sensitive to the inner world of the Helpers.) Lao Tzu, in the *Tao Te Ching*, referred to this way of taking inner action through saying an inner Yes and an inner No as "doing through non-doing, and yet everything gets done."

Allowing Our True Self to Lead our Personality

We may ask: Can there be leadership that is in accord with the Cosmic Principles of Harmony? What about the Principle of Equality? Obviously, we need a Cosmic definition of leadership. This leadership is based on the true self's knowledge that

- our true place in the Cosmos is one that is equal to every other aspect of the Cosmos
- we are dependent on the Cosmos for all our needs
- the Cosmos gives its blessings, nourishment, protection, support, and furtherance when we are modest and sincere, and free of a demanding or begging attitude

Our true self says an inner Yes to its Cosmic possessions and gifts and an inner No to any attempt of the ego to interfere in our lives; it calls on Cosmic help when in need, and refrains from self-righteously interfering in what the Helpers do.

Our Undertakings Have Success that Endures

When we allow the Helpers to inspire our undertakings and when we also include them in carrying them out, we notice that an enduring success occurs. This is because the goal and its realization are in harmony with the Cosmos. The Helper of Transformation completes our undertaking and imbues it with life force. By contrast, when we work toward an ego-goal with the attitude that we are the ones who do it all, we find the resulting success to be short-lived, even though it may have been a big success for a while. The Law of Fate takes away the gain of ego-tainted achievements.

Until we deprogram old feelings of inferiority, there will be the danger that even after having successfully completed a piece of work free of ego, the ego will attempt to appropriate the success. We recognize its interference in statements such as, "Look what I did" (boasting), or, "Now I have made it" (self-congratulating), or, "Now, I'll become famous/rich" (self-important).

Saying the Inner Yes and Inner No

The words Yes and No are the two basic words in the Cosmic language: We say Yes to what is harmonious, and No to what is disharmonious. "No" is one of the first words a child learns to say. That is because he intuitively knows that saying No to what does not feel harmonious is important to keep his borders intact. Unfortunately, many parents and caretakers have the idea that they have the right to cross over the child's borders as they please. This has two unhealthy results, the first being that the child grows up believing that neither he nor anyone else has a right to their natural borders; the second result is that an unhealthy pattern develops in which the child says No to practically everything, which makes the No lose its meaning.

Many adults have impediments to saying an inner No due to being punished by authority figures during childhood for saying it. This leaves them with no way to protect the *intrinsic space* that surrounds their dignity and self-esteem. It also opens them up to accepting the mistaken ideas and beliefs of the collective ego. (Also see Chapter 19, "Stop Chips.")

Saying an inner No to ego-activities in ourselves as well as to ego-interferences coming from others is essential to correcting disharmonious situations.

Allowing the Cosmos to Return Matters to Harmony through Fate

While learning about the Cosmic way of doing things we

may still find ourselves thinking, "wouldn't it be wonderful, if the Cosmos performed a miracle and freed the world from the misery humans have created?" This thought is based on the mistaken idea that the Cosmos works through power. The use of power violates the Cosmic Principles of Harmony.

The use of power, as through some sort of punishment, or threat, or imperious behavior to "correct" disharmonious situations prevents people from learning from their mistakes. Fate, by contrast, is the way the Cosmos, in caring for humans, decreases the ego. Fate is like a blank wall or force field we run into that returns us to the humility we need to get in touch with our inner truth. It is not a punishing force. It stands as a protection to guard the Cosmic Principles of Harmony. The more obstinately we cling to the ego in us, the harder we slam into that wall. Fate thus helps us in more than one respect:

- it frees our inner senses of perception, and thereby frees our commonsense;
- it knocks the ego unconscious for some time, thereby giving us the opportunity to get in touch with our inner truth and reflect on the cause of the fate;
- even if we do not recognize its cause, a fate only runs for a limited amount of time, like a prison sentence;
- as it runs its course, the negative energy that had created the fate is transformed into positive energy, which accrues to our true self;
- the fate need not run its full course — it can be ended any time by our learning its cause (in a mistaken idea, belief, self-image, etc.) and freeing ourselves from it with Cosmic help.

Our own experience of Fate is this: As we progress in our learning, we run into the wall of Fate less often, and with less impact. We also become aware that a fate announces itself in the form of smaller warnings, such as stubbing our toes, or pinching our fingers in a doorway. These events are meant to make us ask ourselves what is it we have been thinking, and then to correct our thinking. Eventually no fate is needed because we have been returned to being sensitive to our inner thoughts. The result is that we choose to live by the Cosmic Principles of Harmony because it feels good to be in harmony and peace.

The Cosmic Principles of Harmony are not to be applied as mental rules we follow. Rather we follow them unconsciously when we are sensitive to what feels harmonious and what does not. Making them into rules is a strategy of the ego to keep us within its way of thinking that if we are diligent in following rules, whatever they are, we will avoid the fate of being punished. This attitude actually invites a fate because it makes the Cosmos into a copy of the collective ego.

Living in Harmony with the Cosmic Order

Saying Yes to living in the Cosmic reality does not mean that the Cosmos requires that we make any *changes* in the way we have been living our lives. We still go to work, pay our taxes, shop at the supermarket, and use the Internet. However, since we began our inner journey, we may have noticed that certain things have changed for us from within: we may no longer enjoy the company of certain people, laugh at the same kinds of jokes, watch the same programs on TV, or listen to certain types of music. These things have simply lost their attraction. We may prefer instead to spend more time alone, or being in Nature; or, we may have started to learn to play an instrument we always wanted to learn.

In spending more time with ourselves, we notice that we are not lonely. This contrasts with the loneliness we felt during those times when we joined others in "pleasures" that betrayed our true nature and dignity.

The *I Ching* acknowledges that there are times when a person who is bringing his true self to maturity is placed in difficult situations. People formerly in his circle resent that he no longer takes part in their ego-activities. They misunderstand his behavior and challenge him to explain or defend himself. The correct response to such challenges is to say an inner No to the others' incorrect demands, and to ask the Sage-in-their-presence to intervene with the ego in them. Thereafter, he remains reserved with them until the Sage has intervened.

Challenges may not only come to a person from other people but also from his own thinking mind as it puts forward all kinds of reasons why he should pull back into conformity with other members of his family, his friends, or other social contacts. Objections such as, "you'll become a loner," "no one will want to have anything to do with you anymore," or, "you must have gone crazy," need to be rejected with a firm inner No. He also needs to be careful not to share his unique experiences of the inner world with people who are not receptive enough. Such people only want to ridicule or denigrate the Helpers. Gradually, he finds new friends with whom he can joyfully share his inner experiences.

Dissolving our Bond with Our Group Identity

Both family and friends tend to form the closest bonds, and accordingly make the strongest demands on our loyalty and adherence. Under this umbrella, demands are made on how we ought to feel, think, and behave. Behind this umbrella is the larger societal structure, which has defined the loyalties we owe to our family and friends. These demands are secured by the threats mentioned above of being isolated, ridiculed, and becoming guilty. The fact that they demand adherence through subtle and hidden threats is an indicator that the natural attraction that exists between people's true selves has been replaced by an ego structure. The development and maturation of our true self means being loyal to our inner truth, even to the point of retreating from our closest relationships when those relationships require compromising our inner truth. It means going on our way alone so as to avoid involving ourselves in energy exchanges contrived by the egos around us. By this we do not mean we necessarily outwardly leave our association with family and friends, but rather that we inwardly dissolve our group identity with them. Thus, we reserve ourselves until such time as their true selves are present.

During times of misunderstandings and conflict between family members, we can ask the Sage to help us understand the inner truth of the situation. For example, if we find that the conflicts are caused by chips or spells, we can ask if it is appropriate for us to deprogram them on their behalf. This can be a great help in restoring family peace and fellowship.

Epilogue

Normally, we would not write an epilogue to a book like this, concerned, as it is, with the inner life. However, because we are keenly aware of the many people who are now facing great difficulties as dire as those that faced us in our darkest hour, it is with them in mind that we are adding this epilogue. For both of us, our cries for help not only brought us the *I Ching*, they brought us the opportunities we needed to find our true paths. In Chapter 1 we presented the "before"; here, we present the "after."

The Perfect Fit for All My Needs

When I, Carol, realized I would be alone in bringing up my four teenagers, I looked at what I had to offer an employer and realized there was probably no way I could get a job that would adequately provide for us. Before becoming a full-time mother, I had been a privileged young woman. I took the courses in college that I hoped would hone my skills as a creative writer. I quickly married and never had a job except to run the office and do the bookkeeping for my husband's business. My husband, on leaving, and knowing my circumstances, expected me to fall back on my "advantaged family," to sell our house, which we had just finished paying for, and to pay him his half. To me, the idea of falling back on my parents was out of the question; therefore, my outlook was bleak. In this situation, I cried out to the Cosmos for help. Help came in the most unexpected way.

To understand this, I need to give a little background: Although my husband had a job for several years in a big industry as a personnel manager, he left it to buy and sell used Volkswagens. He had always been a lover of cars, especially odd ones. When the Volkswagen came along in the 1960's, he began to buy and sell them on the side. Ten years after doing this full time, and seeing our savings dwindle gradually, he took a job elsewhere and made me aware he had left for good. It happened that he also left me with four used Volkswagens, which I was not sure I could sell, having never sold a car. In this moment of great uncertainty, a Frenchman called me, wanting to buy one with the idea of selling it back to me in three months. He was here for training with a growing computer firm in our area. I asked him how much he expected this to cost him, and it came out to $5.00 per day. I realized immediately that rather than sell him a car, I might be able to rent it to him. He agreed, and then mentioned that many more people would soon be coming from various countries to train at the same company, and that they would all like stick-shift cars to rent while they were here.

In a flash, I now saw a possibility that could save me. Within a week I had rented the remaining cars to people he knew, and soon, I had a waiting list for more. To make a long story short, within two years I had sixty-four Volkswagens constantly in rental and three employees. After four more years, I had paid my husband for his half of the house, had paid for all the cars, and had even paid the lawyer who handled my divorce. Meanwhile, my children were raised, and had become self-sufficient.

My business was the "learning ground" for practicing *I Ching* principles. During the first ten years, I kept notes of the insights I gathered along the way. They became the material for my first book, *A Guide to the I Ching,* which I published in 1980. The *I Ching* was a great teacher of how to run a business, as well as how to relate to all the different people and circumstances I met while renting cars. After founding my own publishing company, the car rentals supported it until it was firmly established three years later. By that time, the computer firm had moved its training school away, competing rental companies had moved in, and the choice customers I had for my business were gone. I realized that I had been given precisely the opportunities and support I needed to be launched into doing what really suited me. I had become self-sufficient, my children had completed their educations, and I had thirteen years of experience in being helped by the *I Ching.*

Fulfilling My Cosmic Destiny

When I, Hanna, went to the Canary Islands, the Wilhelm translation of the *I Ching* was the only book I carried in my backpack. Being a total novice to it, my understanding of its messages was gradually increased by my allowing them to reveal their meanings through my everyday experiences. It was often only in retrospect that I understood what the words had been referring to.

Shortly after my return to Germany, I was approached by the publisher of the Wilhelm *I Ching*. His plan was to publish an anthology of articles written on the *I Ching* by famous authors, such as Carl G. Jung and Hermann Hesse, on the one hand, and living people with first hand experiences in consulting the *I Ching*, on the other. My reflections on "My journey with the *I Ching*" were published in his book.[1] This soon led to another request to share my *I Ching* experiences, this time in an interview for a film on the *I Ching* produced by a German TV station.

I had returned from my backpack trip with a trust in the unknown, but with no clear road to follow. Consulting the *I Ching* to learn more about my "vocation" as I called it, I had received Hexagram 5, *Waiting*. The oracle text reads:

> Waiting. If you are sincere,
> You have light and success.
> Perseverance brings good fortune.
> It furthers one to cross the great water.

Wilhelm's commentary states:
> Waiting is not mere empty hoping. It has the inner certainty of reaching the goal. Such certainty alone gives that light which leads to success. This leads to the perseverance that brings good fortune ... One is faced with a danger that has to be overcome. Weakness and impatience can do nothing ... This strength shows itself in uncompromising truthfulness [with himself]. It is only when we have the courage to face things exactly as they are, without any sort of self-deception or illusion, that a light will develop out of events by which the path to success may be recognized. This recognition must be followed by resolute and persevering action. For only the man who goes to meet his fate resolutely is equipped to deal with it adequately. Then he will be able to cross the great water — that is to say, he will be capable of making the necessary decision and of surmounting the danger.

1 *Erfahrungen mit dem I Ging*, herausgegeben von Ulf Diederichs, Eugen Diederichs Verlag, Köln, 1984.

The image connected with "Waiting" describes the person consulting the oracle in these words: "Thus the superior man eats and drinks, is joyous and of good cheer."

Wilhelm comments:

"When clouds rise in the sky, it is a sign that it will rain. There is nothing to do but to wait until the rain falls. It is the same in life when destiny is at work. We should not worry and seek to shape the future by interfering in things before the time is ripe. We should quietly fortify the body with food and drink and the mind with gladness and good cheer."

Taking the words of the *I Ching* as counsel that the time was not yet ripe for my vocation to show itself, I contented myself with taking a part time job that would pay for my immediate needs. The remaining free time was to provide the openness needed for whatever new thing wanted to come into my life.

About three years later, I received a call from the publisher: Would I be interested in taking a job as an editor for his company? I was totally surprised. What, I thought to myself, qualified *me* to work as an editor? I had a master's degree in national economics, and not in the German Language, which I thought was needed as a prerequisite to be an editor. Nevertheless, I agreed to the job interview. It turned out to be an interview with reversed roles: I found myself listening to the publisher's telling me what, in his mind, qualified me for the job: my good way of relating to people, my good writing style, my knowledge of the French and English languages, and last but not least my "life experience," which spoke for my being open to new areas of knowledge. He also shared with me what had prompted him to think of me for this position. The idea had occurred to him only after having done a considerable number of job interviews with candidates who had at least two Ph.D's in the subject matters published by his company. The problem, he said, was that they possessed an intellectual knowledge of the subject matters, but they lacked life experience.

Thereafter, I worked as a free-lance editor for his company for thirteen years, until I moved to the United States to join forces with Carol. During this time I was allowed to edit and translate newer books on the *I Ching*, among which were Carol's *A Guide* to the *I Ching* and *A Philosophy of the I Ching*. These were later followed by her other two books. All along, on the side, I was asked to give lectures on the *I Ching* in bookstores, and teach others in seminars how to consult the oracle.

My inner and outer journeys had converged into what I had asked to be shown: my vocation.

Appendix 1
Using the Retrospective-Three-Coin Method
(rtcm)

The Retrospective-Three-Coin Method is our main means of communicating with the Sage to investigate the causes of an inner or outer conflict, a stress, a worry, a fear, a nervous or emotional condition, or other disturbance. It involves the use of three identical coins such as pennies. One side of the coin, as for example the head side, is designated as saying "Yes," and the tail side as "No." A question is put to the Sage, with the understanding that the Sage will determine the outcome of the toss.

Carol discovered this method in 1994, when, on needing a quick answer to an emergency situation, she simply tossed the three coins she normally used to develop a hexagram, to get a Yes or No answer from the Sage. It was so helpful that she then began to regularly use this method to ask the Sage, after pondering the meaning of a hexagram, "Have I understood the message correctly?" Without realizing it, the Sage had given her a way of not only clarifying the hexagram message, but enabling the Sage to develop new understandings.

While this method led to exciting new discoveries, the fact that it was not orthodox made Carol uneasy that it might not be correct to have such an easy access to the Sage. This doubt prompted her one day to ask the Sage, tossing ten coins for the answer, "Is this a correct method of consulting the Sage?" Nine of the ten coins came up heads. From that time on, she regularly used the method to create a dialog with the Sage.

When the coins indicated that she had not understood the message, it often meant that the Sage wanted to go beyond the narrower understanding implied in the Wilhelm text, which she regularly used at the time. The dialog then required her to propose hypotheses of what the text might mean. It was this use that led to calling the method, the "Retrospective-Three-Coin Method."

Much later, Carol happened to re-read Richard Wilhelm's

introduction to his translation of the *I Ching* and saw that the *I Ching* had developed from just such a method of putting Yes/No questions to the oracle.[1]

Through gaining experience with the method, Carol began to understand that it was used best when she gave the Sage space to explain the Cosmic view of an issue, which she came to understand was the "inner truth" of the matter. This inner truth showed why something was successful (because Cosmic Principles of Harmony were respected), or why it failed (because those principles were disregarded). Asking about why a person was going through difficulties such as sleeplessness, or anxiety, the Sage invariably pointed to the inner thoughts of that person as the cause, or to thoughts coming from people around him that were affecting him negatively. *Never* did the Sage point to the apparent external factors. This fact made her aware that the oracle's answers are always to the inner truth of situations, and that its hexagrams can only be understood correctly when taken in this light.

Through the use of this method, the Sage's messages were no longer a matter of guesswork. Upon experiencing that people began to use the *rtcm* independently of the *I Ching*, and finding that they were using it more to support their existing point of view than to communicate with the Sage, we initially recommended that they use the *rtcm* only to clarify the messages received from hexagrams. However, for the purposes of this book, the Sage answered Yes to using the *rtcm* independently of consulting the *I Ching* to investigate the causes of simple matters.[2] Throughout our use of this method, we need to be aware that the ego can interfere with our questioning process. When this is the case, the answers do not come from the Sage, but instead reflect the

---

1 Wilhelm, Richard, *I Ching*, In his Introduction, Wilhelm writes: At the outset, the Book of Changes was a collection of linear signs to be used as oracles. In antiquity, oracles were everywhere in use: the oldest among them confined themselves to the answers yes and no. This type of oracular pronouncement is likewise the basis of the Book of Changes. "Yes" was indicated by a simple unbroken line (—), and "No" by a broken line (- -). Page xlix.

2 We personally have developed the habit when investigating a matter to ask, "Do I need a hexagram for this purpose?" This practice has proved to be invaluable.

fears, hopes, doubts or preconceived ideas the ego is projecting into the toss of the coins. This creates the need to ask, at times, by tossing the coins, "Has the ego interfered in my questioning?" We will be addressing below the kinds of questions that come from the ego, and questions that lead to confusing answers, or that lead to the retreat of the Sage from the conversation. Investigating a major inner or outer conflict or a major health issue requires using our books, *I Ching, the Oracle of the Cosmic Way*, or *Healing Yourself the Cosmic Way*.

A Toss of Three Coins Can Yield Four Possible Answers:

* three heads, or Yes, Yes, Yes (+++), meaning a definitive Yes
* two heads, or Yes, Yes, No (++-), meaning a relative Yes
* three tails, or No, No, No (- - -), meaning a definitive No
* two tails, or No, No, Yes (- - +), meaning a relative No

For the sake of simplicity, we use the following shorthand when recording the Sage's answers: (+++), (++), (- - -), and (- -).

The Sage Leads Our Investigation

From beginning to end, we allow the Sage to lead our investigation in using the *rtcm*. The primary purpose of investigating is to understand the inner truth of a given problem. Once we find the causes, we then investigate what is necessary to correct it through deprogramming.

The three main phases of any investigation are: (1) Understanding the inner truth and/or the causes of disharmony; (2) Identifying the material for deprogramming, and (3) deprogramming the material found.

Investigating any matter of concern is never a mental process involving only the mind. In order to come to an understanding of the Cosmic perspective, our mind needs to keep in tune with our true feelings. This means that we make sure that our mind is open and receptive. (See below, "Getting Inwardly Prepared.") For the mind to be in a receptive mode also means to stop wanting to lead the investigation, as in looking for a culprit. The Sage is the one leading the way. We keep asking the Sage for guidance and help throughout the questioning process.

The conventional goal of investigating a disturbance, as for example, a conflict we are having with someone, is to attain an outer result (a 'happy ending' to the conflict, or to make a change that allows us to 'function better in the relationship.' By contrast, the Sage's ultimate goal is to help us (1) understand the cause of the conflict, and (2) to dissolve our attachment to the idea(s) that is the cause. The Sage is totally firm in leading us toward this goal, and no other. With each step taken toward the gradual dissolution of our attachment to the disharmonious ideas, we are lifted out of our present difficulties, and at the same time, we make progress on the path of returning to our true nature. The resolution of the conflict or other difficulty is a pleasant side effect in this process.

This description may give the reader who is inexperienced in this approach the impression that it will 'take forever' to get to a tangible result. On the contrary, we experience an instant feeling of relief upon seeing with clarity what has been causing our difficulty. The attainment of this inner clarity already takes us three-quarters of the way to resolving it. The remaining one-quarter is achieved through deprogramming the causes found. Failure to complete this last quarter increases the chance that the cause will be re-installed in our psyche.

Mistaken Beliefs that Block Our Understanding

The Sage cannot effectively help us when we are in the habit of looking up to famous people and spiritual leaders of the day. This is because we then interpret the Sage's words as confirming 'exactly' what those people have been saying 'all along.' The *I Ching* refers to these habits as "looking upward" for help and interpretation. The habit of looking outside ourselves for help comes from the mind under the domination of the ego, and causes us to miss the fact that our access to Cosmic help lies within us, and in our personal relationship with the Sage. This route is not to be equated with channeling, which, according to the Sage, happens when a person connects with the spirit of a dead person who has not yet been transformed. The connection with our personal Sage can only be made through asking for help sincerely from the heart, and through being open to what the Sage wants to show us. Each person's relationship with the Sage will be unique, and the Sage will communicate with him the way it works best for him.

Common Blocks to Undertaking Self-Examination

Investigating a disturbance requires that we go within. If the reader finds it difficult to do so, because it makes him feel guilty, he may first need to deprogram the mistaken idea that self-examination is "selfish," "self-indulgent," "silly," or "a waste of time." (Example: "You are not in this life to contemplate your navel.") Such expressions are spells that keep him within the group-we. Similar spells are phrases such as, "You are selfish if you don't support your group," "Loyalty to your family (country, family, class, race, etc.) comes first," or, "Loyalty requires personal sacrifice of your private views on behalf of your group." Such spells are accompanied by a guilt spell that adds, "You are guilty, if your first loyalty is not to the group," or, "You become guilty, if you do things that are selfish." These spells can inhibit us from questioning ideas and beliefs that are surrounded by taboos, or that have been pronounced as true by recognized wise people, or spiritual leaders.

What Are the Specific Uses of the RTCM in the Context of this Book?

We use it:
- to assess whether we will be able, simply through using the *rtcm*, to successfully identify the cause of a disturbance in the psyche, or a physical condition caused by that disturbance. (Example: "Can the simple use of the *rtcm* lead me to a good enough understanding of the cause of my loss of energy?" If No is the answer, we ask, "Do I need to consult *I Ching, The Oracle of the Cosmic Way?*" or, "Would I find a hint in *Healing Yourself the Cosmic Way?* (One can use the coins to identify the chapter and the exact section of the chapter.)

- to work with the Sage to discover the inner truth of a situation, and what we can do on the inner plane to correct it.
- to determine whether something we have been told to be true is actually true. This question needs to be asked especially when a prognosis is given. (Here, we need to be aware that the Sage does not simply replace a bad prognosis with a good one. It will say, "You have the potential to get well if you bring yourself into harmony with your nature.")
- to avoid merely assuming we have understood correctly
- to check whether we have been deluded by an ego-enthusiasm, such as when the ego has presented us with a "magic bullet," a once-and-for-all solution
- to investigate what has caused a disturbance and its source
- to determine which deprogramming method is appropriate for the particular cause
- to determine whether we need to correct our attitude toward the Sage or the Helpers, or to find any other obstructions that are blocking our communication with the Sage, or our engaging the Helpers. (See "Problematic Questions" below.)
- to ask what the No-answers we have received mean, as in, "Are you saying this (or that) by giving me a No answer?"

Getting Inwardly Prepared to Ask Questions with the RTCM

Before starting to toss three coins to get Yes/No answers to our questions, it is important to attain inner neutrality. Lack of neutrality unconsciously distorts the answers. These distortions come from preconceived ideas we already have about the way things work, a general skepticism, the desire (or fear) to hear a particular answer, or fears that the answer will require us to do something that would harm us.

Preconceived ideas often enter our questioning process unconsciously because the ego-mindset installed in us has a mechanism that automatically re-fits Cosmic concepts into the framework of our existing belief systems. Each belief system has its own frame of reference, making it possible for a person to come with more than one frame of reference. There will be a frame of reference for religion, the natural sciences, mythology, and New Age thinking, for example. They all have in common that they either keep our minds closed to learning from our inner truth (which is identical with Cosmic truth), or they quickly 'translate' the words of the Sage into the language of their preconceived ideas. To learn our inner truth by consulting the Sage, we need to temporarily suspend any and all of these frames of reference we come with. Suspending them does not mean giving them up. It simply means putting them aside, as if on a shelf, while we learn from the Sage. Failing to do this blocks the possibility of having a new experience, which means we remain caught in the very problem we want to resolve.

Carol remembers a time when she was new to the *I Ching*, and in attempting to understand it, she read other books that might throw a light on it. One of these was D. T. Suzuki's book, *Zen Buddhism*. Some of the ideas seemed to "explain" the *I Ching*. However, all her subsequent lessons with the *I Ching* carried the clear message about her "false enthusiasm" and the warning not to compare the *I Ching* with anything! She was to give the Sage clear room to speak for itself.

How to Suspend Our Frames of Reference

Before consulting the Sage, we ask the Cosmic Helpers to temporarily suspend all frames of reference that would prevent us from understanding what the Sage wants to show us about the inner truth of the matter at hand. The effect of this request lasts for about two days, after which it needs to be renewed.

The effect is temporary because it is not possible for us to give up mistaken beliefs that we have held valid until we have attained sufficient insight to realize they are invalid. Because of this, consulting the Sage is not suitable for everyone at a given time, especially when a person is dead-certain of his existing beliefs. In that case it is proper for him to go his own way.

Creating Inner Neutrality

To attain inner neutrality, we can do a short meditation (no more than ten minutes). First, we sit upright, in a comfortable position. We then close our eyes and ask the Helper of Mind Cleansing to clear our mind of any preconceived ideas of what the causes might be, and of any blame we may have assigned either to ourselves or to another person. Also, we ask the Cosmic Helpers "to suspend all frames of reference we come with." If, after ten minutes we still do not feel neutral enough, we do not proceed, because our questions would be coming from the ego, and the answers we receive would come from the same source. We can recognize non-neutrality by the way it feels: It drives, smolders, rages, or rants, or merely feels muddled. We can also ask the Sage to activate the Helpers needed and turn the matter over to them. We return to our meditation at a later time.

Keeping a Written Record of Our Questions and Answers

It is important to keep a written record of our questions and the answers received. This allows us to keep track of the questions we have asked so that we do not make the mistake of asking the same thing twice. It also allows us to review our questioning process in case we become confused, or lose track of the direction of our questioning.

The End of the Our Session with the Sage

The end is determined by asking, "Is this all I need to know now?" If the answer is Yes (++- or +++), we thank the Sage for the help received. If the answer is No, we ask the Sage for further clarification in a meditation or in a dream. If, however, we have the idea that we must continue in spite of being exhausted, the coins will say Yes to our question, because we are violating our commonsense. This happens when we possess a phrase in our psyche that causes us to regard the Sage as a master, or we believe modesty equals subservience, or because we have some false standard of perfection overriding our commonsense.

General Guidelines

A good way to use the *rtcm* is to follow the path laid out by questions that receive either ++ or +++ answers; this also means to avoid changing the subject, thus to deviate into new, uncharted paths. For example, if we have learned that the damaging thought was a conclusion we drew, it is not helpful to then ask if the damaging thought came from someone else. We also need to check periodically whether the ++ answer is leading us to the cause of the problem we are investigating, or is saying Yes only because our hypothesis is true, although not relevant to our issue. Therefore, we need to ask, when any hesitation enters our mind about an answer, "Was my question to the main point the Sage wants to make?" At all times our questioning needs to proceed toward the *main* point the Sage wants to make. We generally know when a question is beside the main point; nevertheless, the ego likes to pull us aside simply to satisfy curiosity. Such questions invariably lead to confusion.

The Sage communicates with us often in the form of hunches. Following these hunches is very valuable in using the *rtcm*. However, when we have been cut off from our feeling nature for many years because we doubt or do not trust it, practice at asking questions with the *rtcm* will be required before our ability to follow hunches returns to full strength. If we find the *rtcm* initially a bit difficult, we can temporarily free up this ability by saying No three times to the poison arrow, "You can't trust your feelings," or statements such as "thinking and feeling don't go together." We may need to repeat this procedure every time we find ourselves allowing our mind, rather than our feelings, to lead. To deprogram this poison arrow for good, we need to follow the instructions in Appendix 3, "Deprogramming."

Problematic Questions

- Questions about the future that imply it is a pre-written script cannot be answered by the Sage. This is because it is our attitudes and beliefs that shape our future. Attitudes based on disharmonious ideas lead to misfortune, while those that are in harmony with the Cosmos lead to success. Often such questions reflect hopes, which are attempts to counter doubt and fear. An example of a hope-based question is: "Am I going to get well?" The true answer to this question may be, "Yes, If you bring yourself into harmony with your nature," and not because it is written in the stars.

This entails finding the ego elements that are disturbing that harmony, and deprogramming them with Cosmic help. An example of a fear-based question is, "Am I going to be permanently disabled?" Such a question implies that no help is available from the Cosmos. The coins will only reflect our fear, since fear-based questions come from the ego and cannot be answered by the Sage.

- Questions that reflect our wanting assurances: "If I do this, will I have success?" This question can imply that we are seeking to make a deal with the Cosmos; in that case, the question slanders its self-respecting nature, and is against its integrity. If, however, we are asking this question from a sincere effort to gain a greater understanding about how the Cosmos functions, there is no problem. If we are unsure about our attitude, we can ask with the coins whether our question comes from the right place inside us.

- Questions that ask "Should I *do* such and such?" The Sage does not answer such questions directly. It first guides us to attain clarity. That means we may need to ask, "Is my goal in harmony with my inner truth?" If Yes, we may need to ask, "Is there anything in my attitude that needs to be corrected first?" In this case we may need to deprogram something. We need to keep aware that asking "should I do" questions can be motivated by doubting our commonsense. If, for example, we are angry with someone and think we should outwardly tell them what is wrong, we are ignoring that the situation first requires finding the inner truth of the matter and doing the necessary inner work to correct it. Then we will know whether an outer No also needs to be said. Inner responses avoid coming into conflict with the ego.

- Questions that reflect a slavish dependency on the Sage. The Sage does not answer questions that violate our commonsense. Example: "Is it time to get out of bed now?" or, "Should I eat such and such?"

- Questions that put our nature down, or are based on how we believe others may view us. Examples are "Am I a *bad* person?" or, "Is something wrong with me?" Such questions come from having adopted negative judgments about ourselves and from self-doubt. Such judgments are untrue and need to be deprogrammed as poison arrows.

- Cross-questioning (also called "begging the question") occurs when we ask the same question twice, either because we did not like the first answer, or doubted it. Or, we forgot that we already asked that question. When we beg the question, the Sage simply withdraws because the ego is doing the asking. If we recognize this might be the case, we can ask the Sage if we were begging the question. If we are sincere, the Sage will answer. We also beg the question when we ask a question that violates our commonsense, or what we already know through many experiences. When we receive answers that violate our commonsense, the Sage, through retreating, is saying, "Trust your commonsense!"
- Questions that arise from fears, such as the fear of being punished by the Sage for making a mistake, a belief that the Sage is difficult to communicate with, or that we might be communicating with the devil. Such fears can stop us from asking questions altogether. The Sage teaches us that making mistakes is part of the learning process. What counts is that we approach the Sage with sincerity and are willing to correct our mistakes.
- Questions that presume existing ideas or beliefs are true.
- Questions that seek the Sage to confirm our favorite beliefs, or actions we desire to take, or have already decided to take. In asking such questions we are not neutral.

Helpful Questions to Check Where We Are in Our Questioning Process:

- "Am I still on the track that leads to the main point?"
- "Is there more I need to understand in this matter, now?"
- "Do I need to look for something to deprogram?"
- "Is it time to proceed to the deprogramming?"

Receiving Confusing Answers

Receiving confusing answers indicates that we are stuck in

our questioning process. At this point, we stop to find out what has caused this situation. The Sage will help us clarify the cause. Here are possible questions we can ask:

- "Does my question contain an incorrect presumption that prevents me from understanding the Sage's answer?" (An example is when we ask the Sage what needs to be done, based on thinking that all help involves external procedures. The Cosmic Way is to correct things first and foremost on the inner plane, in the realm of consciousness. Usually, this is sufficient to end the difficulty.)
- "Have the answers been coming from the ego because my questions were inspired by the ego?" (If we receive a Yes we can go back over each answer to ask which ones have been coming from the ego.)
- "Have I used a word in my question that has no Cosmic basis?" Sometimes we use a word that would mislead us. (If Yes, we need to look for ideas or words in our question that we take for granted as true. We can ask the Sage, pointing to each word, if an incorrect presumption is involved.) Examples are words such as special, evil, or culprit.
- "Is my approach too mental or mechanical?" If Yes, we ask, "would it help to ask the Sage to bring helpful questions to mind?"
- "Is it better to stop asking questions, and do something else, such as sleep on it, or meditate and ask for help?"
- "Would it be helpful to ask the Sage to activate the Helpers needed to unblock the situation?"
- "Would it be helpful to ask the Sage for a dream?"
- "Is there any hint to be found in this book that would help me now?" If so, use the *rtcm* to narrow down the page, paragraph, or sentence.
- "Is there an obstruction in my attitude?" (See possible obstructions below.)

Among such obstructions are the following:

- Having doubts about the answer, even before asking.
- Having already decided to do something, then asking the Sage just to get a confirmation.

- Presuming that the Sage will protect us from harm no matter what. (We are protected by the Cosmos only as long as we are sincere in our efforts to correct ourselves.)
- Is a demonic element (demon, dragon, or imp) causing the obstruction?

Here are some examples:

- a dragon of fear of what the Sage is going to say. This will only cause the coins to reflect the fear; the answer, therefore, does not come from the Sage.
- an imp of idle curiosity is active, causing the Sage to retreat.
- an imp, demon, or dragon of "knowing better"
- an imp, demon, or dragon of impatience
- an imp, or dragon of ambition
- an imp, or dragon of spirituality

To free yourself from these demonic elements, see the instructions given in Appendix 3, "Deprogramming." Then apologize to the Sage without ceremony, and refrain from blaming yourself or thinking the Sage has abandoned you because you have "been bad," or are "undeserving of the Sage's help." The ideas behind these views need to be seen as belonging to the collective ego, and deprogrammed. This work on yourself corrects the mistake.

What "No" Answers Can Mean

Getting two "No's" for an answer can mean:

- "no to your hypothesis"
- "your question is going in the wrong direction"
- "I cannot answer your question because it contains a word that has no Cosmic basis"
- "I cannot answer your question with a simple Yes or No answer because it would create a misunderstanding; the answer requires a hexagram to show you the subject of your question from the Cosmic perspective"
- "Your question is coming from the ego in you" (meaning it is coming from an incorrect attitude"; see the possibilities listed under "Problematic Questions" above)

A toss of three tails, (meaning No, No, No) can be saying:
• a full and complete "No"
• "You have asked that question already and now are importuning by trying to get a Yes answer"
• "You are allowing the ego to make you doubt the answer I have already given you"
• "Your question is off the main track indicated"

In all cases, we can ask the Sage, "Does your No answer mean any one of these possibilities?" We then clarify which of them applies.

When we receive a whole series of "No" answers, it may mean that the Sage is trying to get something through to us that is outside all the possibilities we now have in mind. When this is the case, we need to stop asking questions and ask the Sage to help us ask the helpful question. A short meditation can bring this question to mind. We then ask if this is the point the Sage wants to make.

A series of "No" answers can also mean that the Sage has retreated. We can ask directly whether that is the case, and the Sage will answer that question. The Sage retreats when we have an attitude of superiority or arrogance, as when we treat the Sage as a servant that can be commanded, or we have an attitude of knowing better. The Sage also retreats when we become ambitious, as in seeking to be the "most spiritual." Once we become aware of a mistake and correct our attitude, the Sage is once more available to us.

Appendix 2
Investigating a Disturbance

It would surpass the scope of this book to show how to investigate and heal a multi-layered psychological disorder. Doing so takes experience in using the methods outlined in this book, and time. The goal of this section is rather to give some general guidelines for investigating a relatively simple matter of psychological concern, and to provide examples of investigations.

Chips containing traumatic memories often are the cause of psychological disturbances over which the mind has no control.

The possible causes for any matter of psychological concern are many, and they can be intertwined in different ways in different people. However, in all instances, we look for them in the realm of demonic consciousness created by the ego, and not as lying in the person's nature. The goal is to identify these causes (in the form of phrases, images, self-images, and/or demonic elements, including ego-complexes) so that we can deprogram them in a second step. Deprogramming them with Cosmic help removes them once and for all from our psyche, body, or brain, wherever they had been stored. The longer a person has been suffering from a psychological disturbance, the more things may have been added to its original cause, such as:

(a) guilt for having the disturbance

(b) doubt that it will be possible to free ourselves from the disturbance through deprogramming with Cosmic help

(c) heroic self-images based on the disturbance

(d) prognoses regarding the possibility of freeing oneself from the disturbance

(e) a spell in the form of the name given the disturbance, if that name merely describes its symptoms

(f) coping mechanisms (ODE's)

(g) conclusions drawn due to the disturbance

Although relatively simple psychological issues are usually not surrounded by all the above-mentioned elements, some of them may apply, which is the reason why we have listed them here.

315

All that apply need to be deprogrammed *in the order described above, before we can successfully deprogram the actual cause(s).* The reason for this procedure is that the elements mentioned under (a-g) have formed a defensive wall around the original cause(s). We can look at them as forming a kind of computer program that has self-protective features. If not dealt with first, these elements would re-install the causes after we have deprogrammed them. In fact, certain demonic elements connected with guilt or doubt are activated when the program is threatened. This is why we need to pay close attention to them as part of our deprogramming effort.

The Result of Doing an Investigation and Deprogramming the Causes of a Disturbance

The successful completion of an investigation and the deprogramming connected with it transforms the situation from within. The ego-elements that created the disturbance are discredited and removed with Cosmic help.[1]

Transformations show themselves in myriad ways: The person feels relieved and released from an inner prison; a person who normally does no small acts of kindness suddenly does them; a person's viewpoint has suddenly become moderate and fair; an outer conflict receives no more fuel. In sum, the transformation that has taken place feels phenomenal, and, unlike the result of mere external changes, it results in an enduring solution. The Sage discourages us from calling it a miracle because it is the ordinary way the Cosmos works.

"No Blame"

The words "no blame" are frequently used in the *I Ching* to indicate that the purpose of an investigation is not to find out 'who is to blame' for the difficulty we are experiencing, *but to free ourselves from blame.*

When we realize that the issues we are investigating are due to childhood conditioning and traumas that all of us have ex-

---

1 See Hexagram 64, *Before Completion*. This hexagram makes clear that we can only go so far in our efforts to correct a situation. At this point, we need to call on the Helper of Transformation to complete our work.

perienced, there is no real blame to be found. Regret might be a more proper word. Thus, we are not looking for who is to blame, but for understanding. This kind of understanding is attained when we look at the negative things that happened to us in "the yellow light of moderation," as compared to the "harsh white light of judgment."[2] Further, it is important not to be afraid of finding the causes in thoughts or actions that originated either in ourselves or in those closest to us, such as our parents. We need to remember that they, too, were subjected to the same kinds of harmful conditioning, and possess(ed) the same kinds of demonic elements in their psyche that we find in ourselves. Finding these causes leads us ultimately to the wisdom we would like to see operating in the world. While we do not blame them, we also do not excuse them, or in any way accept behavior that is not in harmony with the Cosmos. Doing this would only increase the energy of the collective ego, since acceptance or accommodation of incorrect behavior enables what we see as "evil in the world." We say a firm inner No to such behaviors and thereby strengthen the true self in people.

The *I Ching* makes it clear that making mistakes is part of our learning process, and has to do with the fact that our thinking mind is the most inexperienced of all the aspects that make up our personality. Like a good teacher, the Cosmos wants us to learn from our experiences, and does not hold our mistakes against us. In fact, a mistake can sometimes provide a profound lesson, and be the source we need for further growth.

As long as we are willing to correct our thinking, we receive the help we need to learn these lessons and to carry out the necessary corrections. When we are unwilling to do so, we isolate ourselves from Cosmic protection and help by our own free will.

The reader who is inexperienced in the approach presented here will inevitably make mistakes during his questioning process. However, his sincere desire to understand what the Sage wants to point out will compensate for this deficiency and bring the Sage's help. Therefore, we need not have blame or shame for what, in the end, can greatly promote our progress

---

2 See Hexagram 30, *Attaining Clarity*, Line 2.

Investigating a Psychological Problem on Behalf of Another Person

Investigating a psychological problem on behalf of someone else is basically permissible. The restriction is that we need to respect that person's integrity and dignity, meaning our motivation to help must not come from the ego in us, as when we suffer from a 'helper syndrome,' or when we want a person to 'change' in order to satisfy our ego desires, or when we seek to gain power over him. We may also need to respect his decision to allow the ego to rule his life. If the person has openly declared that this is his decision, any interference on our part would be coming from the ego in us. This increases the ego in both. Likewise, any attempt to explain things to a person dominated by the ego only gives energy to the egos involved. Instead, we withdraw into inner neutrality and allow the Cosmos to take care of the situation.

In cases where no such open declaration has been made, we need to ask the Sage whether it is correct to help a person become free from a psychological problem. If so, the investigation and the resulting deprogramming may be carried out with or without that person's knowledge. (See the examples below.) In all these cases, the goal is to bring that person one step closer to his true nature with the help of the Sage and the other Helpers.

If, in doing this work on behalf of another person, we need to find a specific phrase stored in his psyche, we can actually ask the "Finding Helper" in our own psyche to bring that phrase to mind. This is possible thanks to an inner connection the Sage creates between us and the other person.

General Guidelines

The first question is: "Can I investigate the issue at hand only with the help of the *rtcm*?" If the answer is Yes (two or three heads), proceed according to the guidelines given below. Feel free to reverse the order of the steps, if that feels appropriate.

Step 1: *What? Identify the actual harmful cause*
Do I need to look for a phrase? Or, do I need to look for an

image, or a self-image? Or, do I need to look for a demonic element or a chip?

If the harmful element is a phrase and/or image, and does not come to mind easily, you can ask the Finding Helper of your psyche, in a short meditation, to bring it to mind. When you have inwardly heard the phrase, or seen the image, verify with the *rtcm* that it, indeed, is the phrasing or image you are seeking, and whether it is sufficiently identified. Then ask if there is more to find in regard to the cause. If the answer is yes, it usually refers to a related phrase or image.

If the cause is a demonic element, find out whether it is an imp, demon, or dragon, an ODE[3], a changeling[4], or an ego-complex.[5]

If the cause is a chip, identify the kind of chip involved (microchip, memory chip, ego chip, birth chip, conception chip, or stop chip). Then see "Identifying a Chip" at the end of Chapter 20 for suggestions as to what components to look for in a chip.

Step 2: *From Whom? Identify the Source of the Cause*

If you are the source, you can go to the next question below. If the source is someone else, start with those closest to you: Is it a member of my family? If not: A friend? Someone from work? Or, is it a group? The culture I belong to? Or, is it from something I have read? Heard on the radio? Seen on TV? In rare cases, the source can also be a dead person who is still clinging through some unfinished business, or to whom you are still attached. Sometimes, it is easier to remember the kinds of negative things that were either expressed, or thought, once you have identified their source.

Step 3: *When? The time element*

It may be helpful to find out when the cause was created. You can start with questions such as, "Is it an old item?" "Did it happen recently?" The following possibilities exist: at conception; *in utero*; at birth; 0-10 years old; 11-20, 21-30, etc, up to the present

3 Examples of ODE's are given in Chapter 16.
4 Examples of changelings are given in Chapter 12.
5 Examples of ego-complexes are given in Chapter 13.

time. It helps to pin it down to the exact year by asking further questions. Once you have identified the year, the upsetting thing often comes quickly to mind, along with the conclusions you drew from it, and the damaging things people may have said about you at the time.

Examples of Investigating Situations

Doubting the Answers Received

When Tom attended one of our seminars we noticed that he was constantly doubting the answers he received through the *rtcm*, which led to his receiving confusing answers. To understand the cause of his doubt, he asked these questions:

Is the cause to be found in a phrase? (++) After asking his Finding Helper, he came up with the phrase, "You will never be good enough." (++) Do I need to look for any other cause? (- -)

Tom clearly recognized this phrase as having come from his father, so there was no need to look for another source.

A Sudden Bad Mood

A woman in her early twenties sought our help to understand her periodic mood changes. We helped her ask the following questions:

Do I need to look for a phrase? (- -) Is the cause a DDI? (- -) Is the cause a fear? (++) Does the fear come from a source outside of me? (+++) From a particular person? (- -) From something I read in the paper? (- -) From something I saw on TV? (++) Was it the advertisement for the XYZ drug? (++)

The woman deprogrammed: (1) the image of the depressed looking woman used in the ad, (2) the message that bad moods are typical for the days that precede menstruation, and (3) her fear of "being stuck with this condition until she would come into her menopause."

A Headache Caused by Guilt

Dora had noticed that every time she did things purely for

herself, she would get a headache. To get to the root of the matter, she asked these questions:

Is the source for the guilt to be found in me? (- -) Is it to be found in a member of my family? (+++) My mother? (++) Anyone else besides her? (- -) Do I need to look for a phrase? (- -) A chip? (++) Is it a memory chip? (++) Is it also a microchip? (++) Was it created when I was ten years or younger? (- -) Between eleven and twenty? (++) Fifteen or under? (++) Was I fifteen? (++) Does it have to do with my running away from home to live with my boyfriend? (++) (At this point, Dora was able to recollect her mother's words):

"How dare you run away!"

"We were worried to death!"

"Don't ever do that again!"

Then Dora asked with the *rtcm*, "Is there anything else my mother said that needs to be added?" (- -) Is guilt stored in the chips? (+++) Is anything else stored in the chips? (++) A fear on my part? (- -) Anger on my part? (++) A conclusion I drew? (- -) Is there anything else I need to look for? (++) An ego-emotion? (++) Resentment? (++) Is there anything else I need to look for? (- -)

To prepare her findings for deprogramming, Dora asked: Is there a changeling connected with any of the chips? (- -) Do both chips contain all the same components? (- -)

She then went over the list of her findings with the *rtcm* and sorted out which of the components belonged in the memory chip, and which belonged in the microchip. Then she asked: Can I use the same deprogramming method for both chips? (- - -) For the memory chip, do I use the "water-meditation?" (- -) The "fire-meditation?" (++) For the microchip, do I use the "water-meditation?" (++)

Looking into a Cause of Sleeplessness

John, an executive in his mid-forties, wanted to get to the root of a habit that caused him a lot of sleeplessness before corporate meetings: he found himself constantly preparing mentally for what he was going to say in response to possible questions. The

Sage had indicated that he did not need a hexagram to find the cause. Here are the questions John asked with the *rtcm*:

Is the cause to be found in a phrase? (++) (John closed his eyes and asked the Finding Helper in his psyche to bring the phrase to mind.) Is it the phrase, "You don't know anything unless you are prepared?" (++) Would it be helpful to find out when I took that phrase into my psyche? (- -) Would it be helpful to next find out the source of that phrase? (++) Did it come from school? (- -) from college? (- -) from a book I read? (++) (John identified the book.) Do I need to look for any other cause? (++) Another phrase? (++) From the same book? (++) Is it the phrase, "To avoid humiliation, you need to have an answer?" (++) Is there anything else I need to look for from that book? (- -) Do I need to look for any other cause? (- - -)

Noticing a Sudden Personality Disturbance in a Child

A 3-1/2 year-old girl, Madeleine, had returned from her grandparents where she had spent the Christmas holidays. Her mother noticed a sudden change in Madeleine's personality that caused her concern. After a temper tantrum, her mother said to her, "This is not the Madeleine I know." Madeleine had an immediate fear reaction and was extremely upset, begging her mother, "Don't send me away!" Her mother realized that Madeleine had taken her very literally, concluding that "since mommy doesn't know me anymore, she'll give me away." The extreme reaction and change in her personality surprised her mother, causing her to ask us to investigate the cause.

We put the following questions to the Sage:

Do we need a hexagram to understand the cause of the sudden change in Madeleine's personality? (- -)

Did the grandparents say, "If you don't behave we'll send you away." (+++)

Did they also say, "This is not the Madeleine I know." (++)

Did she interpret it that they would give her to a stranger? (++)

Has she developed an ego-complex? (- -)

Has she changed her personality because she thinks that will protect her? (+++) Is this new personality triggered by the words,

"This is not the Madeleine I know"? (+++)
Does it simply need to be deprogrammed? (- -)
Do we need to understand it more? (++) Did she draw false conclusions because of the phrase, "this is not the Madeleine I know"? (++) about herself as being defective? (++) Has anyone else supported that conclusion in her? (- -)
Is there anything else they said that intensified her fear? (++) another threat? (- -) guilt? (- -) blame? (++) Did they say she was a bad girl? (++) Did they say what would happen to bad girls? (- -) Is there more they said that we need to know? (++) Did they actually punish her in some way? (- -) Did they say, "You are horrible?" (++) "Nobody will want you like that." (+++)

Did Madeleine conclude that she would be sent out to a stranger who also would not want her so that she would be all alone? (++) Did she put the spell on herself: "I have to become someone else?" (++)

Do we need to know what she did to cause the grandparents to say these things to her? (++)

Did she want to do something and they wouldn't allow it? (++)

Did it have to do with touching her genitals? (+++) anything else? (+++)

Did she conclude it is terrible to do that? (++)

Doing something else with her body? (++) go without clothes? (- -) would her mother know what that is? (++)

Was all this from the grandmother? (++) Did anything come from the grandfather? (- -)

Would this be the beginning of an ODE if not deprogrammed? (++) Is that ODE the doubter? (++)

(The Doubter creates the ego. It haunts the psyche, saying, "You are not good enough," causing all kinds of problems in the psyche. See Chapter 11, "The Darkening of the Light.")

Extracting what needed to be deprogrammed
What the grandmother said after Madeleine touched her genitals:
• The spell, projection, and poison arrow: "You are a bad girl;

if you don't behave we'll send you away."
* The projection and poison arrow: "This is not the Madeleine I know."
* The spell: "You are horrible."
* The spell: "Nobody will want you like that."
  Madeleine's conclusions to be deprogrammed:
* "They will give me to a stranger."
* The spell created by seeing herself as being defective: "Something is wrong with me."
* A self-blame spell and projection to the effect, "I am to blame because I touched myself."
* The spell and projection: "I will be sent away; nobody will want me and I will be all alone."
* The decision that changing herself to be someone else would protect her, created the spell, "I have to become someone else."

Helping Madeleine to process public attitudes about sexuality at age 3-1/2

The question arises, what would have been the Cosmic way to help Madeleine realize that touching her genitals is not a public thing to do?

One way would be for her mother to explain to her, "Every family has a different way of seeing things. Your grandparents see things as good or bad. We don't think that way. Your body is not bad. No one's body is bad. But, because they think that way, it is best not to touch your body when you are with them."

As a result of this investigation, and the ensuing processing and deprogramming, all changes in Madeleine's personality ceased and she returned to her normal self within a very short time.

Understanding Strange Behavior in a Partner

Beth's partner approached us to achieve an understanding as to why Beth, a woman in her thirties, tended to force her way when she felt obstructed. The Sage gave us permission to investigate the issue with her partner's help. We asked:

Is Beth doing this from a self image? (- -) From a pact she made with herself at some time? (- -) Is it an ego-complex?

(+++) Is it something that comes from her youth? (++) We learned that it was a complex not known to us. With the Sage's help we identified it as the "You-Have-to-Elbow-Your-Way" Complex. We then found that this complex was based on these spells: "You have to be vigorous in standing your ground!" "You have to use your elbows in life." "You have to fight for your place in life."

To find out where the roots of the complex were to be found, we asked: Was it *in utero*? (+++) Knowing this, we did not need to seek further. This caused Beth's partner to suggest that she had been a possible twin, which the Sage confirmed. We then asked, "Is it that Beth wanted to get the twin out of her space?" (++) This was the extent of the complex. Her partner, after asking the Sage if it was a correct thing to do and getting (+++), deprogrammed the complex for her.

Understanding the Meaning of a Dream

Example 1: A blockage on the path of returning

I, Hanna, was driving a car on a dirt path that led away from the main road. The path led downhill. At some point, I realized I had to get back onto the main road, and thought of putting the car in reverse gear. It was getting dark. A man was sitting next to me. As I started backing up, the man said there was a log on the dirt path behind me and that I could not simply drive over it. I thought it would be best to turn the car around so that I could see better what was in my way. However, the car started rolling downhill, and the brakes were not working properly. Actually, I could not tell anymore whether the car was rolling forward or backward, but in any case, it was out of control.

Hanna asked: Is the dream about me? (++) Does the car stand for the Helpers of my body? (- -) Does the car have something to do with my psyche?++ Can one say that the downward leading dirt path was a 'slippery slope?' (++) Was I trying to return to the path of my Cosmic destiny (the main road)? (++) Did the log stand for a spell that was blocking my ability to return? (++) (Hanna then asked the Finding Helper in her psyche to bring the spell to mind.) The phrase was, "There is no way to

roll things back. All you can do is go forward." (++) Do I need
to identify anything else that needs to be deprogrammed? (- -)
Hanna realized that the 'man' sitting next to her had been helpful by making her aware of the log she was unable to see in her
rear view mirror. Was the man the Sage? (- -) Was it a Helper
of my psyche? (++) The Helper of Remorse? (++) Was the
spell blocking the remorse function in my psyche? (+++) The
remorse function automatically puts one back into accord with
the Cosmos. The spell represented by the log, had blocked this
function by making her feel she could not "back up" to correct
her mistake.

Example 2: Discovering a microchip

In 2004, Hanna had this dream: I was at a convention. At
first, it reminded me of the convention of the Liberal Party in
Germany in my early twenties; the scene then blended into a
women's convention that seemed to be about women's rights.
Women were being asked to volunteer to sit on the board. At
first, I held back, but after almost all the seats were taken, I came
forward because I thought, "I should." Immediately, one of the
women on the board leaned over to me, and said, "That means,
of course, that you will be supporting my position?" I was taken
aback by her approach, and did not say yes or no.

To understand the message of the dream Hanna asked the
following questions: Does the dream want to make me aware
of something in my psyche that needs to be deprogrammed?
(++) Did I put it on myself? (++) In the last ten years? (++) (She
found that it was in 2002, the year when *I Ching, The Oracle of
the Cosmic Way*, came out.) Did it have something to do with
the publication of that book? (++) Did it have something to do
with my understanding of 'taking position' in the sense of taking a stance? (++) Do I need to look for a spell? (++) Hanna's
Finding Helper brought the phrase to mind, "I must make up
my mind." (+++) Was this spell created when the Sage made
me aware that the time had come to make a decision whether I
wanted to live in the Cosmic reality or in the parallel reality of
the collective ego? (+++) Is there more I need to understand
about this spell? (++) About its effect on my mind? (++) Did it

create the image in my mind that making that decision meant taking a stance in opposition to the collective ego? (++) Do I understand it correctly that the ego interfered at that decisive moment in order to keep opposition going? (+++) Are any other ego-elements involved in this? (++) Is it a chip? (++) A memory chip? (- -) A microchip? (++) (Hanna was puzzled, because a microchip is stored in the body, not in the mind. But then it occurred to her that the mind also has a physical aspect.) Is it a microchip that was stored in the cells of my mind? (++) Did it activate the image of opposition when I compared myself with people who did not use the *I Ching*? (++)

Hanna was shocked to learn that she had fallen into this ego-trap; she had assumed she was protected from falling into such traps. While the Sage did not protect her from falling into that trap, through the dream, it made her aware of the danger so that she could free herself from the chip.

Using the Method of "Asking Your Inner Senses of Perception" in Combination with the RTCM[6]

This method involves our five *inner* senses of perception, which are: our inner senses of smell, taste, sound, sight, and feeling. We possess these inner senses to tell us the inner truth of a matter, be it in the form of a word, a phrase, an image, or an emotional influence active in a situation.

Hanna wanted to investigate what was causing her eyes to water whenever she walked out into the slightest cold. She sat down to do a meditation with the help of her inner senses of perception. The Sage confirmed that all five senses were free and could be included in the investigation. She asked each sense for its perception, and received the following answers:

- How does it smell? — "Awful."
- How does it taste? — "A bitter experience."
- How does it sound? — "Unheard of," and "fast."
- What does it look like? — The image was that of piles of rubble after the bombings of World War II. A few women and children were standing forlorn between the rubble.

---

6 Also see Appendix 4, "Exercises."

• How does it feel? — "Like an entangled ball of thread."
Hanna then used the *rtcm* to identify more precisely what she had learned:

Is this pointing to something I experienced in Germany soon after the war? (++) Is it contained in a chip? (++) Was it when I was 3-4 years old? (++) Do I need to look for anything my parents said? (++) Both parents? (- -) Only my mother? (+++)

Hanna asked the Helper of that stored memory to bring her mother's words to mind. The words came, "That they made us leave (Czechoslovakia) is a bitter experience." And, "It is unheard of to make us leave the country so fast, within 48 hours." Hanna found that these were the words that needed to be deprogrammed. There was nothing else her mother had said.

She then identified the feeling that was stored in the chip as *confusion* (the 'entangled ball of thread').

She further asked whether she needed to identify anything she had put on herself at the time. (++) She found the words, "I must be brave now." "I must not cry."

She asked whether any other content of the chip needed to be identified, and received (- -).

Next, Hanna needed to find out what kind of chip this had formed: Was it a memory chip? (- -) A microchip? (- -) An ego chip? (++) The fact that it was an ego chip made her realize that it had contributed to forming a family identity — that of being a member of a refugee family.* She then assembled the following components of the ego chip for deprogramming:

• the image of women and children lost among the rubble
• her mother's words, "That they made us leave is a bitter experience." "It is unheard of to make us leave the country so fast, within 48 hours."
• the feeling of confusion
• the phrases she had put on herself, "I must be brave now." "I must not cry."

One changeling was guarding this ego chip.

*This identification with a refugee family explained to Hanna the fact that she had lived a kind of 'nomadic' life. She had never, for any extended period of time, created her 'own home.'

Appendix 3
Deprogramming

Deprogramming is essential to freeing the mind, psyche, and body from the conditioning that creates and maintains the ego. Its primary purpose is to restore our wholeness. It requires saying a firm No to the phrases and images that create and maintain mistaken ideas, beliefs, self-images and demonic elements of all sorts. It also requires Cosmic help. We will give a list of Helpers needed for deprogramming.

Deprogramming is not to be thought of as something we do for a month or two and then are finished. It is something we do, like good daily housecleaning, to remove dust, dirt, and disorder, even from the dark corners of our mind and psyche. It is true that by nature we are protected from disharmonious thoughts and ego-emotions, even those coming from outside; however, conditioning has created holes in this protection, so that disharmonious thoughts enter without our notice. Additional holes have been created by chips that contain stored traumatic memories. These trigger ego-reactions in us to what others say and do.

We also receive harmful thoughts and ego-reactions from others. This is a sign that we have either entertained harmful thoughts about them, to which they are reacting, or that we have adopted a self-image that invites the ego in them to attack the ego in us. For example, a self-image in us of being inferior invites the ego in another to take advantage of us. Deprogramming involves identifying and freeing ourselves from these harmful things.

Indeed, when we begin this inner housecleaning, we may find the house full of trash. After all, trash that has not been cleaned out accumulates year after year, causing both emotional and physical problems. Returning our inner house to order may, in fact, require months or even longer, but all the while we do this work, we become more unburdened, with joy returning to our lives. The starting point for returning is always an obstruction, or a conflict, or a problem of some sort. They are giving us the message that it is necessary to begin to look for their cause.

Deprogramming is a way of removing everything that does not belong in our inner house. Doing so frees up our Cosmic possessions, which have been abused by the ego. If we have suffered a burnout, or find our life full of problems, this is the time to investigate the causes. It is neither necessary nor desirable, when things are going well, to look for things to deprogram. Deprogramming is not to be tackled ambitiously. Ambition indicates that the ego has taken over both our introspection and our deprogramming. When the ego leads the way, it protects itself. Furthermore, it falsely makes us see the Sage, which we think is helping us, into a taskmaster.

At the end of the day we may want to spend a few minutes reflecting on whether disharmonious thoughts and feelings are present. If we met someone during the day, how did we feel? Was it clear and nourishing, or disappointing? If the latter, we can ask the Sage, through the *rtcm*, if we need to investigate the matter further. If so, "Did I feel better or lesser than they? Did they make me feel inferior, or flattered?" If, by investigating with the *rtcm*, we find that an ego-element was involved, we deprogram these elements. We also deprogram the cause of a sudden pain or a negative emotion, such as a bad mood. All this is done with the Sage's and the Helpers' help.

Deprogramming Harmful Thoughts We Have of Others

As part of our self-respect, we make sure not to harm others. Such harm occurs when we put projections, judgments, blame, condemnations, fears, or doubts on them, or when we entertain ego-emotions, such as resentment, envy, or hatred. Examples: "He is hopeless," or using words such as "villain," or "culprit," or "insensitive," "uncaring," "selfish," or "too proud" or "stuck" to describe them. Indeed, all these descriptions may apply to the ego that is dominating them, but by judging them as such, we are making statements about their *nature*, and thereby are fixing them in those behaviors. On seeing such behavior, it is important to say an inner No to it and ask the Cosmos to come to their aid. As soon as we become aware that we have put a harmful thought or ego-emotion onto another, we can deprogram them; doing so with Cosmic help undoes any negative effects these things have caused the other even in the past!

What Do We Mean by Deprogramming?

What basically happens in deprogramming is this: Saying a firm inner No to a phrase or image that is untrue deletes a previous Yes we have said to it. Even if we do not remember having accepted that phrase or image consciously, the fact that it is in our psyche is proof that we took it in by some sort of agreement. Taking things in by default amounts to saying Yes to them. This is true for many commonly accepted ideas and beliefs we are taught in childhood that are actually in conflict with our true nature. Saying an inner No has the effect of reversing our former acceptance, much the way a "–1" in mathematics eliminates a "+1."

We wish to emphasize that deprogramming works best when we say the inner No to a phrase that is as much as possible in its original wording. Otherwise the mathematical equation may remain incomplete. Also, it is best to build the habit of saying No to phrases in this way: "No" to, "I am a failure," rather than stating, "I reject being a failure," or, "I am not a failure."

Deprogramming, as we describe it here, initiates the transformations that are needed to remove the harmful phrases, images, ego-complexes, chips, etc., from our psyche for all time.

Over the years, the Sage has shown us different methods of deprogramming. Some people have dismissed the methods as "too complicated," and have said that it should be only a matter of saying No. However, the Sage has explained that this attitude is actually immodest and lacking in sincerity, and therefore does not engage the Helpers.

Deprogramming on Behalf of Others

While the primary purpose of deprogramming is to bring oneself back to wholeness, and to maintain that wholeness, we also have occasions when we deprogram things for other people. This is especially so for children, or the ill, or persons who lack the knowledge or energy to do it for themselves. We can assume that this is true for children. For adults, we need to ask the Sage if it is appropriate. If we get No for an answer, we need to remember that the Sage's answers are always relevant to the time of our asking. It is No for now, or for this particular situation. The Sage may answer No when a person is so rigidly set in his mind, that he needs to experience his fate to burn out on the idea or belief that has caused the fate.

Parents need to deprogram whatever negative attributes they have assigned to their children, however late in life that is.

We can always ask for Cosmic help to protect and heal children we hear about who are being abused. As for the abusers, we need to ask the Sage whether we are meant to deprogram anything on their behalf. Sometimes, the Sage makes us aware that the fates such people create need to run their course.

The Sage's Role in the Deprogramming Process

In all matters of deprogramming we need to ask the Sage via the *rtcm* to guide us (1) to determine the phrasing of a statement we want to deprogram; (2) to indicate the most appropriate method to use (fire, water, shredder, etc., as described below); (3) to find which Helpers are needed to make it successful, and (4) to know when we may discontinue our deprogramming effort.

Note: The deprogramming methods suggested below are from our personal experience and have been successful both for ourselves and the people who have worked with us. We are sure that there are other methods that fit the needs of one person more than another. People need to check with the Sage whether the method they want to use is suitable for this purpose.

Deprogramming as a Combined Effort Between Our Hearts and Minds

Deprogramming cannot be carried out in a ritualistic way that excludes our feelings. This is because Cosmic Helpers only respond to feelings; they are not able to respond to a purely mental or mechanical approach. For this reason, rituals are counter-productive.

The Helpers Needed to Make Our Deprogramming Successful

Deprogramming requires the aid of certain Helpers of our nature as well as Cosmic Helpers. They are referred to in the *I Ching* as "friends," and "specialists in their fields."

The following is a list of such Helpers that may be needed to make your deprogramming efforts successful. We ask the Sage which Helpers we need in each case. Although we give a long list, only a few of these may be needed. The most usual ones are listed first: The Sage, our Personal Helper of Deprogramming, the Cosmic Helpers (unspecific), the Cosmic Army, the Helper of Transformation, the Cosmic Doctor, the Cosmic Surgeon, our Health Helpers, our Feeling Manager, the Helper of Dissolution, the Helper that Cleanses Our Psyche, the Helper that Cleanses our Body, our Personal Helper, the Helper of Freeing, the Helpers of Inner Truth, the Helper that Ends Fate, the Helper that Removes Self-Images, the Helper that Breaks Spells, the Helper that Removes Poison Arrows, the Helper that Removes Projections, the Helper that Kills Imps, the Helper that Kills Demons, the Helper that Kills Dragons. When we are unable to identify the appropriate Helpers, we can ask the Sage to bring the Helpers needed, without needing to know their names.

Other Helpful Means to Free Ourselves from Ego-Aspects

In the early days before we knew about what we now call deprogramming, Carol frequently received Hexagram 50, *The Ting*. She understood that it pointed to "sacrificing" something that was causing obstructions in her life. In a meditation she understood that this referred, at the time, to anger that had been stored up over the years. She saw herself putting the anger on a Cosmic altar, whereupon it quickly disappeared. Furthermore, she noticed the great relief she felt on becoming entirely free of it. Not long after, when she was to sacrifice a number of ego-emotions, she found that the altar disappeared and was replaced with a "Cosmic dumpster" that was big enough to hold her emotional trash. In another meditation, in which she had seen her inner house as quite dirty, she was given a "Cosmic vacuum cleaner," which she then used to clean out all troubling thoughts

and "daily trash" in her mind, The benefit of these homey men
tal devices was enormous. When, much later, her two-year-old
granddaughter came to live with her for several years, and suffered from nightmares, Carol would have her granddaughter
imagine that her head had "cellar doors" that opened up, and
Carol would vacuum out all the horrible images, while making
the "whooshing" noise of a vacuum sweeping up dirt. Immediately, all the images disappeared and her granddaughter felt
happy to return to her bed. Later, when the granddaughter was
age thirteen and lived elsewhere, she experienced her younger
brother complaining that the video game he was playing got
"stuck" in his mind, and he couldn't get it out. She called Carol
and asked her to vacuum out her brother's mind. Carol repeated
the exercise over the phone. Immediately, he was "unstuck."
When he asked if he could still safely play the video game, Carol
told him that there would always be the danger of getting stuck
again. Within a year, the boy stopped all video games of his own
free will. This example is given to show that the Sage and the
other Helpers, can use the homeliest of means to free us of the
harmful images created by words.

The Deprogramming Process

Generally, deprogramming takes three days, during which we
go through the procedure once a day. It then takes another three
days for the Helpers to carry out the transformations in the realm
of consciousness. The effect of the transformations is to return
the psychic functions that had become blocked or perverted
to their healthy functioning. In the case of chips that contain
the memory of a traumatic event, they become removed in an
enduring way. In cases where the chromosomes have become
disturbed, they are returned to normal.

The process of deprogramming consists of two parts: (1)
saying No three times to the word, phrase, image, etc., and (2)
asking the Helpers to complete our effort. If the phrase was
placed in you by someone else, you also say an inner No three
times to that person for having done so. If you learn through
the *rtcm* that you have the ability to effectively say No, you can

simply follow these steps.

The methods given below for deprogramming differ from this description in that they have been adapted to enable people who have an impediment to saying No (due to stop chips) to successfully do their deprogramming. These methods allow the Helpers to say the necessary No on their behalf.

Killing as Part of Deprogramming

Demonic elements in the psyche need to be *killed*. This task is carried out by certain Helpers such as the Helper that Kills Imps, the Helper that Kills Demons, the Helper that Kills Dragons, and the Helpers that are specialized on killing the different kinds of ODE's. Some people hesitate to ask for something to be killed because they believe they are killing off parts of themselves. Or, they hesitate because of the commandment, "Thou shalt not kill." We need to realize that demonic elements are parasites in the psyche that are created by disharmonious ideas that have taken on a life of their own. They use the idea that they are part of our nature, and the commandment not to kill, to give them safe haven in our psyche. So long as they exist, they imprison the Helpers of our true nature.

The reader who wants to free himself of them may first need to deprogram the belief that they are a part of him, along with the phrase, "Thou shalt not kill" in relation to these elements.

Deprogramming Guilt and Doubt

It has been our experience that in some cases, the deprogramming can be undone by guilt or doubt, if these have not been removed first. In regard to guilt, you may first need to free yourself from the false concept of 'guilt as an inextinguishable stain on your nature', and possibly also from the idea of original guilt/sin. We have listed these below. In order to be able to deprogram them successfully, you need to first attain clarity about their falseness. (See Chapter 4 to understand the difference between guilt and Cosmic blame.) Once these two basic ideas related to guilt/sin have been successfully deprogrammed, we do not need to concern ourselves with them any longer. However, we will still need to deprogram guilt when it is connected with something else we are deprogramming, such as a chip, certain self-images, mistaken ideas and beliefs, or ego-complexes. If the guilt connected with these things is not also deprogrammed, it will undo the deprogramming of those things.

Sometimes, in deprogramming an issue, we may have a doubt that the thing can be removed by deprogramming. In that case, that doubt must be deprogrammed in advance.

A Step-by-Step Guide to Deprogramming:

Step 1: Write down the things you wish to deprogram.

Example: (a) The phrase, "I never do things right." (b) The self-image of "the helpless person." (c) Unspecific feelings of guilt.

Step 2: Ask for each point on your list, which of the deprogramming methods mentioned below is suitable.

Step 3: Ask for each point on your list whether a changeling is connected with it. If yes, find out how many. It is sufficient to know their number.

Step 4 (only applicable for your first experience with deprogramming): Start by deprogramming the false concept of guilt under (1) below. Then ask the Sage whether you need to also deprogram the spell of original guilt/sin mentioned under (2) below. You may have taken on this spell simply by being part of a culture, without your conscious awareness.

Step 5: Proceed with the deprogramming by using the methods indicated by the Sage.

Step 6: The next day, ask for each item whether you need to repeat the deprogramming. Continue this exercise once per day until the Sage confirms you are finished. Deprogramming is generally complete in three days. If you learn that you can discontinue after only one day, you can safely discontinue.

Mini-Meditations Used for Deprogramming

By mini-meditations we mean short meditations in which we

put the harmful phrases or images either in water, fire, a Cosmic vacuum cleaner, a Cosmic shredder, or other such means that give us the feeling of extinguishing them. We *do* need to ask the Sage which means that comes to mind is most appropriate for the matter at hand. The deprogramming occurs in the realm of consciousness. No part of our nature or psyche gets injured or harmed in this process; on the contrary, they get freed from an oppressive energy.

Keeping a Daily Notes Record

We recommend keeping a daily notebook or computer document in which you keep a record of your investigation, the items needing to be deprogrammed, and the method(s) to be used. It is helpful to separate out the items for deprogramming at the bottom of your document so that they can be addressed until such time as the deprogramming is finished for each item. Then you can delete those items that are finished.

Methods of Deprogramming

(1) Deprogramming the False Concept of Guilt

To free yourself from the false concept of guilt as an inextinguishable stain on your nature, do a mini-meditation in which you ask the Helper that Frees People from Guilt to free you from the concept of guilt; also ask the Cosmic Doctor to do what is necessary to erase the harm the guilt has done to your body.

(2) Deprogramming the Spell of "Original Guilt/Sin"

You can picture the phrase, "humans are born with original sin/guilt," and the image of an inextinguishable stain on human nature as being dunked in water until the stain is removed. Or, you can use any other image the Sage approves of. Then ask your Personal Helper of Deprogramming to deprogram this spell on your behalf.

(3) Deprogramming Feelings of Guilt

When you find that you feel guilty for something, say No

three times to whatever it is, and ask your Personal Helper of Deprogramming to deprogram the guilt on your behalf.

If you have a whole list of things for which you feel guilty, do the Mini-Meditation Using the Image of Water. After dunking the whole list, ask the same Helper to free you from it.

4) Deprogramming Changelings

(a) If we want to stop the creation of ever-new changelings that support the ego's mindset, we deprogram the two basic changelings that are behind the production of new ones. These are "The Inventor of Rationales" and "The Inventor of Counter-Rationales." They become active when we come close to being freed of the ego. After having said No three times to the following phrases, we can ask the Helper that Kills Changelings to kill them. These phrases are: "We have nothing other than the rational mind to give us answers." "Things have to make sense" (when the ego appropriates the word "sense" to refer to its reasoning). The phrase connected with the Inventor of Counter-Rationales is, "There is always another reason that explains why things are the way they are."

Even though no new rationales will now be created, we will still need to detect and deprogram changelings that are connected with things stored in our psyche as these things come up for deprogramming.

"The Guardian of Ancient Wisdom" calls up old rationales that, being cryptic, are half-truths. (An example is the phrase, "Life is suffering." The reason this is a half-truth is that it is pronounced as an *absolute truth*, whereas, it becomes true only so long as we leave out of our recognition the multitude of Cosmic Helpers that are available to us.) The single phrase of the guardian changeling is, "You can't disregard the wisdom of the past." We say No three times to this phrase before asking for the changeling to be killed. (This kind of wisdom is also falsely referred to by the ego as "commonsense.") By deprogramming it, the psyche is freed from relying on the old wisdom sayings, and to instead rely on the feelings of harmony and disharmony coming from our inner truth.

(b) Freeing ourselves from individual changelings
In Chapter 12 we have given the names of many changelings. Changelings are the hidden rationales behind ego-phrases, ego-inspired images, ego-complexes, chips, etc. In deprogramming such items, it is common for one or more changelings to be connected with them. There can be up to nine changelings connected with one item. You do not need to identify them by their name or rationale, but find out, with the *rtcm*, how many changelings are connected with the thing being deprogrammed. Then ask the Sage to bring the Helpers needed to kill the number you have discovered.

Changelings can also exist independently as specific rationales. They are responsible for re-installing things we have deprogrammed. We can ask the Sage to identify the changelings involved without needing to know their names, and to bring the Helper that kills them.

(c) Free-floating changelings
These changelings become active when we have deprogrammed something without realizing that a changeling was connected with that thing. We become aware of the presence of one or more when we experience pains that travel from one part of the body to another. The Helper needed to kill them is the Helper that Kills Free-Floating Changelings.

(5) Mini-Meditations Using Suggested Means

Using the image of water
When water is indicated for deprogramming, here are some suggestions: if it is a self-image, see it as a mask which you splash with water; if it is a memory you want to let go of, picture putting it in a stream and letting it flow away. If it is a negative thought ascribed to you, picture it being washed away by your standing in a shower, or under a waterfall. When the item is a chip, you can dunk the whole chip in water.

Using the image of fire
When this method is indicated, picture putting the phrase (written on a piece of paper) and/or image (as a drawing, painting, photograph, or mask) into a fire.

Using a 'Cosmic vacuum cleaner'

This meditation is useful for things that want to stick in your psyche, and also to give the psyche a good cleansing of nondescript roaming negative thoughts. Picture a Cosmic vacuum cleaner sucking up into a bag whatever you have identified.

Using the image of a Cosmic shredder

In this meditation picture the phrase(s) as written on a piece of paper that you put in a Cosmic shredder.

(6) Deprogramming "Other Demonic Elements" (ODE's)

ODE's need to be killed. First say No three times to the ODE you have identified, then ask the Helper that kills this kind of ODE to kill it. For example: to kill a "doubter" say No three times to it, then ask the Helper that Kills Doubters to kill it.

Also ask the Sage if any changelings are connected with the ODE you have identified. If Yes, ask the Sage to bring the specific Helper(s) needed to kill the number of changelings indicated.

(7) Deprogramming an Ego-Complex

Ego-complexes are deprogrammed by using a fire meditation in which we picture its phrases written on a piece of paper that is then burned. Self-images that are part of the complex are pictured as a mask that gets burned. Then we ask the Sage to kill the changeling that has been guarding the complex, and to extinguish any other demonic elements that belong to it. We also ask the Helper of Transformation to complete the process, and the Helpers of Healing to heal the damage done by the complex to our psyche and body.

Note: When freeing yourself from *The Superiority Complex*, you need to take into consideration that it owes its existence to *The Inferiority Complex*. The bigger the *Superiority Complex* the bigger the *Inferiority Complex* that underlies it. Any attempt to only deprogram the Superiority Complex, would plunge us into the traumatic experience of feeling that 'nothing of worth is left of us'. The correct order would be to deprogram both complexes at the same time, and only after having gained enough clarity to see the falseness of the *Inferiority Complex*. To make sure that we do not make such mistakes that would harm our psyche, we need to follow the Sage's guidance.

(8) Deprogramming a Ball-of-Conflict

A ball-of-conflict is based on the idea that there is such a thing as a 'culprit.' This word has no validity in the Cosmic order. Say No three times to the word 'culprit', and ask the Helper of Dissolution to free you from the whole ball-of-conflict.

(9) Deprogramming Crystallized Ego-Emotions or a Crystallized Memory

Picture putting the crystallized thing in liquid light (like the bright white light that emanates from a big waterfall), and ask the Helper of Transformation to transform it into light.

What to Do When the Deprogramming Exceeds Three Days

Deprogramming is usually finished in three days, but there are exceptions. When the Sage confirms that you need to continue, it is helpful to inquire into the reason, as for example:

"Have I been deprogramming only from my head, leaving out my feelings?" If the answer is Yes, do the following: Every time before you start deprogramming a single point or a whole list, say No three times to being disconnected from your feelings. Also, ask the Sage to assist you in your deprogramming effort.

"Is there a changeling (one or more) connected with the point I want to deprogram, which I have overlooked?" (A changeling that got overlooked can undo your deprogramming.)

"Do I need to correct the phrasing of what I want to deprogram?" or "Is there a phrase I have missed?"

"Are other Helpers needed to deprogram it?"

"Is there an imp or a dragon of guilt interfering with my deprogramming effort?" If yes, these will need to be deprogrammed before you can continue with the rest.

What to Do When Some of Your Deprogramming Has Been Undone by Guilt or Doubt

When you notice that symptoms have returned, it may mean

that your deprogramming has been undone by guilt connected with the material that was overlooked at the time. Do not despair: find out what you feel guilty for, and deprogram this guilt according to the instructions given under (3) above. Next, you can ask the Helper that Deprograms Reinstalled Things to deprogram them again on your behalf. You do not have to remember what those things are. Ask each following day whether you need to repeat this procedure until the answer is No. Then thank the Helper for its aid.

If you find that *doubts in the effectiveness of the deprogramming* have undone your work, you need to ask for help to deprogram an "imp and dragon of doubt in the effectiveness of deprogramming." Follow the instructions for the "Mini-meditation using the image of a vacuum cleaner bag" described under (5).

Next, ask the Helper that Deprograms Reinstalled Things to deprogram them again on your behalf as described above.

Appendix 4
Helpful Exercises

A Good Daily Practice

Before starting a new day, we ask the Sage to help us through-out the day, and to gather all the other Helpers needed. This alleviates the need to ask for specific Helpers for various tasks. We still, however, need to ask for specific Helpers in our depro-gramming activity.

Seeing A Person's True Self

This is not so much an exercise as keeping in mind, when the ego is dominating someone, that his true self is oppressed and needs to be seen. This has a strengthening effect on his true self. It also prevents us from giving up on him as hopeless, which, in *I Ching* terms, is to mentally "execute" him.

Asking the Sage to Control the Ego in Us

When we notice that the ego is dominant in us, we ask the Sage to control it. The effect lasts for 2-3 days. Then we may need to repeat our request.

Asking the Sage to Control the Ego in Another Person

When we know that we will be meeting with someone we think of as "difficult," we can ask the Sage-in-his-presence to control the ego in him. This also applies to groups of people when we are preparing for a business conference or a public lecture.

It is best to make our request on the day before the meeting takes place, or at least one hour before the meeting.

It is important that we not view the others as "opponents," "rivals," "competitors," or "culprits," since that keeps us in the realm of demonic consciousness, and the Sage cannot intervene. If that is our view of them, we need to deprogram the negative image by saying "No, No, No" to it and then turning it over to the Sage. The deprogramming needs to be repeated once per day until the Sage confirms that we have done enough.

343

Asking the Sage to Bring Someone Back to Himself

When a child or adult is in a state of rage as expressed by the word "outraged," or in a state of deep depression, anyone who is present can ask the Sage to call the child or person by his name. Then the Sage calls him back to himself.

A Mind-Cleansing Meditation

In addition to being a helpful meditation in itself, its purpose is to come to a state of inner neutrality, so that the Sage can communicate with us. Once we have cleansed our mind, we can ask for the Sage to help us solve the problem of the moment.

First, sit upright in a comfortable position. Close your eyes and ask the Helper of Mind Cleansing to clear your mind of all preconceived ideas, worries, preoccupations, and ego-emotions. This can take from three to ten minutes. Then, if you still do not feel neutral, do not proceed. You can recognize non-neutrality by the way it feels: it drives, smolders, rages, rants, or feels muddled. To bring help, ask the Sage to activate the Helpers needed to resolve this for you and turn the matter over to them. Return to your meditation at a later time.

A Heart Meditation

A heart meditation is needed when we are lacking in energy. Returning your heart to a healthy condition is of primary importance because heart-chi is needed to invigorate your body.

First, ask the Helper of Mind Cleansing to cleanse your mind. Allow about three minutes until your mind is free from all thoughts and/or expectations. Then, ask the Sage to show you the condition of your heart. Do not judge what you see. If you see that anything is "abnormal," ask the Helper of your Heart to do whatever is necessary to return your heart to a healthy condition. This meditation need not exceed fifteen minutes, nor need to be repeated for more than three days.

A Meditation in Which You "Sit in Your Original Image"

We use this meditation for several purposes: to get in touch with our true nature, to be made aware of a chip, a self-image, or a projection, spell, or poison arrow, or to help heal a damaged part of the body.

First, ask the Helper of Mind Cleansing to cleanse your mind. Allow about three minutes for this to happen, or until your mind is free from all thoughts and/or expectations. Then, ask the Helper of Your Original Image (it is a holographic image) to allow you to sit in it. Feel how that feels: Does it feel fitting? If not, explore the cause, after your meditation. (See Appendix 2.)

When we do this meditation to heal a damaged body part, we ask the Helper of Our Original Image to remove our damaged image of it and replace it with the image that shows it whole.

Allow fifteen minutes for the entire meditation.

Centering Yourself / A Meditation to Attain Clarity about a Concern

This exercise brings you back into your center, thus enabling the Sage to teach you whatever you need to know about your situation, and to deepen your understanding of the nature of things, and of the Cosmic Way. It can also be used to enable you to sleep. It is achieved through a brief meditation in which you turn over to the Helpers everything that is bothering you at the moment.

Step 1: Suspending your disbelief: This means stopping the "yes, but..." thoughts of disbelief that attempt to fill up your inner space and crowd out the Sage, by saying the inner No to them. If these thoughts appear in meditation as figures, regardless of size, ask the Helpers to take care of them.

Step 2: Loading things onto the wagon of the Helper of Transformation. This is a reference to the wagon mentioned in Line 2 of Hexagram 14, *Possession in Great Measure.* You may see it in a different image that is personal to you; allow whatever other image comes to your mind that serves the same purpose of "removing" from you whatever is bothering you at the moment, and let go of it. This frees up your inner space, enabling the Sage to reply and address the problems in the most efficient way. Turn over any of the following kinds of mental elements:

• self-images, including being the rescuer of others

- all arguments, criticisms, and analyses
- ego-emotions such as worry, anger, desire, vindictiveness, hate, grief, and melancholy
- the fear of doing something that will make you guilty
- all fears of not knowing how to meditate
- self-blame, guilt, and blame of others. Turn over the idea of there being a culprit—be it yourself, others, or anything. Not even the ego is a culprit.
- all ambition, and the image of striving upward toward some degree of perfection
- the idea that freeing your true self is hard work and/or an ascetic practice
- images that show your body in a degraded way

After turning over these things, you then envision your inner space as a circle around you, or a room which you have cleaned out. This is your intrinsic space. Now possess it as yours, as not belonging to anybody but yourself. At this point you are free of attachment. Having come to this point, remain quietly in your inner space to allow the Sage to enter, if and when the Sage will. Leave that entirely up to the Sage.

Continue until you feel it is time to stop meditating. If this time exceeds twenty minutes and nothing has happened, it is enough. Inner cleansing is the most important thing you have achieved. Continuing the practice each day without expectation that something will happen, will make it possible for the Sage to enter. If you stay, through some inner feeling that you have not done enough, the ego has already entered, with its ambition, to control the process. Then it is time to stop and make a renewed effort later. With repeated practice and cleansing, the ego will be successively diminished in its ability to dominate you.

Asking Your Inner Senses of Perception

This exercise can be used:

(1) to get in touch with a stored traumatic memory

(2) to examine the truth or untruth of a statement

The senses referred to are: our inner senses of smell, taste, hearing, seeing and touch. Their function is to perceive the inner truth of a matter. Before doing this exercise, we need to check with the *rtcm* to find which of our five inner senses of perception is free enough to be included.

The exercise is carried out in a short meditation, in which we ask one by one those inner senses of perception which are free, how they perceive the matter at hand:

- How does it smell?
- How does it taste?
- How does it sound?
- What does it look like?
- How does it feel?

Example: Hanna asked her inner senses of perception to assess the truth or untruth of the statement, "You need to become a spiritual person."

- How does that statement smell? Answer: It smells like a dead body.
- How does it taste? Answer: it tastes bitter.
- How does it sound? Answer: crazy.
- What does it look like? Answer: The image of something like an ethereal flame hovering over a dead body.
- How does it feel? Answer: a feeling of pressure in the head that comes from searching with the head, and the feeling of not knowing.

Note: To understand the responses of Hanna's inner senses, we need to realize that the idea of becoming a spiritual person is based on the mistaken belief that our animal nature is "lowly, evil, and the source of guilt, and that therefore we need to develop our higher nature and sacrifice or transcend our lower nature." Her inner senses showed her the consequence of this desire that comes from the ego in the image of "an ethereal flame hovering over a dead body."

Appendix 5
Glossary of Definitions Used in this Book

(Note: References to other glossary entries
are marked with >)

Animal Nature: In the Cosmic sense, humans are part of the animal kingdom. It is our animal nature that gives us our Cosmic dignity and our true place in the Cosmic whole. It is also our animal nature that holds us, through our feelings and our DNA, in a positive, symbiotic relationship with the >*Cosmos*. The human desire to be special because we have language has led to the mistaken idea that our 'self' is divided into a 'higher' (spiritual) and a 'lower' (animal) nature. In this book, the term animal nature is often used as a synonym for our bodily nature, particularly when speaking of our sexuality.

Inasmuch as we have accepted these slanders as true, they have separated us from the Cosmic unity and thus made us susceptible to mental, physical, and emotional illness.

Chi Energy: We have learned to distinguish these different kinds of *chi* energy:
- The *life force* that animates existence
- *Heart chi* as Cosmic love we receive directly through our heart. It differs from the *chi* we receive through other parts of our body in that it invigorates the body and enables us to fulfill our destiny
- *Chi* energy we receive from Nature; our feeling relationship with Nature gives us stamina and emotional energy
- *Chi* energy we receive from sunlight is necessary for a healthy metabolism

These kinds of *chi* energy and others not mentioned here are all part of the Cosmic Consciousness and of Nature.

Collective Ego: This is the name given to the totality of mistaken ideas and beliefs about the >*Cosmos*, Nature, human nature, and the human place in the Cosmos, which have been adopted by different societies and groups. Common to these is the presumption that humans are the special creatures of creation, to which all other things are subservient. Because this view contradicts the Cosmic Principles of Harmony, it has separated humans and their cultures from the Cosmos and its harmonious order. The visible side of the collective ego is found in those social structures and institutions that support this view. The collective ego is the parent of the individual >*ego.*

Commonsense: This is the name for the consensus of all our *inner* and *outer* senses of perception and our *metaphorical* senses. In humans, commonsense is the 'inner judge' that discerns what is in harmony with our inner truth (and therefore also in harmony with the Cosmos) and what is not. Its judgment has the form of a *felt* Yes or No. Because our commonsense is derived from the DNA of our >*animal nature*, it becomes dysfunctional when our animal nature is slandered as having no intelligence and as being the source of evil, and when our feelings are disregarded as unreliable. (Also see below >*Senses.*)

Cosmic blame: We incur Cosmic blame when we follow an idea that violates the Cosmic Principles of Harmony. This is also to go against our true nature. We feel this as *shame.* Our feeling of shame, when not seized by the ego and turned into ego-shame (a permanent stain), gives way to remorse, which, in turn, extinguishes the Cosmic blame. Our return to harmony with the >*Cosmos* is made possible through the *natural self-correcting function* in our psyche. The ego can also interfere with this function by converting our true feelings of remorse into >*guilt.*

When we continue to violate the Cosmic harmony, we create a >*fate.* By deprogramming the idea in question, our fate can be ended and the Cosmic blame extinguished. Even if we do not realize what has caused our fate, it has only a limited duration. When it has run its course, our Cosmic blame is extinguished.

Cosmos (from the Greek) means "the whole universe in its harmonious order." In its entirety, the Cosmos consists of the invisible Cosmic Consciousness and its expression in the visible forms of Nature. The *I Ching* shows us that it achieves its duration through its system of Principles of Harmony.

Among the Cosmic Principles of Harmony are the Principles of Equality, Wholeness, Goodness, Uniqueness, and Modesty of all aspects of the Cosmos. These principles give each thing its Cosmic dignity. All these principles work together to ensure harmony.

The Cosmic Consciousness is composed of several kinds of consciousness, most of which can be characterized as *feeling* consciousnesses. When we are in harmony with the Cosmos, we feel its presence as love. Every manifestation of the Cosmic Consciousness in form, including humans, is an expression of this love. However, because the Cosmic gift of language to humans comes with the freedom to experience what it means to be part of the loving Cosmos, we have the freedom as well to make mistakes in using our gift of language. This happens when we create and use words that have no Cosmic basis. The consequence is disharmony and suffering, both of which create >*Cosmic blame*. Feeling ashamed sets in motion our *natural self-correcting function*.

The disharmonious consciousness created by humans through these mistakes has put humans outside the Cosmic whole, isolated in a *parallel reality* that competes with the Cosmos. From its place of isolation, the negative energy of this sphere, created by the perpetuation of conflict, operates destructively on humans and on Nature like a 'black hole'; it is characterized by conflict, lack, the use of power, and the absence of love, peace and prosperity. The return to unity with the Cosmos is possible for every individual who is willing to recognize that his true home is to be found by turning within and correcting his thinking.

Death: When applied to processes in Nature, death marks the >*transformation* of a person, animal, or plant from its visible form into an invisible form of existence within the Cosmic whole. Applied to humans, this transformation occurs when the individual's uniqueness is fulfilled. His aggregate consciousness continues to live in its unique identity and takes on new tasks. Those who have not developed their uniqueness or fulfilled their destinies are given another opportunity to do so by being returned once more to human form. They return free and clear of all blame; innocent, they are able to make an entirely new start. No burden gets carried forward into the new life in a body.

It may happen that before the transformation has become completed, the deceased contacts a spouse or child to inform him of something that is standing in the way of his transformation. An example is an attachment that person has to the deceased, or feelings of guilt. Holding onto the dead prevents both the living and the dead from making progress. While the living is kept from fulfilling his uniqueness, the dead is kept from the tasks he is to fulfill in the invisible realm. When we say the inner No to the ego-emotions that tie us to the dead, and ask the Helper that Frees us from Ego Emotions to do so, the transformation can be completed.

The fear of death is the result of the body cells having been led to falsely believe that death is "the end of life." This is generally accompanied by horrible images. This fear, like all fears, is promoted by the ego for its purposes of control. The ego is the only thing that dies when our life *in the body* ends. To deceive itself about the inevitability of its own death, the ego has created the idea of an immortal soul, which it hopes to inhabit after death.

When we have fulfilled our Cosmic destiny, we will feel that our time to die has come. We need no help in this process; it occurs peacefully when we are not ill. However, a person who is dying from an illness can usually be helped by calling upon a team of >Helpers to help him make that step in harmony with Nature. These Helpers are: the Helper of Transformation, the Helper to Make Death Swift and Easy (to overcome the effects of the platitude that death is difficult and hard), the Helper of the Acceptance of Death, and the Helper of Seeing One's Inner Truth. Before we can help another in this way we always need to ask the Sage whether it is correct to do so. If we go ahead without asking, the ego has taken charge of the action, which creates blame. Doing this would not harm the dying person, because the Helpers do not associate with the ego.

Ego: The individual ego is a composite of negative and positive self-images we develop in the course of childhood conditioning. The seeds for its development are put into our psyche at a very early age by being made to doubt the wholeness and total goodness of our nature. This self-doubt causes our >*true self* to become repressed and replaced with the ego as a false self that looks to its parent, the collective ego, for all our needs, including the authorization of our very existence. This authorization is given under the condition that we accept the rules and values of the collective ego and its institutions. This acceptance is called "developing our higher nature by suppressing our lower/animal nature."

Since adopting the self-images, roles, pretenses, mistaken beliefs, and ego emotions conflicts with our true nature, they are the main causes of mental, emotional, and physical illness.

Fate: Fate is the Cosmic Principle of Harmony that brings humans down to earth when they have exceeded their natural limits. It is the natural consequence created by thoughts and beliefs that are in conflict with our true nature (which is in harmony with the Cosmos). Such thoughts and beliefs create a negative energy trajectory that returns to us like a boomerang when unimpeded by the interference of others. Fate makes us aware of the disharmonious ideas and beliefs we harbor that have created the fate, thus giving us an opportunity to correct our thinking and attitudes. Fate always has a limited duration, like a prison sentence. It is not to be confounded with our Cosmic destiny. Rather, its purpose is to return us to the path of our Cosmic destiny.

Guilt: The *I Ching* makes it clear that the word guilt and all ideas related to it do not have a Cosmic basis. This includes the concept of original guilt or sin. The association of the word guilt with the image of an inextinguishable stain on our nature serves to keep us under the control of the >*collective ego.*

The justification used for guilt is that it "gives us a conscience and protects us from the evil in us." Therefore, the threat of becoming guilty is attached to all *roles and virtuous self-images* given to us by the collective ego. If guilt is not deprogrammed together with the things to which it is attached, it will reinstall what we have deprogrammed. Guilt is both the cause of disturbances, and the factor that can keep us caught in them.

Guilt generally has to do with going against the collective ego, whereas >*Cosmic blame* occurs when we go against the harmonious order of the Cosmos.

Helpers: Helpers are individualized energies of the Cosmic Consciousness and of Nature, including our human animal nature. Being energies, they are invisible. However, as the photo shown on page 23 indicates, the Helpers will sometimes show themselves in digital photographs. Each Helper is a "specialist in his field" that fulfills a specific function within the Cosmos as a whole. The Helpers are not invisible human beings like ghosts, although a human can, once transformed, become a Helper. Helpers can give their help *through* humans, as for example, through a doctor, therapist, lawyer, employer, state official, etc. Helpers are feeling consciousnesses, not 'spirits'. (Spirits are the products of disharmonious ideas about the invisible world and the way it works.) The Helpers perform many of their tasks through >*transformations* in the realm of the atom. Because the Helpers can help in ways that humans cannot, it is important to abstain from trying to imagine how they accomplish their tasks, how much or how little time they need to complete them, and in what form the result will manifest.

Mind: The mind is composed of two parts: the thinking mind and the imaging mind.

Poison Arrows, Spells, Projections: These words refer to phrases that are not in harmony with the >*Cosmos*, and there-fore create a negative energy that harms the psyche and/or body of the human being, animal, plant, or other thing in Nature to which they are applied. They are the main causes of mental, emotional, and physical illness. We can project them onto ourselves (our body or psyche) or onto others. Their harmful effects can be ended when we identify the words, phrases and/or images that make them up, and thoroughly reject them by deprogramming them with Cosmic help. Once the >*Helpers* transform them, their harmful effects end.

Psyche: Our psyche is the invisible aspect of our being. It is mistakenly called "soul" as something apart from our body, and which uses the body as its "vehicle." The *I Ching* informs us that psyche and body form an inseparable harmonious whole. The psyche comprises all the *consciousnesses that make up our invisible existence.* Central among these are our feeling consciousness, our thinking consciousness that forms language, our reflective consciousness that attracts insight-flashes, and our intuitive consciousness that forms images. Our psyche is the meeting place for all these kinds of consciousness. It has functions that enable them to exchange their experiences and learn from each other. It is also the 'library' where all memories of our experiences are stored in a coded, or 'mini-form.' It also stores there all our unprocessed traumatic memories that create mental and emotional dysfunctions and disorders. Processing these negative memories and deprogramming them with Cosmic help frees us from their harmful effects. The psyche also contains the > *subconscious* chamber, or prison created by the development of the ego, into which the true self is locked (repressed) and guarded by the threats and taboos that have assumed demonic forms.

Senses: The senses include our five outer senses of perception (seeing, hearing, smell, taste, touch), our five inner senses of perception that produce insight, inner hearing, and inner smelling, inner taste, and inner touch. They also include metaphorical senses such as our sense of wholeness, our sense of appropriateness, our sense of caution, and also our will, to name a few. The function of our inner senses of perception is to tell us the *inner* truth of matters, as when we say that "something smells foul," "a behavior is tasteless," "an information sounds horrible," "an outcome feels rough," or "an outcome looks bright."

Even though a suspicious odor or taste may not be noticeable to the outer senses, it triggers our inner senses unless these senses have been turned off by devaluing them at one time or another. Renewing our respect for them enables us to detect sick-making thoughts and ego emotions that can lead to illness.

Renewing our conscious connection to our inner senses requires practice in paying attention to our inner sense of hearing. Its function is to bring what has been smelled or tasted into our conscious mind. When this sense gives the message that something does not "sound" right, our inner sense of touch comes into play; it compares this feeling with our sense of inner truth, (our memory of what Cosmic harmony *feels* like). Then what does not sound right is perceived as a dissonance, an inner feeling that something does not "feel" right.

Our *metaphorical senses*, when functioning, automatically trigger the correct response to disharmonious situations. These senses also include our sense of loyalty to our inner truth, our sense of fairness or neutrality, our sense of integrity, our sense of inner quiet, our sense of innocence, our sense of the dignity of all things, and our general sensitivity toward everything around us. Egotism shuts down these senses, making us vulnerable to the tactics of the ego, such as flattery. One of the main characteristics of the metaphorical senses is their *simplicity*. They guide us from within to conduct ourselves appropriately in every circumstance and thereby keep us *centered and complete within ourselves*. We enjoy their full abilities when we consciously pay them our full respect. The result is self-respect in its true meaning.

Subconscious: The subconscious (unlike the >*unconscious*) is not a natural part of our makeup. It is a dungeon created in our psyche during the development of the ego into which the true self is thrown, once the ego has taken over the leadership of the personality. Thereafter, it is held there by the illusion of the ego's power, self-doubt, and the fear of self-expression.

Transformation: Transformation is the word for the way the >*Cosmos* brings everything about through the attraction between its complementary aspects. The most basic attraction occurs between the forces of the dark of Nature and the light of the Cosmic Consciousness. All processes of growth and death in Nature require transformations — growth being the result of transformations from non-form into form, and death being the transformation from form into non-form.

The forces of the light and the dark, as the two primary aspects of the Cosmos that create transformations, are inseparable. The Chinese ideogram for "I" in *I Ching* means transformation, not "changes," as it has been falsely translated. Transformation is indicated by the fact that the Chinese ideogram is based on the image of a chameleon. Seeing it as meaning *change* has created the assumption that life is ruled by changes, that is, through something that is mechanically induced. This incorrect assumption supports the human-centered view of the universe whereby we humans think "we do it all."

In this view, the forces of the light and the dark are incorrectly seen as competing with each other for dominance. This view prevents transformations both within our body cells and in our relationship with Nature. The transformations that are necessary to renew our life force occur in the realm of the atom. Humans cannot achieve transformations by any conscious effort. Transformations are the function of a particular >*Helper* that operates on the plane of feelings. Deprogramming a mistaken idea or belief with Cosmic help brings about transformation, which erases the disharmonious words or images from our psyche, along with their effects.

Saying an inner No to the idea that the Cosmos operates through changes, and to all other ideas and beliefs that are in conflict with the Cosmos, engages the Helper of Transformation and enables the Cosmos to correct matters. Saying a conscious Yes to what feels harmonious also engages the Helper of Transformation and enables the Cosmos to manifest it in form.

True Self. We have a "thinking sense of self" and a "feeling sense of self." The latter is referred to as our *true self*. As a result of childhood conditioning our true self becomes repressed into the >*subconscious* once the false self we refer to as the individual >*ego* takes over the leadership of the personality. Freeing our true self from its imprisonment in the subconscious is the purpose of making the inner journey into our psyche. Our true self, not the ego, is the rightful leader of our personality.

Unconscious. What is referred to as the unconscious is the feeling consciousness of our body, and of our psyche. In performing its multitudinous functions, it operates outside the consciousness of the >*mind*.

Index

H

of, 83-91; the organizing function, 83, 145, 156; the processing function, 84, 155; the active transforming function, 85, 151, 160; the transmitting function, 86; the focusing function, 87, 159; the linking/harmonizing function, 87, 156, 159; the remorse function, 87, 151; our natural self-correcting function, 87, 145, 151, 349, 350; the categorizing and searching function, 89; the premonition function, 90; the mind's cooperation with, 90; the causes of dysfunctions in the psyche, 91-94, Chapter 13; definition, 354

Q

Questions, using the *rtcm* to communicate with the Sage, see Appendix 1(301-314)

R

RTCM: Retrospective-Three-Coin Method, Appendix 1; using the rtcm, 301-314; discovery of the method, 301-303; the Sage leads the investigation, 303-304; beliefs that block our understanding, 304; common blocks to self-examination, 305; use of, 305; inner preparation for its use, 306-307; problematic questions, 309; helpful questions, 311; confusing answers, 311; the meaning of No answers, 313

S

Sage, x-xi, 7-8; its functions in the psyche, 50-51; questions about its identity, 60-61; our relationship with it, 75-76; as our Cosmic Teacher, 79, Appendices 1-4; the psyche as facilitator for the Sage, 81; as a Helper of our psyche, 168

"Seeing the Great Man," 109

Self-image, as cause of a fate, 12; its inevitable downfall, 44; example of, 70; types of, 92; aspect of the ego and its effects on the psyche, 95-100, in ego-complexes, Chapter 13; in dramatic literature, 198; creating demonic elements, 203; deprogramming, 339-340; in glossary entry "ego", 352

Senses, as part of our Cosmic possessions, 17-18; how they are changed to suit the ego, 191; asking our inner senses of perception to show us the inner truth of a matter, 327-328; definition, 354-355

Sexual abuse, 263-266

Shock, as part of Fate and as breaking spells, Chapter 2; as bringing us back to Earth, 44-47; knocking the ego temporarily unconscious, 51

Shocking and/or traumatic events stored in chips, Chapters 18